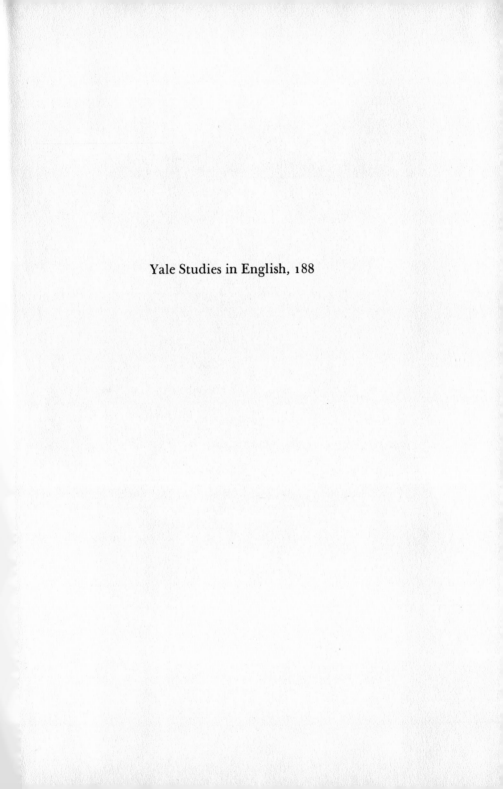

Yale Studies in English, 188

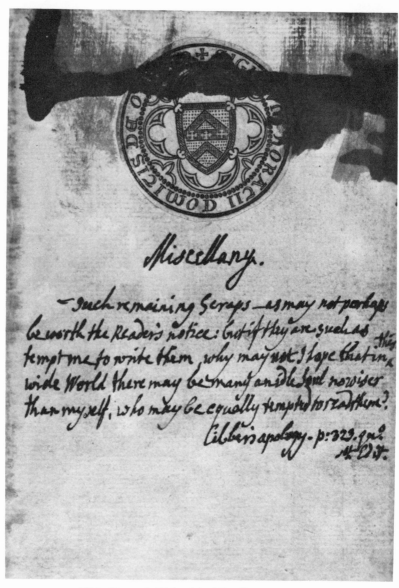

Title Page of Walpole's *Miscellany* 1786–1795

Horace Walpole's *Miscellany* 1786–1795

edited, introduced,
and annotated by

Lars E. Troide

New Haven and London, Yale University Press, 1978

Designed by John O. C. McCrillis
and set in Baskerville type.
Printed in the United States of America by
The Vail-Ballou Press, Inc., Binghamton, New York.

Published in Great Britain, Europe, Africa, and
Asia (except Japan) by Yale University Press,
Ltd., London. Distributed in Latin America by
Kaiman & Polon, Inc., New York City; in
Australia and New Zealand by Book & Film
Services, Artarmon, N.S.W., Australia; and in
Japan by Harper & Row, Publishers, Tokyo
Office.

Library of Congress Cataloging in Publication Data

Walpole, Horace, 4th Earl of Orford, 1717–1797.
   Horace Walpole's Miscellany, 1786–1795.

   (Yale studies in English ; 188)
   Originally presented as the editor's thesis, Yale.
   Includes bibliographical references and index.
   I. Troide, Lars E., 1942–   II. Title.
III. Series.
PR3757.W2M5   828'.6'09   77-14117
ISBN 0-300-02105-4

To W. S. Lewis
and my wife,
Teresa

Contents

Foreword

This is the first of Horace Walpole's three most important notebooks to be edited and published in full. The first two, which Walpole called 'Books of Materials,' were begun in 1759 and 1771. Extracts have been printed from them, but they await the editors of their full texts. All three show the range of Walpole's interests and the pleasure he took in them. This is seen in the *Miscellany* from its epigraph, in which Walpole expresses his desire to inform and entertain us, to his final note on the fine Gothic church at Batalha in Portugal, built after a design of Stephen Stephenson, an Englishman.

Dr. Troide served a Walpolian apprenticeship of ten years, notably as coeditor of the Conway and Hertford Correspondences in the Yale Edition of Horace Walpole's Correspondence. It therefore gives me particular pleasure to welcome this book for its delightful self and for its full and admirable editing by an erstwhile colleague who has made a notable contribution to Walpolian studies.

Wilmarth S. Lewis

Acknowledgments

First and foremost I wish to thank W. S. Lewis, Esq., of Farmington, Connecticut, for placing at my disposal the manuscript of the *Miscellany* and for giving me every assistance and encouragement in my labors on it; my editing the *Miscellany* caps over ten years of the most warm and rewarding association with the Dean of Walpolians. Secondly I wish to thank my wife Teresa for the invaluable moral support she gave me during the year it took me to do the edition. Since the edition was originally done as a Ph.D. dissertation in the English department at Yale, I next wish to thank my dissertation advisor, Professor Martin Price, who gave me many helpful criticisms and suggestions. Acknowledgment is also due to Professors Frank Ellis of Smith College, Robert Halsband of the University of Illinois at Urbana-Champaign, and Morris Golden of the University of Massachusetts at Amherst. Professor Ellis while in England checked for me the copy of *La Vie et les amours de Charles Louis Electeur Palatin* in the British Library, as well as Craven Ord's manuscript extracts from Henry VII's books of payments; Professor Halsband kindly answered a query from me about Lord Hervey's poems in the *Miscellany;* while Professor Golden had many helpful comments to offer as reader of my manuscript for the Yale University Press.

Most of my work on the *Miscellany* was done in the offices of the Yale Walpole Edition in the Yale Library, where I occasionally tapped the great collective knowledge and wisdom of my sometime colleagues Doctors Warren H. Smith, Edwine M. Martz, and John C. Riely: all thanks to them. I also wish to thank the staff of the Inter-Library Loan Office in the Yale Library for their almost entirely successful efforts in procuring the infrequent items not available at Yale. Finally

I wish to express my appreciation to Patricia Woodruff, Editor at the Yale Press, who gave me much valuable assistance and advice in the preparation of the *Miscellany* for publication.

L. E. T.

McGill University
Montreal, Quebec, Canada

Introduction

Horace Walpole began to make entries in his notebook *Miscellany* sometime in the spring or early summer of 1786. As writer and connoisseur he could look back upon a long life filled with achievement in diverse areas. In literary history his *Catalogue of the Royal and Noble Authors in England* (1758) had been a pioneering effort. In art history his four-volume *Anecdotes of Painting* (1762–71), supplemented by a *Catalogue of Engravers* (1764), was the first detailed and systematic account of painting in England. Strawberry Hill, his house in Twickenham, was a pioneer in the Gothic Revival in architecture that spread throughout England and America.[1] His novel *The Castle of Otranto* (1765) inaugurated the genre of the Gothic tale of terror and the supernatural, while his passionate Gothic drama *The Mysterious Mother* (1768) despite its shocking theme[2] met with strong critical approval and was later to be praised by Byron as "the last tragedy of our language."[3] In the field of historical inquiry his *Historic Doubts on the Life and Reign of King Richard III* (1768), by questioning the Lancastrian accounts of Richard's guilt, renewed a controversy which continues to this day.[4] In landscape gardening his *Essay on Modern Gardening* (1771) broke away from Elizabethan formalism to

1. At Strawberry Hill Walpole also established one of the earliest private printing presses in England and amassed a notable collection of objets d'art and antiquarian curiosities which attracted numerous visitors. See his *Journal of the Printing-Office at Strawberry Hill,* ed. P. Toynbee (London, 1931), and his "Description of . . . Strawberry Hill" in Vol. II of his *Works* (London, 1798).

2. See below, p. 127.

3. Preface to *Marino Faliero* (1821).

4. See below, p. 136, n. 3.

advocate a more natural or "picturesque" style.[5] In addition, Walpole was the author of voluminous memoirs which, upon their publication after his death, would make him a chief source for the political history of his times.[6] He also of course wrote thousands of lively and perceptive letters which gave a vivid chronicle of his age. These, although unpublished in his lifetime, were handed about freely among his friends and had already gone far towards establishing his reputation as perhaps the most brilliant letter writer of the eighteenth century.[7]

Walpole began making entries in the *Miscellany* in his sixty-ninth year; he was to continue to do so until late in 1795, just some fifteen months before his death in March 1797 at the age of seventy-nine. This last decade of Walpole's life was marked by a gradual but steady physical decline which all but eliminated his once active social life. Added to the inroads of advancing age were the weakness and decrepitude caused by recurrent attacks of the gout, a condition from which he suffered over half his life.[8] The effects of the gout on Walpole's constitution are apparent in those passages in the *Miscellany* where he plainly had to struggle to

5. For these works see Allen T. Hazen, *A Bibliography of Horace Walpole* (New Haven, 1948), pp. 52–67, 69–74, and *A Bibliography of the Strawberry Hill Press,* new ed. (New York, 1973), pp. 33–37, 55–68, 79–85, 129–32.

6. *Memoires of the Last Ten Years of the Reign of George the Second,* ed. Lord Holland (London, 1822), 2 vols., royal 4to; *Memoirs of the Reign of King George the Third,* ed. Sir Denis Le Marchant (London, 1845), 4 vols., 8vo; *Journal of the Reign of King George the Third, from the Year 1771 to 1783,* ed. Dr. Doran (London, 1859), 2 vols., 8vo (reprinted in 1910 as *Last Journals of Horace Walpole*). For later editions of these works see Hazen, *Bibl. of HW,* p. 95. Forthcoming is the definitive *Yale Edition of Horace Walpole's Memoirs,* edited by John Brooke.

7. After his death his letters would be published in four major editions: *The Letters of Horace Walpole, Earl of Orford,* ed. John Wright (London, 1840), 6 vols., 8vo; *Letters,* ed. Peter Cunningham (London, 1857), 9 vols., 8vo; *Letters,* ed. Mrs. Paget Toynbee (Oxford, 1903–5), 16 vols., 8vo (with three supplementary volumes edited by Paget Toynbee, 1918–25); and *The Yale Edition of Horace Walpole's Correspondence,* ed. W. S. Lewis (New Haven, 1937–).

8. He had his first attack in 1755 at the age of thirty-eight (see *YWE,* XXXV, 259).

form his letters legibly. Occasionally the struggle has been too much for him, and he either blotches his words beyond recognition or his crippled hand goes completely haywire, leaving an unreadable scrawl on the page. Walpole's growing weakness in these last years of his life is evident in the decreasing number of entries he makes. Those for the abbreviated year 1786 fill some twenty manuscript pages, while those for the whole of 1795 fill less than three. After 1795, although he wrote isolated notes elsewhere,[9] Walpole made no further attempt to write in the *Miscellany;* he may have felt that his final entry there, on the Gothic church of Batalha in Portugal, was a particularly fitting item with which to conclude.

Though he became almost totally infirm in body, there is ample contemporary testimony to the fact that Walpole remained mentally alert until the very end. Joseph Farington, while noting Walpole's physical frailty in his diary for 13 July 1793, marks his nonetheless being "lively and attentive in mind."[10] Edmond Malone's record of his final conversation with Walpole just two months before his death reveals no lessening of Walpole's mental powers.[11] If such testimony did not exist, there would be in any case the evidence of Walpole's own writings; his last letters are as witty, charming, and spontaneous as any he wrote.[12] The *Miscellany* itself shows in a graphic manner the continued wide range of his interests and the continuing agility and inventiveness of his mind during these final years of his life.

That the *Miscellany* was regarded as special by Walpole is evident in the handsome red morocco binding with clasps and the gilt edging he gave it, as well as in the epigraph from Cibber which he prefixed to it: "Such remaining Scraps—as may not perhaps be worth the Reader's notice: but if they

9. See, for instance, the verses dated 1796 in his "Book of Visitors at Strawberry Hill," ibid., XII, 271.

10. Cited ibid., XV, 316.

11. The conversation is recorded in Sir James Prior, *The Life of Edmond Malone* (London, 1860), pp. 229–31.

12. See, for instance, one of his very last letters, to Lady Ossory, 15 Jan. 1797 (*YWE*, XXXIV, 230–31).

are such as tempt me to write them, why may not I hope that in this wide World there may be many an idle Soul no wiser than myself, who may be equally tempted to read them?" Aware that the *Miscellany* contained much that would seem trivial to later generations, Walpole nevertheless hoped that it would not be completely neglected. In keeping with the attractive exterior of the *Miscellany,* Walpole made a special effort to keep the interior neat. Unlike his two earlier notebooks or "Books of Materials," as he called them (covering the years 1759 through 1785), the *Miscellany* has no pages disfigured by lengthy cross-outs or pasted-in newspaper cuttings. (Cuttings for the period are pasted instead into the back of the "Book of Materials" for 1771–85.) The diminutive size itself of the *Miscellany* (small octavo as opposed to quarto for the earlier volumes) supports the notion that it was not regarded by Walpole as just another notebook, but rather that he intended it from the outset as a last memento to the posterity of which he was so conscious.[13]

Except for extracts (indicated in the notes to this edition), the *Miscellany* has not been previously published. The volume measures $6\frac{3}{4} \times 4\frac{1}{2}$ inches, and contains 103 leaves of good quality paper, the last 56 of which are blank (excluding some pencil memoranda on the verso of the last leaf; see Appendix A). The first leaf has Walpole's signature and the date "1786" in large characters on the verso, while facing these on the recto of the second leaf is the title "Miscellany" in large letters with Walpole's seal as Lord Orford affixed above and the epigraph from Cibber written below (see the frontispiece). The seal is the first of two that Walpole had designed after succeeding to the earldom of Orford in December 1791; bearing the Walpole family arms and the words, "Sigillum Horatii Comitis de Orford," it was designed in 1792 and probably added to the *Miscellany* in the same year.[14] The text proper of the *Miscellany* fills both sides

13. For references to posterity in Walpole see his *Memoirs of the Reign of King George the Second,* 2d ed., ed. Lord Holland (London, 1847), I, 237, and *YWE,* X, 95, 197; XXII, 303; XXVIII, 292; XXIX, 207, et passim.

14. See Allen T. Hazen, *A Catalogue of Horace Walpole's Library* (New Haven, 1969), I, p. xxv and facing illustration.

of 44 leaves, and the recto of a 45th. The red morocco binding is overly tight, which has resulted over the years in several sprung signatures; the tightness of the binding must
have made it especially difficult for Walpole to hold the
volume open with one gouty hand while making his entries
with the other. In addition to the smaller ink blotches mentioned above there are several large stains both inside and
on the edges; these were evidently made when Walpole's
shaky hand caused him to spill ink from the bottle. The
writing is almost entirely in ink, though there remain some
faint pencil notations which Walpole neglected to erase; some
of these have been copied over in ink, while others were apparently fragments of poems or the germs of ideas which he
did not bother to develop (for instance, see the lines from
Virgil, below, p. 10). Besides these notations there are other
assorted pencil markings, such as brackets in the margins, the
significance of which is no longer apparent, and arabesques
in ink which Walpole used as added punctuation at the ends
of items. (These ambiguous pencil markings and arabesques
are omitted in the present text.)

Upon Walpole's death the *Miscellany,* along with the other
books of materials, passed to his residuary legatee and executrix Anne Seymour Damer, a sculptress famous in her day,
who was the only daughter of Walpole's cousin and lifelong
friend, Field Marshal Henry Seymour Conway. Upon Mrs.
Damer's death in 1828 the *Miscellany* and other books passed
in turn to her friend Sir Wathen Waller, first Baronet, in
whose family they remained until December 1921, when they
were sold in the first Waller Sale at Sotheby's to the dealer
Maggs. Maggs sold them in turn to H. C. Folger, the Shakespeare collector, who was mainly interested in the Shakespearian references in them. They remained in the Folger
Shakespeare Library in Washington, D.C. until 1950, when
W. S. Lewis acquired them by exchange and brought them
to his library at Farmington, Connecticut (the Lewis Walpole
Library), where they are now in the section reserved for
books from Walpole's own library.

The *Miscellany* is a microcosm of Walpole's life and

thought. In its pages he appears for a last time in most of
the familiar roles with which posterity has come to associate
him: we see him here as antiquarian, minor poet, raconteur,
literary critic and historian, political observer, and connoisseur of the arts. Even his career as a letter writer is represented briefly by his fragment of a letter to Lady Craven
(p. 6). We see him also in the less familiar but equally
characteristic roles of moralist and philosopher: as will be
noted, his political observations in the *Miscellany* as elsewhere have a decidedly moralistic tinge, while scattered
throughout the volume are moral and philosophical observations in the vein of his "Detached Thoughts," first published
in the posthumous *Works*.[15] The *Miscellany* reveals Walpole
primarily as the Augustan man of sense, emphasizing man's
social role and responsibilities while advocating the Horatian
ideal of reason and restraint in human relations;[16] but it also
shows his penchant for the romantic, particularly in the numerous antiquarian jottings that reflect his interest in the
pageantry and customs of past ages. In addition, the *Miscellany* displays that curious mixture of elegance and ob-
scenity so characteristic of the eighteenth century; for instance, Walpole's delicate and whimsical mock elegy on the
death of a piping bullfinch (p. 26) is followed shortly by his
transcription of an off-color bon mot by George Selwyn on
the alleged impotence of Sir William Duncan, physician to
George III (p. 26).[17]

In all of Walpole's writings on poets and poetry his assumption is that the poet properly performs a social func-
tion and that "sense," "good sense," or "common sense"
should be both his guide and his goal: as a man of culture
addressing other men of culture, the poet is expected to ex-

15. *The Works of Horatio Walpole, Earl of Orford* (London, 1798), 5 vols.,
royal 4to. The *Works* were nominally edited by Robert Berry but actually
edited by his daughter, Mary Berry (for whom see below, p. 79, n. 6). "Detached Thoughts" are in Vol. IV, pp. 368–72.

16. Walpole called Horace "my namesake" and "my godfather" (see *YWE*,
XIII, 87; XXXII, 172).

17. Walpole himself was capable on at least one occasion of writing gross
pornography: see his verses, "Little Peggy," printed ibid., XXX, 307–10.

press timeless, self-evident truths in an original but readily
intelligible manner. Walpole's emphasis on sense in poetry
is so strong that in the *Miscellany* he actually defines poetry
as "a beautifull way of spoiling prose, & the laborious art of
exchanging plain sense for harmony" (p. 20).[18] The only
poet in his view to have achieved a perfect union of sense
and harmony seems to have been Pope, who "without neglecting Poetry, introduced good Sense into Verse" (p. 91); his
predecessor Dryden, though "great Master of th'harmonious
art / Coud charm our ear, but seldom touch'd our heart"
(p. 138). Later poets seem content to arrange "poetic phrases
without a plan & almost without a Subject" (p. 91).[19]
Walpole's discontent with the current literary scene is not
limited to the poets; he has no patience with "Pedants" who
"make a great rout about Criticism, as if it were a Science of
great Depth, & required much pains & knowledge," and believes that in theory at least, every cultivated person has the
qualifications to be a critic, since criticism "is only the result
of good Sense, Taste & Judgment" (p. 64).[20]

For Walpole, as for most of his contemporaries, the great
poet of Nature (and therefore the greatest of poets) was
Shakespeare.[21] Actually, it is Shakespeare's dramatic rather
than his poetic art which most commanded Walpole's re-

18. For an exhaustive treatment of Walpole's literary opinions, see Jeanne
Welcher, "The Literary Opinions of Horace Walpole," Diss. Fordham 1955.

19. Walpole elsewhere calls Dryden "the greatest master of the powers of
language" (*Catalogue of the Royal and Noble Authors, Works,* I, 518), while
Pope is the model of "purity and taste" (Walpole to John Pinkerton, 6 Oct.
1789, *YWE,* XVI, 257). His complaint about modern poets dates at least as
far back as 1745 (see his letter to Sir Horace Mann, 29 March 1745 OS, ibid.,
XIX, 27); among the few later poets to meet with his approval was his friend
Thomas Gray (see below, p. 93, n. 9). In the *Miscellany* he also alludes
favorably to the satiric poet Charles Churchill (p. 97) and to Thomas Chatterton (p. 23).

20. In his "Book of Materials," 1759–70, pp. 104–05, Walpole calls taste
"extempore judgment" and "the flower of judgment" and cites Antoine
Houdart de la Motte's definition of taste (in his *Œuvres,* Paris, 1754, VIII,
355) as that sort of judgment which "par des raisonnements soudains" em-
braces "d'une seule vue les défauts & les beautés des choses."

21. See David Nichol Smith, *Shakespeare in the Eighteenth Century* (Oxford, 1928); also, Augustus Ralli, *A History of Shakespearian Criticism* (1932;
rpt. New York, 1959), I, 12–107.

spect. Walpole has reservations about the more metaphorical passages in Shakespeare's plays; he feels that the Bard is most effective when using simple language, the language of the heart.[22] In the *Miscellany* (pp. 44–45) he refers to the "marvellous powers of [Shakespeare's] Genius in drawing & discriminating Characters." Although he admires Voltaire and Racine, "how inadequate woud [they] appear to their Office, were the Characters in their Tragedies to be scrutinized & compared like those of Macbeth & Richard [III]!"

In another passage he is especially hard on French authors for their fear "of offending Delicacy & rules" (pp. 57–58). At the end of that passage he turns significantly to the figure of Falstaff in support of the argument that Shakespeare, had he chosen, could have given us "beautifull delineations" of "absolute Savages" in a "State of Nature": "He who invented such a Compound as Falstaffe, & coud make every feature of such a fictitious character perfectly natural, coud not have failed in painting simple Natures."[23] This observation points up the fact that Walpole regarded comedy, not tragedy, as "the chef-[d']oeuvre of human genius."[24] Tragedy he objected to on the grounds that "it is an unnatural elevation of nature. Its sentiments are exaggerated,"[25] and so in the end it is the richly developed but relatively earthbound comic figure of Falstaff, rather than Shakespeare's superhuman tragic heroes, that most excites his admiration.[26] Walpole

22. For instance, he wrote to the playwright Robert Jephson (8 Nov. 1777): "I believe the most figurative passages in Shakespeare are not the most admired. . . . Indubitably Shakespeare is never so superior to all mankind as when he is most simple and natural" (Toynbee, X, 155).

23. By "compound" Walpole seems to mean made up of several passions, precisely balanced, rather than just one "ruling passion," while "fictitious" means artificial. Falstaff's contending passions are his "wit" and his "humour"; he is a being "of artificial habitude," not an entity "that would exist in a state of nature," but is rendered "natural" (that is, credible) by Shakespeare's genius. See below, and Walpole's "Thoughts on Comedy," *Works*, II, 318–20.

24. Walpole to Robert Jephson, 24 Feb. 1775 (Toynbee, *Supplement*, I, 247).

25. Walpole to Jephson, 8 Nov. 1777 (Toynbee, X, 156).

26. Walpole wrote to Lady Ossory, 3 Dec. 1776: "I believe firmly that fifty *Iliads* and *Æneids* could be written sooner than such a character as Falstaffe's" (*YWE*, XXXII, 334). After Falstaff Walpole considered Addison's Sir Roger de

was less interested in human nature as it manifests itself in
extreme situations than in its more mundane operations
within the framework and limitations imposed by society;
less concerned with the naked passions of tyrants or savages,
who act outside the constraints of civilized law, than with
the complicated evasions and artifices of the "man of society." In other words, the norm of nature for Walpole was
human nature as he saw it operating about him in the circle
of eighteenth-century London society. Since the aim of art
for him was the just imitation of nature, the highest art was
that of the comic writer, who sought to capture faithfully
the shades of character arising within that society, or in
similar societies past or present.

Although Walpole looked for sense in the best poetry and
aimed for it in his own more serious efforts, he also had
"a partiality for professed nonsense"[27] and in his lighter mo-
ments turned out a good deal of ephemeral verse of a whimsical and humorous nature. (Indeed, not being a Pope he was
much better at this latter kind and knew it.) An example of
his "nonsense" verse in the *Miscellany* is his "Ode" on p. 19
("Love sits enthron'd in Clara's eyes") while perhaps his best
lines there are found in his epitaph on a piping bullfinch
mentioned above. Also noteworthy, though uneven, are his
lines "On the portraits of Henry 8th & his Queens" (pp. 27–
28). Walpole's verses in the *Miscellany* and elsewhere reveal
that at times he could be a successful minor poet, in the
charming vein of a Campion or Herrick.[28]

Walpole's interest in literary sources and in literary history
is well represented in the *Miscellany*. With regard to sources,
he suggests that the name of Ben Jonson's character, Captain
Bobadill, in *Every Man in His Humour*, was derived from

Coverley to be "the best drawn character" in literature ("Book of Materials,"
1771–85, p. 6; see also below, p. 151, n. 1).

27. Walpole to Lady Ossory, 4 July 1785 (*YWE*, XXXIII, 476).

28. See F. L. Lucas, *The Art of Living* (London, 1959), p. 93. Most of Walpole's light and serious verse is gathered in *Horace Walpole's Fugitive Verses*,
ed. W. S. Lewis (New York, 1931). For an extended study of his poetry, see
Paul Yvon, *Horace Walpole as a Poet* (Paris, 1924).

the name of a Spanish soldier in a treatise on warfare, a translation of which was published at London the year before Jonson's play was first performed (in 1598) (p. 7); that a passage in Froissart was the source of the Roan Barbary passage in Shakespeare's *Richard II* (pp. 11–12); that the informing idea in Matthew Prior's poem "Alma" was taken from Montaigne's essay "De l'Yvrognerie" (pp. 51–52); and that the plot of Molière's *Mariage forcé* was suggested by an episode in the life of Philibert, Comte de Gramont (p. 113). The first and third suggestions seem to be original with Walpole; the latter is canonical today in Prior criticism, although William Jackson, and not Walpole, is credited with the discovery. (Jackson's suggestion does not appear until 1798, in his *Four Ages*.) With respect to literary history, Walpole notes with surprise that "Plays & Mysteries" were performed at Newcastle as late as the middle of the sixteenth century (p. 107), and he lists an additional fifteen authors not mentioned in his *Catalogue of the Royal and Noble Authors*.[29] His listing of these authors (all noble) suggests that he may have been considering bringing out a revised and updated edition of his *Catalogue*. With one exception (Lady Conway) the authors are all contemporary; among the works cited are several items apparently otherwise unrecorded, namely, Priscilla, Lady Willoughby's manuscript verses (including "several pretty Stanzas to Lord Mansfield on his birthday. 1788") (p. 100), and a volume of poems by the Marquess of Salisbury which the Marquess had privately printed in 1792 (p. 142). For the most part the works themselves seem to have been of slight interest to Walpole; he apparently owned copies of only five of them, and of these one was a presentation copy from the author (Lord Carlisle's *Verses to Sir Joshua Reynolds*), one

29. These additional authors are Earl Stanhope (pp. 84, 115, 138); Viscount Dudley and Ward (p. 92); Baroness Willoughby (p. 100); the Dowager Countess of Carlisle (p. 109); Baron Petre (p. 117); the Earl of Carlisle (p. 118); the Earl of Charlemont (p. 129); Baron Muncaster (p. 130); the Marquess of Salisbury (pp. 131, 142–43); Viscount Mountmorres (p. 137); Baron Sempill (p. 141); the Earl of Abingdon (p. 144); the Earl of Dundonald (p. 153); Viscountess Conway (p. 154); and Baron Auckland (p. 154).

was the work of a friend (the Dowager Countess Carlisle's *Thoughts in the Form of Maxims*) and two (Stanhope's *Letter to Edmund Burke* and Petre's *Letter to Doctor Horsley*) were political pamphlets which he dutifully added to his extensive collection of tracts of the reign of George III.[30] The remaining item, Mountmorres's *History of the Principal Transactions of the Irish Parliament, from the Year 1634 to 1666*, was undoubtedly of genuine interest to Walpole because of its historical and antiquarian contents.

Mention should be made of the numerous bons mots, anecdotes, charades, and conundrums, some of them in verse, which occur throughout the *Miscellany*. These jeux d'esprit show Walpole the raconteur, the witty man of fashion sure to be entertaining in company, and reflect the great emphasis placed on wit in eighteenth-century upper-class circles, where a cardinal sin was to be dull or solemn.[31] Besides Walpole's own witticisms (such as his pun, made to Hannah More, about the Bishop of London's being "Sugar-candied," p. 73), there are bons mots uttered by the famous wits George Selwyn and James Hare (pp. 26, 48, 87, et passim), a charade in French made by the historian Edward Gibbon (p. 139), and a host of clever sayings by a wide range of individuals, male and female, which tempt one to paraphrase Pope and characterize the upper-class inhabitants of the eighteenth century as "the mob of gentlefolk who quipped with ease."

Walpole's attitude towards art is epitomized in the *Miscellany* by his suggestion of a subject for the picture (now in the Hermitage Museum, Leningrad) which Catherine the Great commissioned Sir Joshua Reynolds to paint for her

30. These tracts and his parallel collections of plays and poems were part of Walpole's effort to be the chronicler of his age. The tracts and a majority of the plays are now in the Lewis Walpole Library, while the poems are at Harvard.

31. In his "Book of Materials," 1759–70, p. 105, Walpole defines wit as "the flower of sense," and in the *Miscellany*, p. 20, he describes the genius of wit as an acquired talent: "A man of sense, tho born without wit, often lives to have wit. His memory treasures up ideas & reflexions; he compares them with new occurrencies, & strikes out new lights from the Collision. The consequence is sometimes bon mots, & sometimes apothegms."

in 1785 (pp. 17–18). Walpole objected to Reynolds's choice of "the Infant Hercules strangling the Serpents from Pindar's description," and vainly suggested to him that he portray instead the subject of Peter the Great addressing himself to work as a shipwright in the dockyard at Deptford. Walpole's discussion of the reasons for his choice reveals both his criteria for art and the continuing fertility of his imagination. First of all he feels that Sir Joshua "ought to have chosen a Subject that either related to Russian or English History." Walpole's subject

> woud have embraced both Countries & complimented Both. . . . What a fine Contrast might have been drawn, as Peter threw off the imperial Mantle, & prepared to put on Trowzers, between the sullen Indignation of his Russian Attendants, & the joy of the English Tars at seeing Majesty adopt their garb! Peter learning Navigation here in order to give a Navy to his own Country—how flattering to both Nations! how superior to the passions of a Nursery & the common expressions of affrighted parents! . . . the pencil that can only represent Nature, can give no Novelty to such an Occurrence. The parents woud feel the same emotions if two large rats had got into a Cradle. Their being serpents does not exalt the accident.

Elsewhere Walpole exclaims, in criticizing allegorical figures in art: "How much more genius is there in expressing the passions of the soul in the lineaments of the countenance!"[32] These and other examples indicate that, in art as in literature, Walpole looked primarily for verisimilitude in the depiction of human nature; in portraits and history paintings and drawings, he was interested mainly in the psychological, dramatic, and narrative content, and only secondarily in matters of composition and technique. Again, Walpole's discussion

---

32. *Anecdotes of Painting, Works,* III, 48. In the *Miscellany* Walpole, discussing a painting at Broome Park attributed to Pordenone, praises the expressions of the Pharisees in it as "very natural, of the Virgin, not so well" (p. 14).

shows his distaste for the "naked passions"; as an appropriate
subject for a work of art the "common expressions of affrighted parents" are eschewed for the more complex, "social"
emotions of the English tars and Russian attendants.[33]

In landscape painting Walpole characteristically looked for
the "picturesque," or irregular and rugged beauty, as opposed
to formal regularity of composition. He also sought the
picturesque in the natural world, for instance in the settings
of country seats. In the *Miscellany* he remarks approvingly
of "Broome a Seat of Sr Henry Oxenden in Kent" that "it
stands well at the head of a descending Val" (p. 13), and observes that the situation of "Chilham Castle, seat of Mr
Heron" is "high & fine" (p. 15). With regard to the latter
seat, however, he observes significantly that its situation "has
not been assisted by modern Art." The picturesque for Walpole of course did not mean a surrender to the anarchy of
nature, but rather a compromise between natural wildness
and the tendency of the human mind to impose a pattern on
its environment. Such a compromise is at the heart of the
concept of landscape gardening expressed in Walpole's *Essay
on Modern Gardening.*[34] While rejecting geometric formalism
in favor of a more natural style, Walpole does not mean to
imply there that anything more than a *simulation* of nature
is desired: the element of artifice and calculation, designed to
heighten and surprise, is never supposed to be totally absent.

Walpole's great contribution to the history of art is his
Anecdotes of Painting in England, which he skilfully edited
from a morass of manuscript materials left by the antiquary

33. As he objected to depictions of the more common or primitive emotions, so Walpole objected to representations of the coarser aspects of man's
physical nature: for instance, the Flemish school of painters he dismisses as
"those drudging mimics of nature's most uncomely coarsenesses" (*Ædes Wal-
polianæ, Works,* II, 226). In painting Walpole preferred above all the com-
bination of psychological penetration and ethereal beauty found in the works
of Raphael (see ibid., II, 236).

34. For a thorough study of the *Essay* and its influence on English landscape architecture, see Isabel Chase, *Horace Walpole: Gardenist* (Princeton,
1943).

George Vertue.[35] "Anecdotes" in the title means "unpublished . . . details of history";[36] as Walpole himself described it to the painter Hogarth,[37] the work is essentially an "antiquarian history" in which are amassed a host of details about painters in England from the earliest times through the reign of George II. Walpole's motive in compiling the work was largely patriotic: without setting up English painters as rivals of the continental masters, he wished to demonstrate that nonetheless there were figures among them worthy of regard.[38] While the work is valuable mainly for the facts it gives, it also contains perceptive comments by Walpole which render it more than just an antiquarian catalogue.

In the *Miscellany* Walpole corrects one item in the *Anecdotes* regarding the authoress of a life of Van Dyck (p. 121), and he cites a work supporting his argument there that oil painting was invented long before the Van Eyck brothers (p. 138). He also records death notices and other accounts of contemporary painters, draftsmen, and engravers (including Sir Joshua Reynolds, who died in 1792),[39] as well as noting items he has come across on artists of past ages;[40] three artists in this latter group (the limner Mark Bilford and the painters Melchior Salaboss and "Poutie of Harley Castle") are apparently unknown to history except for the brief mentions of them in the antiquarian works which Walpole cites. In addition to painters, draftsmen, and engravers, Walpole enters items on the contemporary architects James Paine, Francis

35. See Lawrence Lipking's study of the *Anecdotes* in his *Ordering of the Arts in Eighteenth-Century England* (Princeton, 1970), pp. 127–63.

36. *Oxford English Dictionary*, s.v. Anecdote 1.

37. See *YWE*, IX, 366.

38. In the preface he notes: "This country, which does not always err in vaunting its own productions, has not a single volume to show on the works of its painters" (*Works*, III, 3).

39. The other artists are Tilly Kettle (p. 43); Alexander Cozens (p. 47); Giovanni Cipriani (p. 47); John Astley (p. 62); Jeremiah Meyer (pp. 92, 116); Richard Dalton (pp. 97[?], 125, 157); Francesco Zuccarelli (p. 100); François-Germain Aliamet (p. 115); John Brown (p. 116); John Keyse Sherwin (p. 122); Richard Paton (p. 124); Jacob C. Schnebbelie (p. 129); and William Peckitt (p. 154).

40. Henry Winstanley (p. 114); Mark Bilford (p. 120); Daniel Fournier, Jean-Baptiste-Claude Chatelain, N. Tull, Thomas Worlidge, Wenceslaus

Hiorne, and Robert Adam, the sculptor Thomas Banks, the bridge builder William Edwards, and, from the past, the carvers and statuaries John and Mathias Christmas and the tapestry manufacturer Sir Francis Crane (pp. 109, 121, 130, 140–41). None of this material was included in the edition of the *Anecdotes* in the posthumous *Works,* but in 1937 Frederick W. Hilles and Philip B. Daghlian brought out a supplementary volume to the *Anecdotes,* "Volume the Fifth and Last," covering the period 1760 through 1795 and compiled from Walpole's materials on that period in the *Miscellany* and the two earlier "Books of Materials."[41]

The lighthearted manner which Walpole affected in society and the gentlemanly pose of nonchalance he usually maintains in his writings have tended to obscure the fact that he was an acute and thoughtful man. Not a profound thinker, as he himself was the first to admit,[42] he nonetheless had an agile and inquisitive mind which could not accept facile answers to the fundamental problems of existence. The *Miscellany* reveals this serious side of his nature in the moral and philosophical observations running through it, as well as in the decidedly moralistic turn of his political and historical observations.

As for religion Walpole was early in life weaned from the Church of England, in which he had been raised, by the deistical teachings of his chief mentor at Cambridge, the controversial divine Dr. Conyers Middleton. From Middleton Walpole learned a rationalistic approach to religious ques-

Hollar, Augustin Heckel, Francis Perry, John Smith, Hans Holbein the elder, Hans Holbein the younger, Sigmund Holbein, and Christoph Amberger (pp. 137–38); Melchior Salaboss (p. 139); Willem Wissing (p. 141); and ——— Poutie (p. 148).

41. *Anecdotes of Painting in England; [1760–1795] with Some Account of the Principal Artists; and Incidental Notes on Other Arts . . . Volume the Fifth and Last,* ed. Frederick W. Hilles and Philip B. Daghlian (New Haven, 1937). The items in the *Miscellany* previously printed by Hilles and Daghlian are so indicated in the footnotes.

42. For instance, modestly exaggerating the shortcomings of his intellect, he wrote to John Pinkerton (19 Aug. 1789): "I hold my own [understanding] to be of a very inferior kind, and know it to be incapable of sound, deep application . . . " (*YWE,* XVI, 308).

tions which ultimately led him to doubt whether we can know anything about God except the testimony to his existence to be found in the design of his creation.[43] Walpole's rationalism led him to reject the claims of both revelation and inspiration;[44] however, it also told him that the atheism of certain rationalists (such as some of the more "arrogant" of the French philosophes, whom he despised)[45] was itself "unnatural and irrational" since it refused to concede that the order of the natural world implied a creator.[46] Walpole's religious stance reveals him to have not so much a rationalist as an empiricist; in all matters religious or otherwise the final authority for Walpole was the evidence of his senses, the concrete particulars of everyday experience.[47]

Walpole once remarked to his friend John Pinkerton: "I go to church sometimes, in order to induce my servants to go to church. I am no hypocrite. I do not go in order to persuade them to believe what I do not believe myself. A good moral sermon may instruct and benefit them. I only set them an example of listening, not of believing."[48] Although he rejected the supernatural doctrines of Christianity, Walpole accepted the Christian ethic. He felt strongly the need for an explicit moral code to counter man's brutal and tyrannical propensities; without such a code civilization would quickly relapse into a savage Hobbesian state of nature. Walpole's

43. See, for instance, Walpole's letters to William Cole, 12 July 1778 and 7 Aug. 1781, and to William Mason, 8 Nov. 1783 (ibid., II, 99–100, 283; XXIX, 315–16); also John Pinkerton, *Walpoliana* (London, 1799), I, 76.

44. See *Miscellany*, pp. 23, 64, 70–71, 125.

45. For example, in his letter to Sir Horace Mann, 7 July 1779, he calls them "arrogant, dictatorial coxcombs" (*YWE*, XXIV, 498).

46. Pinkerton, *Walpoliana*, I, 75–76.

47. In *Anecdotes of Painting* Walpole expresses his contempt for all "fables, researches, conjectures, hypotheses, disputes, blunders and dissertations, that library of human impertinence" (*Works*, III, 92); the discoveries of the natural philosophers, however, he regarded with the highest respect (see *YWE*, XXIV, 498; XXXIII, 128; below, p. 55, n. 8). On the other hand, it should be noted that Walpole himself was not given to careful generalizing from the particular, as the natural philosophers were; rather, he tended to look for truth as an immediate intuition through the portals of the senses.

48. Pinkerton, *Walpoliana*, I, 76.

writings are full of diatribes against the tyrants and conquerors
of history who have spilled oceans of blood in order to further
their own ambitions. In the *Miscellany* he shows his low opinion of the understandings of the shifty and dishonest: "Cunning is neither the consequence of Sense, nor does it give
Sense . . . "; "Art is the filigraine of a little mind, & is
twisted, and involved & curled, but woud reach farther if
laid out in a strait line" (pp. 23, 38).

Walpole's reading of the political scene and of history is
essentially moralistic in its tenor. With an Augustan penchant
for antithesis that manifests itself time and again in his style,
he tends to divide the world into two camps. On the one side
are ranged the righteous heroes and "apostles of humanity,"[49]
such as John Cockburn, valiantly defending Hume Castle
against the forces of Oliver Cromwell (*Miscellany*, p. 120), or
Henry IV of France, who sheathed his sword as soon as a
just peace was won (p. 106 and n. 4). On the other side are
the villains and destroyers: Catherine "Slayczar" (p. 142 and
n. 7); Warren Hastings, who plundered India (p. 51 et passim); the "monster" Philip II of Spain and the obsequious
French minister to his Court, the Comte de Cheverny
(pp. 105–06); and so on.[50] Chief among Walpole's heroes is
his father, Sir Robert Walpole, the great Whig statesman and
first prime minister. One of the longest items in the *Miscellany*, occupying two full manuscript pages (pp. 66–68) in the
present text), is devoted to an account of a "singular Adventure" that befell Sir Robert after his retirement; the burden
of this account is to assert and demonstrate Sir Robert's
"goodness, good nature & great sense." W. S. Lewis has plau-
sibly portrayed Walpole, the youngest son of estranged par-

49. Walpole uses this phrase in his letter to Michael Lort, 5 July 1789
(*YWE*, XVI, 217).

50. A striking example of Walpole's antithetical thinking is his juxtaposi-
tion, in one of his portfolios of English portraits, of prints of the virtuous
Lord Chief Justice Hale and the villainous Chancellor Jeffreys, with the motto
beneath, "Quantum vertice in auras atherias [sic]—tantum radice in Tartara
tendit" (freely translated, "as one reaches to heaven, so the other plunges to
hell") (*Miscellany*, p. 82).

ents, as a "mama's boy" who, removed from his father, was brought up and spoiled by his mother.[51] The intimacy with his father did not begin until Walpole returned from the Grand Tour in 1741 and as a member of Parliament threw himself into the last months of Sir Robert's administration. Thus Walpole knew his father not as the all-powerful political manipulator but as a man who after twenty years of faithful service had been toppled by his enemies; his long-suppressed feelings of filial devotion, at last given an outlet, were intensified by his instinctive sympathy for the underdog. After his father's death Walpole was unswerving in his devotion to his memory; conversely he was relentless in his antipathy to Sir Robert's enemies, whom he attacks repeatedly in his letters and memoirs.[52]

A chief villain in the *Miscellany* is Walpole's own king, George III. According to Walpole's version of the "Whig myth of history" George, initially urged on by his mother the Princess of Wales and her alleged lover Lord Bute, attempted throughout his reign to effect unlawful extensions of the royal prerogative in a frontal assault on the individual liberties of his subjects.[53] Walpole, on the other hand, as a "True Blue Whig"[54] believed in the supremacy of the English constitution as established by the Glorious Revolution of 1688. He was vehemently opposed to the extremes of absolute monarchy and democracy (that is, government "by the Mob") (see *Miscellany*, pp. 63–64). Of the types of government between these extremes, after constitutional monarchy[55] he

51. W. S. Lewis, *Horace Walpole* (New York, 1961), pp. 11 ff.

52. Walpole's chief targets are the Duke of Newcastle, the Earl of Hardwicke, and William Pulteney. In the *Miscellany* he repeats a story in which Pulteney is accused of trying to cheat the Duchess of Buckingham out of her estate and charges Newcastle and Hardwicke with being the authors of the Seven Years' War (pp. 20–21, 89).

53. See below, p. 80, n. 7. The pioneering work on the Whig myth is Herbert Butterfield, *The Whig Interpretation of History* (London, 1931).

54. See Archibald S. Foord, "'The Only Unadulterated Whig,'" in *Horace Walpole: Writer, Politician, and Connoisseur*, ed. W. H. Smith (New Haven, 1967), pp. 25–43.

55. In *Mem. Geo. II*, I, 376–77, Walpole wrote: "My reflections led me early towards, I cannot quite say republicanism, but to most limited monarchy.

probably sympathized most with the American brand of republicanism, where the passions of the mob were held in
check by such wise and virtuous leaders as George Washington.[56] By contrast French republicanism, as it took shape
during the Revolution, aroused Walpole's horror and loathing; his last years were darkened by the bloody events of the
French Revolution which seemed to him, as it did to so many
of his fellow Englishmen, to be threatening the very foundations of Western civilization.[57]

But even in the dark days of the Revolution and its after-
math, the Revolutionary Wars, Walpole had available as always a ready-made escape from the dismal realities of the
present: his antiquarian studies.[58] The second-to-last item in
the *Miscellany* is Walpole's notation of Lord Auckland's
pamphlet, *Some Remarks on the Apparent Circumstances of
the War in the Fourth Week of October 1795* (p. 154); the
last item (as noted above) is his query about the fourteenth-
century architect of the Gothic church of Batalha in Portugal
(p. 155). In 1766 Walpole wrote to his friend George
Montagu: "Visions, you know, have always been my pasture;
and so far from growing old enough to quarrel with their emp-
tiness, I almost think there is no wisdom comparable to that
of exchanging what is called the realities of life for dreams.
Old castles, old pictures, old histories, and the babble of old
people make one live back into centuries, that cannot disap-
point one. One holds fast and surely what is past. The dead
have exhausted their power of deceiving—one can trust

. . . . a quiet republican, who does not dislike to see the shadow of monarchy, like Banquo's ghost, fill the empty chair of state, that the ambitious,
the murderer, the tyrant, may not aspire to it; in short, who approves the
name of a king, when it excludes the essence: a man of such principles, I
hope, may be a good man and an honest. . . . "

56. Walpole calls Washington a "great" man in his letter to Henry Seymour
Conway, 7 July 1790 (*YWE*, XXXIX, 478). For Walpole's sympathy with the
American Revolution, see below, p. 50, n. 8.

57. See below, p. 115, n. 1, et passim.

58. See W. S. Lewis, "Horace Walpole, Antiquary," in *Essays Presented to
Sir Lewis Namier*, ed. R. Pares and A. J. P. Taylor (London, 1956), pp. 178–
203.

Catherine of Medicis now."[59] Not content with merely reading about and observing the past, Walpole attempted to make
it live again in his own writings: his *Catalogue of the Royal
and Noble Authors, Anecdotes of Painting,* and *Historic
Doubts on Richard III* are all attempts to preserve or recreate
past ages, while his most important imaginative efforts, *The
Castle of Otranto* and *The Mysterious Mother,* are set repec-
tively at the time of the Crusades and in the early days of the
Reformation. Walpole's consuming interest in the Gothic,
which found its most striking expression in Strawberry Hill,
can be seen as an attempt by him to escape from the restraint
to which his reason and common sense committed him. Without surrendering to Gothic passion and excess in his own life,
he could experience them vicariously in the crimes, follies,
and romances of historical figures (such as Catherine de
Medici or, in the *Miscellany,* pp. 40–41, Charles Louis Elector Palatine and Mademoiselle Degenfeld) or indulge them
artistically in the irregular accretions of his neo-Gothic house
or in the turbulent lives of the characters in his fictitious
works.[60]

Whatever his temperamental turn towards the Gothic past,
though, Walpole was never under any illusion that the past
was a better time in which to live; in his antiquarian researches he would be met everywhere by instances of bigotry,

59. Walpole to George Montagu, 5 Jan. 1766 (*YWE*, X, 192). The importance of particulars and minutiae to Walpole as a key to understanding per-
sonalities and the spirit of past ages is highlighted in the *Miscellany* by his
extensive extracts from Henry VII's books of payments (pp. 133–36), followed
by the comment: "This little abstract is a tolerable picture both of Henry &
the times; of his Avarice & of the general dearth of elegant amusements [etc.]"
(p. 136). Walpole also looked for accuracy of detail in old paintings; for instance, in the *Miscellany* he notes at Chilham Castle a "piece of two Ladies
in the exact dress & undress of the reign of George 1st" (p. 16).

60. Walpole's greatest departure from the norms of reason and restraint is
to be found in his "Hieroglyphic Tales" (*Works,* IV, 319–52), which he describes as "writings in which the imagination is fettered by no rules" (p. 352).
"Mere whimsical trifles," they contain such surrealistic elements as a princess
who speaks perfect French but was never born, and a prince "who would
have been the most accomplished hero of the age, if he had not been dead"
(p. 331).

superstition, and cruelty that would make him thankful to be alive in the relatively enlightened eighteenth century.[61] Even Shakespeare was tainted for him by the barbarism of his age: "Shakespeare had no Tutors but Nature and Genius. he caught his faults from the bad taste of his Contemporaries. In an age still less civilized Shakespeare might have been wilder, but woud not have been vulgar" (*Miscellany*, p. 57). In his emphasis on "civilization" Walpole shows again his essentially Augustan orientation, his fundamental belief in a society founded on principles of restraint, order, and harmony (and in the supremacy of an art reflecting those values). In the end it is dedication to this ideal, suffused by a strong spirit of humanitarianism, that forms the ground bass of Walpole's life and writings.

61. For example, in the *Miscellany* (p. 108) he records the burning of fifteen witches by the Presbyterians at Newcastle in 1670 (*sic*), as well as an instance of the intolerance of the founder of the Quakers, George Fox, who prevented the erecting of a college there "as it wd teach Pagan learning." Only glancingly touched on in the *Miscellany* is Walpole's deep hatred, imbibed from Dr. Middleton, of the bigotry and superstition of the Roman Catholic Church (see *YWE*, XXXIII, 173; XXXIV, 19; XXXV, 397; et passim).

Editorial Method

The transcription of the text in the present edition is for the most part a literal one, reproducing Walpole's spellings, capitalizations, contractions, superscripts, and punctuation marks. The following exceptions, however, have been made:

1. Regular *s* has been substituted for long *s* (ſ), as in "buſineſs."
2. Spacing and indentations throughout have been made more logical and consistent.
3. Walpole's arabesques and other gratuitous marks at the ends of items (ʔ ſ / etc.) have been omitted.
4. Underlinings have been italicized and have been expanded where Walpole evidently meant the whole word or phrase to be underscored.
5. Walpole's brackets have been changed to parentheses to avoid confusion with editorial brackets (see below), except in the few cases where Walpole made insertions in quotations from other writers.
6. Walpole's own emendations (insertions, deletions, substitutions, and so on) have not been distinguished as such in the text, but are mentioned in the notes where appropriate.
7. Obvious verbal slips by Walpole (such as "orthody" for "orthodox") have been emended by the editor with comment in the notes.

Manuscript page divisions are indicated in square brackets within the text. Significant pencil notations are reproduced and distinguished by a double asterisk. Editorial insertions have been placed within square brackets and conjectural readings within angular brackets.

The main purpose of the annotation in this edition is to

supply as fully as possible the context of Walpole's thoughts
and reading. Both the style and the fullness of the annotation are by and large in conformity with the practice of the
Yale Walpole Edition; however, an attempt has been made
to minimize the total number of notes by consolidating as
many as possible into larger, unified notes. As in the Yale
Walpole Edition French quotations and phrases have been
left untranslated, although some less familiar terms are explained; on the other hand all Latin quotations have been
translated. (The editor's tendency has been towards literal
translations which are at the same time rather more Latinate
themselves than is the usual practice.) With regard to sources,
use of the *Dictionary of National Biography* is assumed
throughout, as is use of Cokayne's *Complete Peerage* and
Baronetage (see the list of cue titles and abbreviations); these
sources are cited only when there is some special reason for
doing so. Standard texts used for verifying quotations and al-
lusions include the Loeb Classical Library, the Authorized
Version of the Bible, the Pelican Shakespeare (revised edition, 1969), and the Twickenham Edition of the Poems of
Alexander Pope.

Bibliographical Note

Among the many works on Walpole certain studies deserve special citation. Of full-length biographies the best remains R. W. Ketton-Cremer's *Horace Walpole* (London, 1940; 3d ed., 1964); the picture Ketton-Cremer gives us is rounded out by W. S. Lewis's 1960 A. W. Mellon Lectures, published as *Horace Walpole* (New York, 1961). Martin Kallich's recent book in the Twayne English Authors Series (*Horace Walpole*, New York, 1971) is a useful introduction and has a helpful selected bibliography at the back (pp. 137–41). A good essay which Kallich does not mention is J. G. Fairfax, "Horace Walpole's Views on Literature," in *Eighteenth-Century English Literature: An Oxford Miscellany* (Oxford, 1909), pp. 103–26. The most comprehensive study of Walpole's literary opinions is Jeanne Welcher, "The Literary Opinions of Horace Walpole," Diss. Fordham 1955. The fullest study of his poetry is Paul Yvon, *Horace Walpole as a Poet* (Paris, 1924). Yvon also wrote a valuable full-scale biography, *La Vie d'un dilettante: Horace Walpole* (Paris, 1924), which highlights the tension between Walpole's social status and his vocation as a writer.

An especially graceful appreciation of Walpole is F. L. Lucas's essay in *The Art of Living: Four Eighteenth Century Minds* (London, 1959), pp. 79–128. *Horace Walpole: Writer, Politician, and Connoisseur*, ed. Warren H. Smith (New Haven, 1967), contains useful essays on various aspects of Walpole. The best study of Walpole as antiquary is W. S. Lewis, "Horace Walpole, Antiquary," in *Essays Presented to Sir Lewis Namier*, ed. R. Pares and A. J. P. Taylor (London, 1956), pp. 178–203. An excellent recent study of the *Anecdotes of Painting* is Lawrence Lipking's chapter in his *Ordering of the Arts in Eighteenth-Century England* (Princeton,

1970), pp. 127–63. Of course, Allen Hazen's bibliographical studies of Walpole are invaluable (see the list of cue titles and abbreviations). Finally, attention should be called to three recent dissertations: D. M. L. Rogers, "Horace Walpole, Amateur Architect and Art Historian," Diss. Minnesota 1968; H. C. Brown, "Horace Walpole as Historiographer and Antiquary: A Study of Enlightenment Anti-Medievalism," Diss. Virginia 1970; and Janet Adele Dolan, "Horace Walpole's *The Mysterious Mother:* A Critical Edition," Diss. Arizona 1970.

Cue Titles and Abbreviations

Anecdotes of Painting, V. *Anecdotes of Painting in England;* [*1760–1795*] *with Some Account of the Principal Artists; and Incidental Notes on Other Arts; Collected by Horace Walpole; and Now Digested and Published from His Original MSS . . . Volume the Fifth and Last.* Ed. Frederick W. Hilles and Philip B. Daghlian. New Haven, 1937.

Army Lists. Great Britain, War Office. *A List of the General and Field Officers as They Rank in the Army.* London, 1740–1841.

Bibl. Nat. Cat. *Catalogue générale des livres imprimés de la Bibliothèque nationale.* Paris, 1897–.

BM Add. MSS. Additional Manuscripts, British Museum.

BM Cat. Catalogue of Printed Books in the British Museum.

Burke's Peerage. Burke's Peerage. Ed. Peter Townend. London, 1970.

Collins, *Peerage.* Arthur Collins. *The Peerage of England.* Ed. Sir Samuel Egerton Brydges. London, 1812. 9 vols.

"Commonplace Book of Verses." Horace Walpole. "A Common Place Book of Verses, Stories, Character, Letters, &c. &c. with Some Particular Memoirs of a Certain Parcel of People." MS in the possession of W. S. Lewis.

"Des. of SH," *Works,* II. Horace Walpole. "A Description of the Villa of Mr Horace Walpole at Strawberry Hill near Twickenham," in Vol. II of *The Works of Horatio Walpole, Earl of Orford.* London, 1798. 5 vols.

DNB. Dictionary of National Biography. Ed. Leslie Stephen and Sidney Lee. London, 1885–1901. 21 vols.

Foster, *Alumni Oxon.* Joseph Foster. *Alumni Oxonienses: The Members of the University of Oxford, 1500–1714.* Oxford and London, 1891–92. 4 vols. *1715–1886.* London, 1887–88. 4 vols.

GEC. George Edward Cokayne. *The Complete Peerage.* Revised by Vicary Gibbs et al. London, 1910–59. 13 vols.

GEC, Baronetage. George Edward Cokayne. *The Complete Baronetage.* Exeter, 1900–09. 6 vols.

GM. The Gentleman's Magazine.

Hazen, *Bibl. of HW.* Allen T. Hazen. *A Bibliography of Horace Walpole.* New Haven, 1948.

Hazen, *Cat. of HW's Lib.* Allen T. Hazen. *A Catalogue of Horace Walpole's Library.* New Haven, 1969. 3 vols.

Hazen, *SH Bibl.* Allen T. Hazen. *A Bibliography of the Strawberry Hill Press.* New ed. New York, 1973.

HW. Horace Walpole.

Isenburg, *Stammtafeln.* Wilhelm Karl, Prinz von Isenburg. *Stammtafeln zur Geschichte der europaeischen Staaten.* Berlin, 1936. 2 vols.

Journals of the House of Commons. Great Britain, Parliament, House of Commons. *Journals of the House of Commons . . . Reprinted by Order of the House of Commons.* London, 1803. 51 vols.

Journals of the House of Lords. Great Britain, Parliament, House of Lords. *Journals of the House of Lords.* London, ca. 1777–1891. 123 vols.

Mem. Geo. II. Horace Walpole. *Memoirs of the Reign of King George the Second.* 2d ed., ed. Henry R. V. Fox, Lord Holland. London, 1847. 3 vols.

Mem. Geo. III. Horace Walpole. *Memoirs of the Reign of King George the Third.* Ed. G. F. Russell Barker. London, 1894. 4 vols.

Namier and Brooke. Sir Lewis Namier and John Brooke. *The History of Parliament: The House of Commons 1754–1790.* London, 1964. 3 vols.

Nat. Union Cat. The National Union Catalogue, Pre-1956 Imprints.

NBG. Nouvelle biographie générale. Ed. Jean-Chrétien-Ferdinand Hoefer. Paris, 1852–66. 46 vols.

OED. A New English Dictionary on Historical Principles. Ed. Sir James A. H. Murray et al. Oxford, 1888–1928. 10 vols.

Partridge. Eric Partridge. *A Dictionary of Slang and Unconventional English.* 7th ed. New York, 1970.

Royal Calendar. The Royal Kalendar; or Complete and Correct Annual Register for England, Scotland, Ireland, and America. . . . London, 1767–1813.

Sedgwick. Romney Sedgwick. *The History of Parliament: The House of Commons 1715–1754.* London, 1970. 2 vols.

Thieme and Becker. Ulrich Thieme and Felix Becker. *Allgemeines Lexikon der bildenden Künstler von der Antike bis zur Gegenwart.* Leipzig, 1907–50. 37 vols.

Toynbee. *The Letter of Horace Walpole.* Ed. Mrs. Paget Toynbee. Oxford, 1903–05. 16 vols.

Toynbee, *Supplement. Supplement to the Letters of Horace Walpole.* Ed. Paget Toynbee. Oxford, 1918–25. 3 vols.

Venn, *Alumni Cantab. Alumni Cantabrigienses.* Part I to 1751. Compiled by John Venn and J. A. Venn. Cambridge, 1922–27. 4 vols. Part II, 1752–1900. Ed. J. A. Venn. Camridge, 1940–54. 6 vols.

Works. The Works of Horatio Walpole, Earl of Orford. London, 1798. 5 vols.

WSL. W. S. Lewis.

YWE. The Yale Edition of Horace Walpole's Correspondence. Ed. W. S. Lewis. New Haven, 1937–.

Horace Walpole's *Miscellany* 1786–1795

Miscellany.

—such remaining Scraps—as may not perhaps be worth the Reader's notice: but if they are such as tempt me to write them, why may not I hope that in this wide World there may be many an idle Soul no wiser than myself, who may be equally tempted to read them?

Cibber's[1] apology. p:323. qu⁰.
1st Edit.

---

1. Colley Cibber (1671–1757), actor and dramatist. His *Apology for the Life of Mr. Colley Cibber, Comedian* was published 1740 in 4to; HWs copy of the first edition, with numerous MS notes by him, is now in the Hugh Walpole Collection at the King's School, Canterbury (Hazen, *Cat. of HW's Lib.*, No. 450). HW was scornful of most of Cibber's writings, but wrote to George Montagu 16 Oct. 1769 that Cibber's "*Careless Husband* and his own Life . . . both deserve immortality" (*YWE*, X, 298). The quotation, adapted slightly, is from the final chapter.

Aubrey[2] in his natural history & Antiquities of Surrey says Vol. 4. p. 152. that in the Parish of Darking, according to an ancient custom, the Lord of the Manour may demand the first night's Lodging of every Bride within that Manour.

S[r] David Dalrymple in a Dissertation at the End of his History of Scotland, controverts such a custom having ever existed.

In p. 129 of the same Vol. it is said from M[r] Evelyn's[3] authority that my Ancestor Edward Darcy, whose first wife was M[r] Evelyn's Aunt (my great-great-grandmother Lady Eliz. Stanhope was his second) ruined himself & his Estate by his dissolute life, & sold the manours of Episham & Horton.

2. John Aubrey (1626–97), antiquary. His *Natural History and Antiquities of the County of Surrey*, edited by Richard Rawlinson, was published posthumously 1718–19 in five volumes, royal 8vo; HW's copy is now *WSL* (Hazen, *Cat. of HW's Lib.*, No. 648). Sir David Dalrymple (1726–92), Bt., of Hailes, was a Scottish judge and antiquary and HW's correspondent (*YWE*, XV, 25, n. 1 bis). The dissertation HW alludes to is "Of the Law of Evenus, and the Mercheta Mulierum," Appendix 1 to the first volume of Dalrymple's *Annals of Scotland* (Edinburgh, 1776–79) (HW's copy, now *WSL*, listed Hazen, *Cat.*, No. 3185). In this dissertation Dalrymple distinguishes between the *mercheta mulierum* of Britain, a pecuniary fee paid by the tenant of a manor to his lord for the marriage of one of the tenant's daughters, and the Continental *jus primae noctis*. The latter was popularly held to have been the right of the lord to lie with the wife of a tenant on her wedding night, but actually refers to an injunction by the early Church against intercourse between husband and wife the first three nights of marriage. This injunction could be waived at a later date by payment of a fee (see *The Dictionary of English Law*, ed. Earl Jowitt and Clifford Walsh, London, 1959, s.v. Jus primae noctis and Marchet). HW, in MS note at the end of Dalrymple's dissertation, writes: "Considering the absurdities and tyranny of dark ages, the custom is not at all improbable. The author has produced gifts of slaves to monasteries: is the mercheta mulierum more shocking to sense and humanity!"

3. John Evelyn (1620–1706), diarist and connoisseur. Edward Darcy, of Dartford, Kent, HW's maternal great-great-grandfather, married first (1632) Elizabeth Evelyn (ca. 1614–34), John Evelyn's sister, not aunt, and married, secondly, Lady Elizabeth Stanhope, daughter of Philip Stanhope, 1st Earl of Chesterfield (Collins, *Peerage*, III, 423; John Evelyn, *Memoirs . . . Comprising his Diary, from the year 1641 to 1705–6*, ed. W. Bray, London, 1818, I, 4, 5; Aubrey, *Natural History*, IV, 129, and n. 1). Evelyn writes further of Darcy in his diary, loc. cit., that he "little deserved so excellent a person" as Evelyn's sister, and calls him "the worst of men."

5

The Countess of Arundel[4] brought over from Italy large Snails for eating. ib. 70. George 1st. had an Escargotoire in the garden at Kensington for the same purpose.

Extract from a letter to xxxx[5]

—I question whether yr voyage to the Greek Isles will answer your Expectation, except in the beautifull but degraded Scenes of Nature. very slight by all accounts seem to be the Relicks of Grecian Art & Taste. Defaced [p. 2] ruins of Architecture & Statuary, like the wrinkles of decrepitude of a once

4. Lady Alathea Talbot (d. 1654), daughter of Gilbert, 7th Earl of Shrewsbury, m. (1606) Thomas Howard (1585–1646), Earl of Arundel, cr. (1644) Earl of Norfolk. Aubrey writes, loc. cit.: "As I rode over Albury Down, I was wonderfully surpriz'd with those prodigious snails there, as big as two or three of ours. Mr. Elias Ashmole (Windsor Herald) told me, they were brought from Italy by the old Countess of Arundel; who did dress them and eat them." In a letter to Aubrey (8 Feb. 1676) prefixed to the *Natural History*, John Evelyn asserts that it was Thomas, Earl of Arundel who brought the snails to England. No other mention of George I's escargotoire at Kensington has been found. The term itself is rare; *OED* cites only Addison's *Remarks on Several Parts of Italy* (London, 1705), p. 473: "Escargotoire . . . a square place boarded in, and filled with a vast quantity of large snails."

5. This is apparently a fragment of an unsent letter of HW to Lady Craven written ca. July 1786. Lady Craven was Elizabeth Berkeley (1750–1828), m. 1 (1767) William Craven, 6th Baron Craven, 1769, from whom she was separated ca. 1783; m. 2 (1791) Christian Friedrich Karl Alexander, Margrave of Brandenburg-Ansbach and Bayreuth; dramatist; HW's correspondent. HW wrote to Sir Horace Mann 22 June 1786 that she had sent him "a letter from Constantinople. . . . She is now gone to the Greek Isles, and bids me next direct to Vienna" (*YWE*, XXV, 654–55). In his letter to Lady Craven 27 Nov. 1786 he implies that he has not answered her letters over the summer because of her failure to supply a specific address (Toynbee, XIII, 418–20). The present fragment, not previously published, was evidently written between the letter to Mann mentioned above, and HW's next dated entry in the *Miscellany* (7 Aug. 1786). Lady Craven visited Athens and Smyrna in May (*The Beautiful Lady Craven*, ed. A. M. Broadley and Lewis Melville, London, 1914, I, xli–xlii; Lady Craven's *Memoirs*, London, 1826, I, 172); she subsequently published an account of her travels as far as Constantinople in her *Journey through the Crimea to Constantinople* (London, 1789) (HW's copy listed Hazen, *Cat. of HW's Lib.*, No. 2168). HW expresses similar sentiments about the futility of viewing ruins in his letters to John Chute 5 Aug. 1771 (*YWE*, XXXV, 127) and to Richard West 16 April 1740 NS: "I am very glad that I see Rome while it exists: before a great number of years are elapsed, I question whether it will be worth seeing" (ibid., XIII, 208).

beautifull Woman, only make one regret that one did not see them when they were enchanting. I never found even in my juvenile hours that it was necessary to go a thousand miles in search of themes for moralizing. Forty years ago I saw the *Angel, Goddess, Montagu*[6] in her decay, & She was as striking a lesson of mortality, tho still gracefull, as the rubbish of what was once the Acropolis of Athens! When Turkish barbarism is added to the Spectacle, it raises Indignation—& why sail to the Ægean, only to be in a passion? xxxxx

Bobadil in Every Man in his humour[7] is a Spanish name. The Theorique & practise of War by Don Bernardino de

6. From Pope, *Sober Advice from Horace* (ll. 161–66):

> Give me a willing Nymph! 'tis all I care,
> Extremely clean, and tolerably fair,
> Her Shape her own, whatever Shape she have,
> And just that White and Red which Nature gave.
> Her I transported touch, transported view,
> And call her *Angel! Goddess! Montagu!*

"Montagu" is Lady Mary Pierrepont (1689–1762), m. (1712) Edward Wortley Montagu; letter writer. HW, though he admired her wit, makes frequent unflattering remarks about her appearance (and her morals); e.g., he wrote to his cousin Henry Seymour Conway from Florence, 25 Sept. 1740 NS: "Did I tell you Lady Mary Wortley is here? . . . She wears a foul mob, that does not cover her greasy black locks that hang loose, never combed or curled. . . . Her face violently swelled on one side with the remains of a pox, partly covered with a plaister, and partly with white paint, which for cheapness she has bought so coarse, that you would not use it to wash a chimney" (*YWE*, XXXVII, 78–79).

7. By Ben Jonson. Don Bernardino de Mendoza (1540 or 41–1604) was a Spanish diplomat and writer; his *Theorica y Practica de Guerra* (Madrid, 1595) was translated into English as the *Theorique and Practise of Warre* (London, 1597) by Sir Edward Hoby (1560–1617), diplomat and controversialist (*DNB; Enciclopedia Universal Ilustrada*, Barcelona, 1905–33, XXXIV, 623; A. Morel-Fatio, "D. Bernardino de Mendoza," in *Études sur l'Espagne*, Paris, 1925, pp. 375, 458–59, 466–74). The censure or approbation of Mendoza's work was given by Don Francisco Arias de Bobadilla (d. 1610), 4th Conde de Puñonrostro, captain of light horse and afterwards field marshal (ibid., p. 468, n. 1). It is possible that Jonson took the name Capt. Bobadill from this source, as Hoby's translation was published just the year before Jonson's play was first acted; however, Bobadilla is a common Spanish name (see Henry Holland Carter, ed., *Every Man in His Humour by Ben Jonson*,

Mendoza was translated by Sr Edward Hoby in 1597. On the last page is the approbation of Don Francisco Arias de *Bobadilla,* Capt. of light horse. Thence probably Ben Johnson took the name.

v. Herbert's Typogr. Antiq^s. enlarged from Ames. V. 2^d. p. 1259.

A book sold by Sam. Shorter at the great north door of Paule's Church.[8] ib. 1232. This is almost the only instance I have found of the name of Shorter, my Grandfather's name. There is Shorter's Court Throgmorton street & Shorter's street, Cable street Ragfair.

[p. 3]   Works of Sr Hugh Platt.[9]

New Haven, 1921, p. 264), and recent scholarship tends to view Bobadill as a variant on Boabdil, the last king of the Moors in Spain, who was expelled by Ferdinand and Isabella in 1492 (C. H. Herford et al., eds., *Ben Jonson,* Oxford, 1925–52, IX, 342, followed by more recent editors). Perhaps the Bobadilla, "Captaine of light horsse" of Mendoza's book was Jonson's immediate inspiration for the name and rank, while the suggestion of the dispossessed Boabdil was intended at a deeper level of resemblance. Hoby's translation is cited in William Herbert (1718–95), *Typographical Antiquities: or an Historical Account of the Origin and Progress of Printing in Great Britain and Ireland* (London, 1785–90), 3 vols., which Herbert enlarged from the first edition (published 1749) by Joseph Ames (1689–1759), bibliographer and antiquary; the second volume of this work appeared early in 1786 (see *GM* May 1786, LVI, Pt. i, 421). HW's copy, now *WSL,* of the second edition is listed Hazen, *Cat. of HW's Lib.,* No. 29.

8. "1598. 'The Making and Use of the Geometricall Instrument called a Sector. —Written by Tho. Hood, Doctor in Physicke, 1598. . . . Printed by [John Windet] and are to be solde at the great North dore of Paules Church by Sam. Shorter' " (Ames and Herbert, loc. cit.). His name on the title page of this book is the only known reference to Samuel Shorter, bookseller, according to R. B. McKerrow et al., *Dictionary of Printers and Booksellers in England, Scotland and Ireland . . . 1557–1640* (London, 1910), p. 245; "Paule's Church" is Old St. Paul's Cathedral, destroyed in the Great Fire of 1666. HW's grandfather on his mother's side was John Shorter (b. ca. 1660) of Bybrook, Kent, timber merchant (*YWE,* XXVIII, 24, n. 5). "Shorter's Court Throgmorton street" and "Shorter's street, Cable street Ragfair" are so listed in *London and its Environs Described* (London, 1761), V, 345, whence HW probably took the reference (see below, p. 108).

9. Sir Hugh Plat (or Platt) (1552–1608), inventor and author of works on agriculture. HW's listing of his works here reflects his interest in gardening,

Hugonis Platti manuale &c 24°. 1584.[1]
v. Herbert's Ames v. 2. 1206.
The Jewel House of Art & nature. 1594.[2] ib. 1207.
Sundrie new & artificial remedies against Famine. 1596.[3]
ib. 1208.
A brief Apologie of certen new Inventions.[4] ib. 1260.

The garden of Eden, or an accurate Description of all flowers & fruits now growing in England, with particular rules how to advance their nature and growth, as well in seeds and herbs, as the secret ordering of trees & plants. By that learned & great Observer Sr Hugh Plat, Knight. the fifth Edition. Lond. printed for W. Leake at the Crown in Fleet street. 1660. 24°. As mine is the 5th Edition, & as S[r] Hugh was an Author in 1584, as appears above, it is most prob. that he was dead in 1660.[5]

One of his nostrums was to make a Peach tree bring forth

to which subject he devoted his *Essay on Modern Gardening*, first printed in his *Anecdotes of Painting*, IV, 1771. See the Introduction.

1. "1584. 'Hugonis Platti armig. Manuale sententias aliquot divinas et morales complectens; partim è sacris patribus partim è Petrarcha philosopho et poeta celeberrimo, decerptas.' Twenty-fours."

2. "The Jewell House of Art and Nature. Conteining divers rare & profitable Inventions, together with sundry new experimentes in the Art of Husbandry, Distillation & Moulding. —by Hugh Platte . . . 1594." HW's copy is listed Hazen, *Cat. of HW's Lib.*, No. 855. See below for a later edition.

3. "1596. 'Sundrie new and Artificiall remedies against Famine. Written by H. P. *(Hugh Platt)* Esq. uppon thoccasion of this present Dearth. Non est quo fugias à Deo irato nisi ad Deum placatum. Aug[ustine]. . . . 1596.'" The first edition had been published in 1595 *(DNB)*.

4. "[Richard Field, printer] had also licenses for the following, viz. . . . In 1592, 'A brief apologie of certen newe invenc'ons côpiled by H. Plot.'" A unique copy of this broadsheet belonged to the Society of Antiquaries ca. 1896 *(DNB)*.

5. He had been dead 52 years (above, p. 8, n. 9). *The Garden of Eden*, first published in 1608 with the title *Floraes Paradise*, was brought out in a revised edition by Charles Bellingham in 1653; the fifth edition included a continuation of the work based on Plat's unpublished notes *(YWE, XXVIII, 275, n. 7)*. HW's copy of the fifth edition is listed Hazen, *Cat. of HW's Lib.*, No. 2928, where the copy is described as 8vo. In the title HW mistakenly

pomgranates by watering it with goats milk for 3 days to-
gether when it beginneth to flower. As great an observer as
Sʳ Hugh was, he scarce ever saw this experiment succeed!⁶
Plots garden of Eden, both parts. 1675.⁷
Plots jewel house of Art & Nature. 1653.⁸

**—pleno se proluit auro
Post alii proceres—⁹

[p. 4] Renè of Anjou¹ painted a picture of his Mistress's
Corpse as he found it eaten by worms on having it opened on
his return from a pilgrimage to Jerusalem. This another in-

transcribed "as herbs" for "and herbs"; "secret ordering" refers to Plat's concealing his "principal secret" of gardening in a "figurative description" (see
YWE, XXVIII, 275, and n. 9). William Leake was a bookseller in London
1635–81 (Henry R. Plomer, *A Dictionary of the Booksellers and Printers . . .
in England, Scotland and Ireland from 1641 to 1667*, London, 1907, p. 115).
    6. HW reported this "nostrum" to William Mason in his letter of 17 Sept.
1776 (*YWE*, XXVIII, 275), and also recorded it in his "Book of Materials,"
1771–85, p. 54. The nostrum is in Pt. II, p. 147 of Plat's work. "Beginneth"
is of course HW's jocular echo of Plat's archaic language.
    7. HW's copy is listed Hazen, *Cat. of HW's Lib.*, No. 3793, where Hazen
suggests that this item was added at a later date than the preceding items
in the Plat bibliography, "presumably from a newly acquired copy."
    8. A revised edition, prepared by "D. B. gent." This item may also have
been added at a later date; if so, it suggests that HW acquired a copy of this
edition as well, perhaps at the same time. However, since there is no other
record of his having done so, Hazen does not admit it to the *Catalogue*.
    9. Virgil, *Aeneid*, I, 739–40: "He [Bitias] drank from the brimming gold
[goblet], and after him the other nobles," from the banquet scene where
Queen Dido passes the cup in honor of Aeneas and his companions. HW
owned numerous copies of Virgil, and quotes him frequently, but admired
individual passages of the *Aeneid* rather than the work as a whole. Prejudiced against epic poetry as "the art of being as long as possible in telling an
uninteresting story," he wrote that "Virgil with every beauty of expression
and harmony that can be conceived has accomplished but an insipid imitation
[of Homer]" (HW to William Mason, 25 June 1782, *YWE*, XXIX, 255–56; see
also ibid., XI, 20; XVI, 22–23, 268–69).
    1. René d'Anjou (1409–80), Duc d'Anjou, 1435; King of Sicily 1435–42
(ibid., XIV, 69, n. 5). HW wrote to Thomas Walpole 3 Jan. 1784 that "I have
long thought of writing a life of René of Anjou . . . (though I probably shall
not now) . . . as he was a royal painter as well as royal author, I am doubly
interested about him" (ibid., XXXVI, 216–17). HW did produce (in 1779) a
brief sketch entitled "Life of René of Anjou, King of Naples" (printed ibid.,

stance of the strange mixture of religion & gallantry in those
ages.
  v. Gough's Sepulchr. Monum^s. Vol. 1 in the Introduct. p.
cxi.
  Richard 2^d. says Froissart had a favourite Greyhound called
Math. who shocked him by fawning on his Successor.^{2} ib. cxxiv.
How beautifully has Shakespeare introduced & dignified this

XXXI, 438–39); for a fuller account of him, see also below, p. 69. "It" in
"having it opened" refers of course to the tomb of René's mistress. Richard
Gough (1735–1809), antiquary, in June 1786 sent HW a copy of the first
volume of his *Sepulchral Monuments in Great Britain*, in which he carried
out HW's project for a "History of the Manners, Customs Habits, Fashions,
Ceremonies, etc. of England," begun by HW in 1762 (see HW to Gough,
21 June 1786, Toynbee, XIII, 388–90; *YWE*, XVI, 27, n. 3); HW's set of the
first two volumes (London, 1786–96; a third volume appeared in 1799) is listed
Hazen, *Cat.*, No. 3644. In Vol. I, p. cxi, Gough, citing J. D. Breval, *Remarks
on Several Parts of Europe* (London, 1726), I, 138, mentions that "René of
Anjou is said to have painted his mistress after he had opened her tomb at
Avignon, as he found her at his return from a pilgrimage to Jerusalem."
HW's friend and correspondent Lady Mary Coke, encouraged by HW, had
seen this painting (in the Church of the Célestins at Avignon) in 1769 (*YWE*,
XXXI, 143, and n. 6). Probably commissioned by René rather than done by
him, it was described by an eyewitness, prior to its disappearance during the
Revolution, as portraying "un grand squelette debout, coiffé à l'antique, re-
couvert de son suaire; les vers mangent le corps d'une manière affreuse; sa
bière est ouverte, appuyée debout contre la croix du cimetière, et pleine de
toiles d'araignée, fort bien imitées" (Comte de Quatrebarbes, ed., *Œuvres
complètes du roi René*, Angers, 1844–46, I, cl–cli). The name of only one of
René's mistresses (Marie de la Chapelle) has survived, and it is uncertain
whether it was she whose corpse René had painted at Avignon (or indeed
whether it was the corpse of a mistress at all). Also, it appears that René
never made a pilgrimage to the Holy Land, although one of his nominal
titles was "King of Jerusalem" (ibid., I, cli; Edgcumbe Staley, *King René
d'Anjou and his Seven Queens*, New York, 1912, pp. 345–46). The "strange
mixture of religion and gallantry" HW mentions is exemplified by the verses
René had inscribed at the bottom of the painting (cited Quatrebarbes, I, cl):

> Une fois sur toute femme belle,
> Mais par la mort, suis devenue telle.
> Ma chair estoit très belle, fraische et tendre,
> Or, est-elle toute tournée en cendre. [etc.]

  2. "King Richard II. had a favourite greyhound, named *Matt*, whose trans-
fer of attachment from him to the usurper of his crown is naturally told by
Froissart." In his chronicle of the year 1399, Froissart writes: "King Rycharde
had a grayhounde called Mathe, who always wayted upon the kynge, and

Anecdote by applying it to the horse on which Bolinbroke rode to his Coronation, & which had belonged to poor Richard. The name of Roan Barbary, instead of Matt, shows how well Shakespeare knew how to improve & exalt little circumstances, when he borrowed them from circumstantial or vulgar historians.

His reviving Richards Queen Anne, in the place of his second Wife Isabel, who was an Infant, is another instance of his judgement to move our Sensibility.[3] When Shakespeare copied Chroniclers verbatim, it was because he knew they were good enough for his Audiences. In a more polished Age

wolde knowe no man els. . . . And as the kyng and the erle of Derby [Bolingbroke] talked togyder in the courte, the grayhounde, who was wont to lepe upon the kyng, left the kynge and came to the erle of Derby. . . . Cosin, quod the kynge, it is a gret good token to you, and an yvell signe to me. . . . the grayhounde maketh you chere this day as kynge of Englande, as ye shal be, and I shal be deposed: the grayhounde hath this knowledge naturally . . . " (*The Chronicle of Froissart translated out of the French by Sir John Bourchier Lord Berners annis 1523–25,* ed. W. P. Ker, Tudor Translations, 1901–03; rpt. New York, 1967, VI, 369; also printed *Richard II,* ed. M. W. Black, Variorum Shakespeare, Philadelphia, 1955, p. 458). Until now George Steevens (1736–1800), the Shakespearian editor and commentator, has been generally credited with having first thought of this passage as a possible source of the Roan Barbary passage in *Richard II* (Act V, scene iv); his suggestion does not appear until 1803, when it was incorporated posthumously from his MS notes into Isaac Reed's edition of Shakespeare's *Plays* (London, 1803), XI, 166, n. 6. HW himself probably took the idea from Thomas Davies (?1712–85), who draws attention to this anecdote in his remarks on *Richard II* in his *Dramatic Miscellanies* (London, 1784), I, 192; HW's copy, with his marginal notes, now *WSL,* is listed Hazen, *Cat. of HW's Lib.,* No. 3918. Davies, I, 191, says of the Roan Barbary passage: "This is one of those scenes which disgrace the tragedy of a great king." HW notes: "Yet this is one of those exquisite and affecting touches of nature, in which Shakespeare excelled all mankind. To criticize it is being as tasteless as Voltaire."

3. Richard married first (1383) Anne (1366–94), daughter of Charles IV, King of Bohemia, Holy Roman Emperor; and second (1396) Isabel (1387–1409), second daughter of Charles VI, King of France (*Burke's Peerage,* p. liv). HW's observation on Richard's queens seems to be original with him. He communicated it to Edmond Malone (in a letter of 30 March 1785), who printed it in his edition of Shakespeare's *Plays and Poems* (London, 1790), V, 29, n. 7 (see James M. Osborn, "Horace Walpole and Edmond Malone," in *Horace Walpole: Writer, Politician, and Connoisseur,* ed. W. H. Smith, New Haven, 1967, pp. 313–15; HW's copy of Malone's Shakespeare, now *WSL,* is listed Hazen, *Cat. of HW's Lib.,* No. 1360). The passages on Roan Barbary and Richard's queens have been printed in *Notes by Horace Walpole on Several Characters of Shakespeare,* ed. W. S. Lewis (Farmington, 1940), pp. 17–18.

he who coud so move our passions, coud surely have performed the easier task of satisfying our Taste.

The Nine Worthies of London &c compiled by Ric. Johnson. imprinted for Hum. Lownes 1592.[4] One of these was the renown'd S[r] Hugh Caverly, temp. Edw. 3[d]. who married a Queen of Arragon. In this book he is called Silk weaver. That is, I suppose, when made free of the City, he was enrolled in that Company. v. Herberts typogr. Antiq. Qu°. Vol. 2. p. 1248.

[p. 5]   Aug. 7. 1786. Saw Broome a Seat of S[r] Henry Oxenden[5] in Kent. It stands well at the head of a descending Val:

4. "1592. The nine Worthies of London; explaining the honourable exercise of Armes, the vertues of the valiant, and the memorable attempts of magnanimous minds," compiled by Richard Johnson (1573–?1659), romance writer, and imprinted for Humphrey Lownes (d. ca. 1630), bookseller and printer in London 1587–1629, "at the west doore of Paules" (cited Ames and Herbert, *Typographical Antiquities*, II, 1248 [see above, p. 7, n. 7]; see also R. B. McKerrow et al., *Dictionary of Printers and Booksellers in England, Scotland and Ireland . . . 1557–1640*, London, 1910, pp. 178–79). Sir Hugh Calveley (d. 1393) was a noted soldier and adventurer. HW wrote in his "Book of Materials," 1771–85, p. 47, that "King in his Vale Royal of Cheshire says, Sr Hugh Caveley Captain of Calais married in times past the late Queen of Arragon" and argues that this queen was Sibila (or Sibilia) of Fortia (d. 1406), widow of Pedro IV, King of Aragon (Isenburg, *Stammtafeln*, II, taf. 45; *Diccionario de historia de España*, 2d ed., Madrid, 1969, III, 658–59; the book HW cites is Daniel King, *The Vale-Royall of England, or, The County Palatine of Chester Illustrated*, London, 1656, Bk. II, p. 53, his copy listed Hazen, *Cat. of HW's Lib.*, No. 628). Calveley's biographer in the *DNB* concludes that this marriage never took place; HW's argument rests in part on the erroneous assumption that Calveley accompanied John of Gaunt on his expedition to Spain in 1386. As for Sir Hugh's being a silk weaver, Johnson writes in *The Nine Worthies*: "In England late yong Caverley did live, / Silke-weavers Honour merited by Deedes" (reprinted *Harleian Miscellany*, London, 1744–46, VIII, 439). However, there is no mention of Sir Hugh as silk weaver in *DNB* or in Frances Consitt's authoritative study, *The London Weavers' Company . . . Volume I. From the Twelfth Century to the Close of the Sixteenth Century* (Oxford, 1933); probably Johnson was following an unfounded tradition.

5. Sir Henry Oxenden (1721–1803), 6th Bt., 1775. HW visited Deane (or Dene Park), another of Sir Henry's seats, in 1780 (*YWE*, XXXIII, 222, and n. 9). Broome Park, his principal seat, 7 miles SE of Canterbury, is described and illustrated in William Angus, *Seats of the Nobility and Gentry in Great Britain and Wales* (Islington, 1787–1815), Plate 18; Charles Latham, *In English Homes* (London, 1904–09), III, 99–102; *Country Life*, 22 (1907), 18–25. "The house contains a good collection of pictures by Italian masters in the

the House is good & handsome, & he has built one fine room
for his pictures; there are 33, most good & a few fine; particularly Christ with the Doctors, by Pordenone,[6] an uncom-
mon picture in a lighter style than usual with the Venetian
masters: the Expressions of the Pharisees are very natural, of
the Virgin, not so well. there are fine small Salvators, two
good Gaspars, a fine Lanfranc,[7] & a curious picture masterly
drawn & coloured, of the young Slave picking the thorn out of
his foot from the Antique Bronze on the Capitol.[8] It is said to
be painted by Correggio, but probably is not, as the colouring is not bright; nor was Correggio ever at Rome, nor was

highest preservation" (Angus, loc. cit.). These pictures have not been more
positively identified, nor are their present whereabouts known (see Dorothy
Gardiner, ed., *The Oxinden Letters 1607–1642*, London, 1933, p. v). This and
the following item on Chilham Castle have been printed in *Anecdotes of
Painting*, V, 166–67.

6. Giovanni de' Sacchis, called Pordenone (ca. 1484–1539) (Thieme and
Becker, XXVII, 271–72; *Enciclopedia italiana*, ed. G. Gentile and C. Tumminelli, Rome, 1929–39, XXVII, 941–42). This picture was at Deane in 1735,
when it was described by John Whaley as "in water colours of Christ disputing with the Doctors" (Whaley to HW, 10 Aug. 1735 OS, Toynbee, *Supplement*, III, 84). The attribution to Pordenone is probably false; no such
work is listed in any of the standard catalogues, e.g., in "Catalogo dello
Opere" in Giuseppe Fiocco, *Giovanni Antonio Pordenone*, 2d ed. (Padua,
1943), pp. 110–15.

7. Salvator Rosa (1615–73); Gaspard Poussin (originally Dughet) (1615–75);
Giovanni Lanfranco (1582–1647) (Thieme and Becker, XXII, 309; XXVIII,
320–21; XXIX, 1).

8. This statue, known as the "spinario" or "cavaspina" and showing a mixture of Greek and Hellenistic elements, is in the Museo dei Conservatori at
Rome (*Enciclopedia dell'arte antica, classica e orientale*, Rome, 1958–65, VII,
453–54). The picture allegedly by Correggio was at Deane in 1735 (Toynbee,
Supplement, III, 84); there is no such work listed in the various catalogues
of Correggio, though, curiously, there is a painting in the Isabella Stewart
Gardner Museum at Boston of a girl picking a thorn out of her foot which
has been attributed, somewhat dubiously, to him (see Corrado Ricci, *Correggio*, London, 1930, p. 154 and Pl. 30; Alberto Bevilacqua and A. C. Quinta-
valle, *L'opera completa del Correggio*, Milan, 1970, p. 112). Through Vasari,
Correggio's earliest biographer, asserts that Correggio had never been to Rome,
modern critics, basing their judgment on the evolution of his style, tend to
feel that such a trip must have taken place, probably sometime between 1517
and 1520 (see Stefano Bottari, "Correggio," *Encyclopedia of World Art*, New
York, 1959–68, III, 822–23, 828).

likely to have seen a Cast or Print of that Statue so early. There are two fine pieces of Nicolò Poussin with many figures finely drawn, but in his worst & coldest colouring. In another room is a good head by Sr Godfrey,⁹ of Edmund Dunch, grandfather of Sr Henry, & who was of the Kitcat Club. In one room a model of the flying Machine invented by Mr Oxenden,¹ only Son of Sr Henry.

Saw also Chilham Castle, seat of Mr Heron.² The Situation is high & fine, but has not been assisted by modern Art. Of the ancient Castle nothing remains but the Keep covered by Ivy. The House adjoining was built by Sr Dudley Digges, in the Style of K. James's time, & from the number of Bow-windows & two kinds of wings with them that retire & advance again, not unpicturesque, but the whole Inside is compleatly ugly & inconvenient, & tho kept in perfect repair, furnished & inhabited, has nothing in it worth notice, but one

9. Sir Godfrey Kneller (1646–1723); see HW's account of him in *Anecdotes of Painting, Works,* III, 359–66. The "head" was probably a replica by Sir Godfrey of his half-length portrait of Edmund Dunch (1657–1719), politician, Sir Henry Oxenden's maternal grandfather, which hung in the meeting room of the Kit-Kat Club; this portrait is reproduced in *The Kit-Cat Club, done from the Original Paintings of Sir Godfrey Kneller,* engraved by John Faber, Jr. (London, 1735), No. 38 (HW's copy, now *WSL,* listed Hazen, *Cat. of HW's Lib.,* No. 3501), in James Caulfield, *Memoirs of the Celebrated Persons Composing the Kit-Cat Club* (London, 1821), facing p. 210 (see also ibid., pp. vii–viii), and in J. D. Stewart, *Godfrey Kneller* (London, 1971), Appendix, p. x. Sir Godfrey's original paintings of the Kit-Cat Club are preserved in the National Portrait Gallery, London.

1. Sir Henry Oxenden (1756–1838), 7th Bt., 1803. No other mention of his "flying machine" has been found. Interest in aviation was especially high at this time because of the recent pioneering balloon ascents of the Montgolfier brothers and others in France and England (see *YWE,* XXV, 449–51, 517, 528).

2. Thomas Heron, onetime town clerk of Newark, who acquired Chilham Castle in the 1770s and resided there until his death in 1794 (*GM* 1794, LXIV, Pt. i, 484; J. P. Neale, *Views of the Seats of Noblemen and Gentlemen, in England, Wales, Scotland, and Ireland,* 2d ser., London, 1824–29, II, s.v. Chilham Castle, Kent). The estate is described and illustrated, ibid., and in *Country Life,* 32 (1912), 126–33. Sir Dudley Digges (1583–1639), diplomat, acquired the estate through his wife, Mary Kempe, and erected the mansion house; their names with the date 1616 are cut on the architrave over the entrance (ibid., p. 130; photograph p. 127). The picture of the two ladies mentioned by HW has not been identified. In the MS HW first wrote "windows" for "wings."

piece of two Ladies in the exact dress & undress of the reign of George 1ˢᵗ. one sitting, the other Standing.

[p. 6]   In Ant. Wood's³ hist. of the Colleges in Oxford, published by Gutch in quarto 1786. there is a most remarkable letter of Henry 8ᵗʰ. to Wolsey admonishing him of the Dissatisfaction occasioned by the Cardinal's suppression of so many religious foundations (to the number of 22) to enrich his new College of Christ Church. p. 417.

On a certain old Lady.

> Furia to God one day in seven allots;
> The other six to Scandal she devotes.
> Satan, by false Devotion never flamm'd,⁴
> Bets six to one, that Furia will be damn'd.

Sept. 27. 1786. Dʳ Lort,⁵ Librarian to the Archbishop, told me that in the Library at Lambeth there is an account of the

3. Anthony à Wood (1632–95), antiquary and historian. His *History and Antiquities of the Colleges and Halls in the University of Oxford*, which had come out in a Latin translation in 1674, was first published in English in a quarto edition by John Gutch (1746–1831), antiquary and divine, at Oxford, 1786. HW mentions reading the work in a letter to Lord Strafford 29 Aug. 1786 (*YWE*, XXXV, 387); his copy is listed Hazen, *Cat. of HW's Lib.*, No. 3219 (see also the review in *GM* Nov. 1786, LVI, Pt. ii, 973–74). Thomas Wolsey (?1475–1530), cardinal and statesman, in 1524 procured a bull from Pope Clement VII allowing him to convert the monastery of St. Frideswide at Oxford into a college; by another bull of March 1525 he was given leave to suppress St. Frideswide and an additional 21 monasteries for the endowment of that college (listed Wood, pp. 414–17). "Much about which time the King, having occasion to write to the Cardinal about various matters, thus tells him of the suppression of the said monasteries: 'As touching the help of religious houses to the building of your college, I would it were more, so it be lawfully; for my intent is none, but that it should so appear to all the world, and the occasion of all their mumbling might be secluded and put away; for surely there is great murmuring at it throughout all the realm, both good and bad [etc.]' " (ibid., p. 417). After the fall of Wolsey his college was suppressed; subsequently it was reconstituted by Henry, who renamed it Christ Church College (see H. L. Thompson, *Christ Church*, London, 1900, pp. 1–11; C. E. Mallet, *A History of the University of Oxford*, London, 1924–27, II, 35–41).

4. "To deceive by a sham story or trick" (*OED*). Cf. *flim-flam*.

5. Michael Lort (1725–90), D.D.; antiquary; librarian to the Archbishop of Canterbury, 1785; HW's correspondent. There is no evidence that Henry VI

Coronation of Henry 6th. in which it is said that he was made a Bishop before he was crowned. This was done, I suppose, to fill him with pious notions, that he might be governed more easily, & probably was directed by his ambitious Uncle Cardinal Beaufort, & was the Origine of Henry's devout Conduct.

In 1785, the Empress of Russia ordered Sr Joshua Reynolds to paint a picture for her, & left the Subject & the price to him. He fixed on the Infant Hercules strangling the Serpents from Pindar's description.[6] It was a miserable [p. 7] Choice,

was ever "made a bishop," but in a contemporary MS account of his coronation in the British Museum (in William Gregory's "Chronicle of London," printed in *The Historical Collections of a Citizen of London in the Fifteenth Century*, ed. J. Gairdner, Camden Society, new ser. 17, 1876; rpt. New York, 1965, pp. 165–70), it is recorded that, before being crowned with the crown of "Kynge Rycharde," Henry was arrayed in episcopal vestments: "And thenne [the bishops] toke hym up and dyspoyled hym of his gere a-yen, and thenne a-rayde hym as a byschoppe that sholde synge a masse, with a dalmadyke lyke unto a tunycule with a stole a bowte hys necke, not crossyd, and a pon hys fete a payre of sandellys as a byschoppe, and a cope and glovys lyke a byschoppe . . ." (pp. 166–67). Henry's piety was proverbial (see Cardinal Gasquet, "*Cultus* and Popular Devotion to the Saintly King Henry," in his *Religious Life of King Henry VI*, London, 1923, pp. 119–34); Henry Beaufort (ca. 1375–1447), cardinal, Henry's great-uncle and godfather, was a major influence in the monarch's life (see Mabel E. Christie, *Henry VI*, London, 1922, pp. 47–49; L. B. Radford, *Henry Beaufort: Bishop, Chancellor, Cardinal*, London, 1908, p. 2 et passim).

6. Sir Joshua mentioned this commission and his choice of subject in a letter to the Duke of Rutland 20 Feb. 1786 (printed in his *Letters*, ed. F. W. Hilles, Cambridge, 1929, p. 149), and mentioned it to HW by April of the same year (see *YWE*, XXXVI, 237; also, F. W. Hilles, "Sir Joshua and the Empress Catherine," in *Eighteenth-Century Studies in Honor of Donald F. Hyde*, ed. W. H. Bond, New York, 1970, p. 269; Hilles, "Horace Walpole and the Knight of the Brush," in *Horace Walpole: Writer, Politician, and Connoisseur*, ed. W. H. Smith, New Haven, 1967, pp. 141–66). HW in turn suggested to him the alternate project of Czar Peter in the dockyard at Deptford (see William Roberts, *Memoirs of the Life and Correspondence of Mrs. Hannah More*, London, 1834, II, 21), but Reynolds ignored his suggestion, and in July was "entirely occupied in contriving the composition of the Hercules" (Reynolds to Lord Ossory 17 July 1786, *Letters*, p. 155). HW saw the painting at Ampthill in Aug. 1787, and "did not admire it" (HW to Lord Ossory 6 Sept. 1787, *YWE*, XXXIII, 571); it was finished in 1788 and is now in the Hermitage Museum, Leningrad (see A. Graves and W. V. Cronin, *A History of the Works of Sir Joshua Reynolds*, London, 1899–1901, III, 1160–64; IV,

not only as the Story is not one of the happiest Instances of
Greek mythology, but is an old threadbare tale. He ought to
have chosen a Subject that either related to Russian or English History. There was one that woud have embraced both
Countries & complimented Both, viz, the moment when Peter
the Great in the Dockyard at Deptford addressed himself to
work as a Shipwright. What a fine Contrast might have been
drawn, as Peter threw off the imperial Mantle, & prepared to
put on Trowzers, between the sullen Indignation of his
Russian Attendants, & the joy of the English Tars at seeing
Majesty adopt their garb! Peter learning Navigation here
in order to give a Navy to his own Country—how flattering to
both Nations! how superior to the passions of a Nursery &
the common expressions of affrighted parents! Pindar's words
coud give dignity to the theme—but the pencil that can only
represent Nature, can give no Novelty to such an Occurrence.
The parents woud feel the same emotions if two large rats
had got into a Cradle. Their being serpents does not exalt the
accident.

D[r] Calder,[7] a Socinian Minister, is the Author of the notes
to Nichols's new Edition of the Tatler in 6 vols. 1786.

Dr Calder said of D[r] Johnston on the publications of Bos-

1480AAA; also, James Northcote, *The Life of Sir Joshua Reynolds*, London,
1819, II, 214–15; Hilles, "Sir Joshua and the Empress Catherine," p. 271).
Hannah More thought HW's suggestion a "great idea" and agreed with him
that Sir Joshua's subject was "nonsensical" and a "stale piece of mythology"
(Roberts, loc. cit.). For Peter the Great's stay at Deptford in 1698, see Eugene
Schuyler, *Peter the Great, Emperor of Russia* (New York, 1884), I, 300–08;
the Imperial ambassador to England, Count Auersperg, wrote to the Emperor
Leopold that "all the time he was here he went about in sailor's clothing"
(ibid., I, 304).

7. John Calder (1733–1815), D.D., who was "bred to the dissenting ministry
. . . but, having long declined the office of a teacher, he became a warm
admirer of the doctrinal system in Essex Street [i.e., Unitarianism or Socin-
ianism]" (John Nichols, *Literary Anecdotes of the Eighteenth Century*, London, 1812–15, IX, 804–05). "During Dr. Calder's residence at Northumberland-
house [as secretary to the Duke of Northumberland], he formed an intimacy
with Dr. [Thomas] Percy, the late venerable Bishop of Dromore [and editor
of the *Reliques of Ancient English Poetry*]; from whom he received the notes
which that learned prelate had collected for illustrating the Tatler, Spec-

well and Mrs Piozzi, that he was like Acteon, torn to pieces
by his own *pack*.

[p. 8]   Ode

    Love sits enthron'd in Clara's eyes,
       The Graces play her lips around,
    And in her cheeks the tendrest dyes
       Of Lilly mix'd with rose are found.

    Where charms so irresistless throng
       What mortal heart can try resistance?
    —But ah! her nose is two feet long,
       And bids our passions keep their distance.

The fair Bargain.
A Dialogue.

Woman.
You tell me my Cruelty makes you despair,
    And you cannot my frowns any longer survive:
But you men are so fickle, that first you shall swear,
    E'er I yeild, that you'll love me as long as you live.

Man.
Tis a bargain, my Love; and my faith here I give:
    But lest to deceive me my charmer shoud mean,

tator, and Guardian. These were afterwards used in the various editions of
those respective works; more particularly in the Tatler, 6 vols. small 8vo.
1786, published by Mr. Nichols, in which the Annotator, wherever mentioned,
designates Dr. Calder" (ibid., IX, 805). HW's copy of this work is listed Hazen,
Cat. of HW's Lib., No. 2963. HW wrote the following couplet "On Dr Johnson's Biographers" ca. July 1785 in his "Book of Visitors at Strawberry Hill"
(*YWE*, XII, 258): "In Johnson's fate Acteon's re-occurs, / Each piecemeal torn
by his own pack of curs." (In the MS here he first wrote "hounds" for "pack.")
Boswell's *Journal of a Tour to the Hebrides with Samuel Johnson LL.D.* was
published 1 Oct. 1785, and Mrs. Hester Lynch Piozzi's *Anecdotes of the Late
Samuel Johnson, LL.D. during the Last Twenty Years of his Life,* 25 March
1786 (ibid., XXV, 634, nn. 38–39); HW, who disliked Johnson for his boorish-
ness and Tory politics, wrote to Thomas Walpole the younger 8 April 1786
that "Dr Johnson's friends . . . out of zeal have exposed the poor man by
relating all his absurdities and brutalities, more than they had blown up the
bladder of his fame before" (ibid., XXVI, 236).

If I promise to love you as long as I live,
   You shall swear in your turn to be always Fifteen.

[p. 9]   Poetry is a beautifull way of spoiling prose, & the laborious art of exchanging plain sense for harmony.

A poet who makes use of a worse word instead of a better, because the former fits the rhyme or the measure, tho it weakens the sense, is like a Jeweller, who cuts a diamond into a brilliant, & diminishes the weight to make it shine more.[8]

A man of sense, tho born without wit, often lives to have wit. His memory treasures up ideas & reflexions; he compares them with new occurrencies, & strikes out new lights from the Collision. The consequence is sometimes bon mots, & sometimes apothegms. I will give two instances:

All the flattery showered on Louis 14. never presumed to ascribe wit to him; yet his Experience dictated this saying, which is as true in common life as in his case: "I never give a place, but I make nineteen discontented, & One ungratefull."[9] In his youth no doubt he credited the immediate professions of those he preferred.

Mr Pulteney,[1] afterwards Earl of Bath, was the great Antagonist of Sr Rob. Walpole. He was also the confidential friend of the Duchess of Buckingham.[2] One time when She

8. See the Introduction for a discussion of the primacy of sense in HW's theory of poetry. Applying a similar metaphor to human nature, HW wrote of Lord Chesterfield that "the diamond owed more to being brillianted and polished, and well set, than to any intrinsic worth or solidity" (HW to William Mason, 7 April 1774, *YWE*, XXVIII, 147).

9. HW quoted this saying to Sir Horace Mann in a letter of 15 May 1774, where he says "twenty discontented" (*YWE*, XXIV, 5). It is attributed to Louis XIV in Voltaire's *Siècle de Louis XIV*, chap. xxvi: "Toutes les fois que je donne une place vacante, je fais cent mécontents et un ingrat" (*Œuvres*, ed. L. Moland, Paris, 1877–85, XIV, 446). HW's copy of Dodsley's reprint of this work, London, 1752, 4to, is listed Hazen, *Cat. of HWs Lib.*, No. 1149. "Occurrencies" is so in the MS, and is a rare form of *occurrences* (*OED*).

1. William Pulteney (1684–1764), cr. (1742) Earl of Bath; statesman. For his rivalry with Sir Robert Walpole, HW's father, see the articles on him in *DNB* and in Sedgwick.

2. Lady Katherine Darnley (ca. 1682–1743), m. 1 (1699) James Annesley, 3d Earl of Anglesey; m. 2 (1706) John Sheffield, cr. (1703) Duke of Buckingham; natural daughter of James II by the Countess of Dorchester; half sister of James Francis Edward (Stuart), "the Old Pretender."

was going to Rome on some Jacobite plot, She made over her Estate to M[r] Pulteney, lest She shoud be discovered & forfeit it. On her return he pretended to have lost the Deed, & never woud produce it, tho Lord Mansfield[3] telling him he coud never show his face if he did not restore [p. 10] it, he did give a release: but the Duchess broke with him, and struck him out of her Will. Soon after Pulteney & the Opposition triumphed over Sr Robert Walpole & he was created an Earl, as Pulteney was too, but did not succeed him as Minister, Lord Oxford[4] told S[r] Robert, then Earl of Orford, in the House of Lords, that the Dss of Buckingham had appointed him one of her Executors, he replied, "then, my Lord, I have got Lord Bath's place before he has got mine."

Duet
by a Soldier & his Mistress.

He
Honour is the Soldier's pay;
And, unlike all other gain,

3. Hon. William Murray (1705–93), cr. (1756) Baron Mansfield and (1776) Earl of Mansfield; solicitor general 1742–54; lord chief justice of the King's Bench 1756–88; the "dear Murray" of Pope's *Imitation of the Sixth Epistle of the First Book of Horace*. HW, repeating this anecdote in his *Reminiscences, Written . . . in 1788*, ed. P. Toynbee (Oxford, 1924), pp. 93–94, says that "at last [Pulteney's] friend Lord Mansfield told him plainly, he coud never show his face unless he satisfied the Duchess." Aside from a friendly concern for Pulteney's reputation, Mansfield was probably motivated to speak up on the Duchess's behalf out of the strict sense of justice for which he was to become famous. Yet another motivation may have been a lingering sympathy for Jacobites and their cause: Mansfield came of a well-known Jacobite family, and had been an adherent of the Old Pretender in his youth. See the article on Mansfield in Sedgwick.

4. Edward Harley (ca. 1699–1755), 3d Earl of Oxford and Earl Mortimer, 1741. HW, in his *Reminiscences,* loc. cit., calls Oxford "one of [the Duchess's] executors"; however, an account in *Genealogisch-historische Nachrichten,* 1st ser., 5 (1743–44), 192, says that "she had appointed the Earl of Orford [Sir Robert] and Lord Hervey executors of her will, and left a legacy of £5,000 to the former who, as we hear, has accepted neither the one, nor the other" (see YWE, XVIII, 213, and n. 3; Robert Halsband, *Lord Hervey: Eighteenth-Century Courtier,* New York, 1974, p. 303). HW also notes, loc. cit., that "the transaction [of Pulteney's withholding the deed and subsequent release of the Duchess's estate] was recorded in print . . . in a pamphlet that had great vogue called, A congratulatory letter." This pamphlet, "A Congratulatory

Must of merit be the prey,
Never of disgrace or stain.[5]

She
Has He then no other hire?
Is a Sound his sole reward!
Cannot recompens'd Desire
With strict Honour too accord?

He
Oh! yes; by Love when Honour's crown'd,
It turns to Substance what was Sound.
Two last lines repeated by Both.

[p. 11]   When George 2[d] died, Mr H. W. wrote this note to
Mr Brand,[6] who was a remarkable Laugher,

Dear Brand
    You love laughing; there is a King dead; can you help
coming to town?

The best conundrum I ever heard, because the most out
of the way, & yet litterally just, was the following (I know
not the Author)

Letter to a Certain Right Honourable Person, upon his Late Disappointment"
(i.e., "his missing the Treasury on Lord Wilmington's death"; see *YWE*, XXX,
315), published Sept. 1743 and attributed to Lord Chesterfield (ibid., n. 48),
contains, as part of an attack on Pulteney's avarice, a passing mention of his
being "forc'd" to give the Duchess "her estate back again" (5th ed., p. 22).
    5. "Of" has been written over "by" in both the third and fourth lines;
also, "be the prey" in the third line has been inserted after a crossed-out
phrase, conjecturally "be displayed" ("be" and the final "d" are clear). It appears that HW first wrote "Must by merit be displayed, / Never by disgrace
or stain," and then, noticing the incorrect rhyme of the third line, was
forced to alter both that line and the following. (He was perhaps also dis-
satisfied with the sense of the original, though the second version can hardly
be considered an improvement.)
    6. Thomas Brand (1718–70) of The Hoo, Herts.; M.P.; HW's "old school-
fellow" and correspondent (*YWE*, I, 198, et passim). HW's note to Brand, of
which this is the only record, was first printed in Toynbee, *Supplement*, I,
96; it was presumably written the day of George II's death, 25 Oct. 1760.
HW of course does not mean that Brand would be amused by the death itself, but rather by all the pomp and political turmoil attendant upon it;
HW called the coronation of George III "a mere puppet-show" (to Lady
Ailesbury 27 Sept. 1761, *YWE*, XXXVIII, 127).

Why is a Blower of Glass the most likely to make the Alphabet gallop?

Dcanter

Answ. Because he has already made a Decanter.

Charade on my Dog *Tonton*.[7]

My first part is thine; my second belongs only to the most fashionable people; & my Whole, tho doubly thine, belongs only to me.

Cunning is neither the consequence of Sense, nor does it give Sense. A proof that it is not Sense, is, that cunning people never imagine that others can see through them. **It is the consequence of weakness.

I believe it has not been noticed that That strange premature Genius Chatterton has couched in one line the quintessence of what Voltaire has said in many pages,

Reason, a thorn in Revelation's side.[8]

    v. Chatt[s]. Defence p. 36 in the Supplement to his miscellanies. Becket. 1784.

7. A black spaniel bequeathed to HW in 1780 by Madame du Deffand, HW's friend and correspondent (see below, p. 84); out of deference to her memory he took affectionate care of it until its death in 1789 (*YWE*, XII, 265; XXXIV, 45; XXXVI, 182, n. 7, et passim). Mme du Deffand also left HW a gold snuffbox with the dog's image on it (now *WSL*). HW sent this charade to his friend Lord Harcourt in a letter of 25 Oct. 1782 (ibid., XXXV, 525).

8.   Happy (if Mortals can be) is the Man,
    Who, not by Priest, but Reason rules his span;
    Reason, to its Possessor a sure guide,
    Reason, a thorn in Revelation's side.
       (Thomas Chatterton, "The Defence," ll. 23–26)

HW placed an asterisk opposite this line in his copy (now *WSL*, listed Hazen, *Cat. of HW's Lib.*, No. 3690) of *A Supplement to the Miscellanies of Thomas Chatterton* (London, 1784, "printed for T. Becket in Pall-Mall"), p. 36, and quoted it to Lady Ossory in a letter of 4 July 1785 (*YWE*, XXXIII, 475). In this letter he calls Chatterton "a gigantic genius" who "might have soared I know no[t] whither" and praises the line "for its depth of thought and comprehensive expression from a lad of eighteen" (ibid.). In a marginal note to Jacob Bryant's *Observations upon the Poems of Thomas Rowley: In Which the Authenticity of Those Poems Is Ascertained* (London, 1781), p. 499 (now *WSL*, listed Hazen, loc. cit.), HW writes that he is "far from being" of Bryant's opinion that the poems Chatterton acknowledged as his own are

[p. 12]   A Card

sent from Strawberry hill to Eliz. Rich, Baroness Dow^r. Lyttelton,[9] to inquire when She will be in town, Nov. 27. 1784.

From a Castle as vast—as the Castles on Signs;
From a Hill that all Africa's—Ant-hills outshines,
This Epistle is sent to a Cottage so small,
That the Door will not ope if you stand in the hall,
To a Lady, who woud be fifteen, if her Knight   (he 67)
And Old Swain were as young as Methusalem quite;
It comes to inquire—not whether her Eyes

"inferior" to the ones he ascribed to Rowley. HW's rebuff of Chatterton for the Rowley imposture, which, with the help of Mason and Gray, he early detected, led to the unjust vilification of him by Chatterton's supporters for having thereby precipitated the poet's suicide in 1770. Thomas Becket, the publisher of the *Supplement* (Chatterton's *Miscellanies* was published in 1778), was bookseller and publisher at "Tully's Head in the Strand" from 1760 (H. R. Plomer et al., *A Dictionary of the Printers and Booksellers . . . in England, Scotland and Ireland from 1726 to 1775,* Oxford, 1932, pp. 20–21). Chatterton's "Defence," first printed in the *Supplement,* was composed Christmas Day, 1769, as a justification of his refusal to accept the authority of priests in matters of faith. HW himself inclined towards deism in his religious views (see the Introduction).

9. Elizabeth Rich (ca. 1716–95), daughter of Field Marshal Sir Robert Rich, 4th Bt., m. (1749) George Lyttelton (1709–73), 5th Bt., 1751, cr. (1756) Baron Lyttelton; HW's correspondent. For an account of Strawberry Hill, HW's house in Twickenham which he rebuilt in the style of the Gothic Revival, see W. S. Lewis, "The Genesis of Strawberry Hill," *Metropolitan Museum Studies,* 5, Pt. 1 (June 1934), 57–92. The MS of these verses which HW sent to Lady Lyttelton (misdated 28 Nov.) is now in the Robert C. Waterston Collection of the Massachusetts Historical Society; HW also transcribed them in a letter to Henry Seymour Conway 28 Nov. 1784 (first printed in *Works,* V, 234–36; reprinted *YWE,* XXXIX, 428–30; the MS is missing). The poem differs slightly in the three versions: "all Africa's—Ant-hills" in line 2 was originally "an African—molehill" in the MS to Lady Lyttelton and transcribed as "all Africa's—mole-hills" in the Conway letter. A copy of Lady Lyttelton's reply in her own hand survives on the MS which HW sent to her; this copy agrees, except in punctuation, with the first printed version, in a note to the Conway letter in *Works* (V, 236, n. 1). Lady Lyttelton died in Portugal Street in 1795 (*GEC*). The Ninon Lenclos (or Lanclos) of line 2 of her reply was a celebrated French courtesan (1620 or 23–1705) supposed to have had affairs well into her old age (see Edgar H. Cohen, *Mademoiselle Libertine: A Portrait of Ninon de Lanclos,* Boston, 1970, pp. 7, 267–70 et passim). Mary Berry, in her note to the Conway letter in *Works* mentioned above, observes that HW's verses were taken "in perfect good humour," and

Are as radiant as ever; but how many Sighs
He must vent to the rocks & the Echoes around
(Tho nor Echo nor rock in the Parish is found)
Before She obdurate his passion will meet—
His Passion to see Her in *Portugal street.

(*Where she lived in London.)

Lady Lyttelton's answer the next day.

Remember'd, tho Old, by a Wit and a Beau!
I shall fancy e'er long I'm a Ninon Lenclos!
I *must* feel impatient such kindness to meet,
And shall hasten my flight into Portugal street.

Ripley Cottage, Nov. 28ᵗʰ.

[p. 13] The Countess of Ossory¹ losing two piping Bull-
finches in one day, & having them buried under a rose tree,
desired Mʳ H. W. to write Epitaphs on them: he sent her the
following.

that HW owned that her answer "was better than his address." The wit and
good humor of her reply are heightened by the fact that she herself had
apparently been *galante* in her youth (see *GEC; YWE,* XXXVIII, 14, and
n. 10). Both HW's verses and Lady Lyttelton's reply are printed in HW's
Fugitive Verses, ed. W. S. Lewis (New York, 1931), pp. 178–79, following
Toynbee, XIII, 222, and *Supplement,* II, 8, which in turn follow the MS in
the Massachusetts Historical Society (HW's lines) and the printed version in
Works (Lady Lyttelton's).

1. Anne Liddell (ca. 1738–1804), daughter of Henry Liddell, 1st Baron
Ravensworth, m. 1 (1756) Augustus Henry Fitzroy, 3d Duke of Grafton, 1757
(divorced 1769); m. 2 (1769) John Fitzpatrick, 2d Earl of Upper Ossory, 1758;
HW's correspondent. HW transcribed the first of these epitaphs in a letter
to William Mason, 22 Sept. 1783 (first printed in *The Correspondence of
Horace Walpole, Earl of Orford, and the Rev. William Mason,* ed. J. Mitford,
London, 1851, II, 351–54), the MS of which no longer survives; both epitaphs
were first printed in HW's "Miscellaneous Verses" in *Works,* IV, 389–90, and
reprinted in his *Fugitive Verses,* ed. W. S. Lewis, p. 85. The transcription in
Mitford differs from both the version here and the version in *Works* in having "I or you" for "I and you" in line 2, and "This little corpse" for "His little
Corpse" in line 10, both probably copying errors; the *Works* transcription is
obviously wrong in having "plume" for "prune" in line 10. HW, according
to his letter to Mason, wrote the epitaphs in 1779 or 1780 (*YWE,* XXIX,
312). Mason, in his missing reply, evidently accused HW of treating a serious
subject (the immortality of the soul) with unbecoming levity, for HW felt

All flesh is grass, and so are feathers too.
Finches must die as well as I and you.
Beneath a damask rose in good old Age
Here lies the Tenant of a noble Cage.
For forty moons He charm'd his Lady's ear,
And piped obedient oft as She drew near,
Tho now stretched out upon a clay-cold bier.
But when the last shrill flageolet shall sound,
And raise all Dicky birds from holy ground,
His little Corpse again its wings shall prune,
And sing eternally the selfsame tune
From everlasting night to everlasting noon.

On the other Bullfinch.

Beneath the same bush rests his Brother:
What serves for One will serve for tother.

When Lady Mary Tufton[2] married D[r] Duncan, an elderly
Physician, Mr George Selwyn said, "how often She will say
with Macbeth
Wake, Duncan, with thy knocking—woud Thou coudst!

constrained to make the following defence (in his letter to Mason of 8 Nov.
1783): "You amaze me by even supposing that the epitaph I sent you could
allude to the immortality of the soul. . . . The last three lines which justly
offended you if you so interpreted them, were intended to laugh at the absurd idea of the beatified sitting on golden thrones and chanting eternal
hallelujahs to golden harps. When men ascribe their own puerile conceptions
to the Almighty Author of all things, what do they but prove that their visions are of human invention? What can be more ridiculous than to suppose
that Omnipotent Goodness and Wisdom created, and will select the most
virtuous of its creatures to sing his praises to all eternity? —it is an idea that
I should think could never have entered but into the head of a king, who
might delight to have his courtiers sing Birthday odes forever" (ibid., XXIX,
315). "All flesh is grass" in line 1 is an echo of I Peter i . 24: "For all flesh
is as grass, and all the glory of man, as the flower of grass. The grass wither-
eth, and the flower thereof falleth away." HW's use of the colloquial "dicky
birds" in line 9 antedates the earliest example in *OED* by over fifty years
(see also *YWE,* XI, 214).

2. Lady Mary Tufton (1723–1806), daughter of the 7th Earl of Thanet,
m. (1763) Sir William Duncan (ca. 1715–74), Bt., 1764, physician to George III
(*YWE,* IX, 359, n. 13). George Augustus Selwyn (1719–91), HW's friend and

[p. 14]   Fragments

of verses designed for an entertainment that was to have been
given to the Duke & Duchess of Gloucester[3] at Strawberry hill,
but which never were finished nor executed. The verses were
to allude to different pictures &c in the House, & to contain
compliments to the Duke & Duchess & the royal Family.

On the beauty room & the portraits of the Duchess & her
three Daughters by Lord Waldegrave.

Behold the Fair Ones of an age of Charms,
Worthy of Jove's, & rais'd to *Charles's arms!   *Ch. 2^d.
Yet lo! they wave with unrepining mien
The throne of Beauty, when at once are seen
The Daughter Graces & the Mother Queen.

On the portraits of Henry 8th. & his Queens.[4]

correspondent, was a politician and noted wit; HW quoted his bon mot
about Lady Mary and Dr. Duncan (whose marriage was rumored to be un-
consummated) in letters to George Montagu 16 April 1761 and to Sir Horace
Mann 6 Oct. 1774 (ibid., IX, 360, XXIV, 49). The line from *Macbeth* (which
Selwyn cleverly amends by making "Duncan" an object of address rather
than of the verb) concludes the second scene of the second act.

3. William Henry (1743–1805), brother of George III, cr. (1764) Duke of
Gloucester, married secretly (1766) Maria Walpole (1736–1807), HW's niece
(she was an illegitimate daughter of Sir Edward Walpole). Her first husband
(whom she married in 1759) was James Waldegrave (1715–63), 2d Earl Waldegrave, 1741, by whom she had three daughters: (1) Elizabeth Laura (1760–
1816), m. (1782) George Waldegrave, 4th Earl Waldegrave, 1784; (2) Charlotte
Maria (1761–1808), m. (1784) George Henry Fitzroy, styled Earl of Euston,
4th Duke of Grafton, 1811; and (3) Anna Horatia (1762–1801), m. (1786) Hon.
Hugh Seymour-Conway, later Lord Hugh Seymour. The marriage of the Duke
and Duchess, when revealed, resulted in their ostracism from the Court. For
the beauty of the Duchess and her daughters, see *YWE*, XXII, 128; XXV, 68,
et passim; portraits of them by Reynolds hung in the Refectory and in the
Gallery at Strawberry Hill ("Des. of SH," *Works*, II, 403, 463), while the pictures in the Beauty Room (or Yellow Bedchamber) included portraits of the
Duchesses of Portsmouth and Cleveland, Charles II's mistresses (ibid., II, 419).

4. Listed in *Works* as hanging over the staircase ("Henry VIII. aged 29, and
Charles V. aged 20, in one picture, from Mr. [James] West's collection"), in
the Holbein Chamber ("Jane Seymour" and "Henry VIII. three quarters; a
present from the reverend Mr. Pennicott"), in the Tribune ("Catherine Parr,

Harry here, a Tudor bold,
Of Giant soul, & giant mould
Swaggers o'er a trembling court,
At once his Instruments & sport,
The savage Sultan of the Fair,
Who never did his passions spare,
And who, with shame the Muse repeats,
Changed his Religion with his sheets.
But when a less intrepid *Prince,   *James 2ᵈ.
Whom Law nor reason coud convince,
Woud have trod back old Harry's path,
And chang'd again our rites & faith;
A Patriot band, immortal Men!
Champions alike with sword & pen,
Withstood the Tyrant to his face,
And chang'd their King to save their race.
Then *William rose, propitious Name,   *Wm. 3ᵈ.
*Still dear to Britons & to fame,   *Wᵐ D. of Cum-
The Hero stamp'd our cause his own,   berland &
United Freedom and the Throne,   Wm D. of
And bad them undivided shine   Gloster
By his dear Choice, the Brunswic Line.

It was a very ingenious reply made by Ld Altham⁵ one of
the prebendaries of Westminster to King William, after

by Holbein; a most scarce head"; "Jane Seymour; by Holbein, in water-
colours"; "Catherine of Arragon . . . an admirable original; by Holbein"),
and in the Great North Bedchamber ("over the chimney, a large picture of
Henry VIII. and his children [attributed to Hans Eworth]; bought out of
the collection of James West, esq. in 1773") ("Des. of SH," *Works*, II, 439,
458, 460, 476–77, 494; see also *YWE*, XXXIII, 472, n. 25). The three-quarters
length of Henry was moved from the Holbein Chamber to the Great North
Bedchamber in 1785 (ibid., XXXIII, 472, and n. 29). William Augustus (1721–
65), Duke of Cumberland, mentioned in HW's gloss, was uncle of George III.
A military commander, he is best remembered for his victory over the rebels
at Culloden in 1746.

5. Richard Annesley (ca. 1655–1701), 3d Baron Altham, ?1700; prebendary
of Westminster, 1679, and of Exeter, 1681; dean of Exeter, 1681. The lord
great chamberlain at the time of William III's coronation (1689) was Robert

whose Coronation there had been some Dispute between
the Chapter and the Lord Great Chamberlain for certain
perquisites of velvet. The King said, "I wonder yr Lordship
who is a man of Quality, shoud have entered into that
squabble; besides, you know it was not allowed to you at
King James's coronation." "It is very true, S[r], said Lord
Altham—but then We crowned him accordingly."

[p. 16]   Lady Sundon, whose Maiden name was Dives,[6] was
Woman of the bedchamber to Queen Caroline, & was a great

Bertie (ca. 1630–1701) 3d Earl of Lindsey, 1666; the chamberlain's duties included the fitting up of Westminster Hall for a coronation, and he himself
was entitled to have "forty ells of crimson velvet for his own robes" for that
event (Robert Beatson, *A Political Index to the Histories of Great Britain
and Ireland,* 3d ed., London, 1806, I, 356). In the MS HW wrote "perquities"
for "perquisites," an obvious slip which has been emended.

6. Charlotte Dyve (d. 1742), m. (before 1714) William Clayton, cr. (1735)
Baron Sundon; appointed 1714, through the influence of the Duchess of Marlborough, woman of the Bedchamber to Caroline, Princess of Wales (subsequently queen consort of George II). HW, in his *Reminiscences,* ed. P. Toynbee (Oxford, 1924), pp. 71–72, calls her "an absurd and pompous simpleton."
Lord Hervey, on the other hand, says that she had "very great, good, and
noble qualities," and was "certainly no fool" (*Memoirs,* ed. R. Sedgwick, London, 1931, II, 605); the severity of HW's remark probably reflects the preju-
dice of his father, who was clearly jealous of Lady Sundon's influence with
the Queen. Shortly after her arrival in England (in 1714), Queen Caroline was
called on by Dr. Samuel Clarke (1675–1729), the controversial divine, whose
Scripture-Doctrine of the Trinity (London, 1712) had been attacked for its
Arian tendency. He presented her with his writings, which she subsequently
declared to be "the finest things in the world" (*Diary of Mary Countess
Cowper,* ed. Spencer Cowper, London, 1864, pp. 14, 17). Another controversial divine whom both the Queen and Lady Sundon patronized was Dr. Benjamin Hoadly (1676–1761), bishop of Winchester, 1734, a follower of Clarke.
HW writes in his *Reminiscences,* p. 71, that "as Sir Robert maintained his
influence over the clergy by [Edmund] Gibson [1669–1748], Bishop of London
[1723–48], he often met with troublesome obstructions from Lady Sundon,"
who "hated" Gibson (HW to Sir Horace Mann 7 Jan. 1742 OS, *YWE,* XVII,
278; for the relations of Sir Robert and Gibson, see J. H. Plumb, *Sir Robert
Walpole: The King's Minister,* London, 1960, pp. 95–96, 299–300; Norman
Sykes, *Edmund Gibson,* London, 1926, passim). As for the secret of the
Queen's rupture, HW writes that "on my mother's death [in 1737], who was
of the Queen's age, her Majesty asked Sir Robert many physical questions—
but he remarked that she oftenest reverted to a rupture, which had not been
the illness of his wife. When he came home, he said to me, 'now, Horace,
I know by possession of what secret Lady Sundon has preserved such an

Pretender to Learning, & tho a very absurd Woman, had very great Influence over the Queen. Some thought it was by affecting to be the Patroness of the Arrian Clergy to whom her Majesty leaned. Sʳ R. W. often found Ly Sundon in his way, when he wanted to promote Orthodox Clergy, as he espoused Gibson Bp of London. Sʳ Robert was always persuaded that Lady Sundon had gained her ascendant, by being privy to some Secret of the Queen. Just before the Queen's death, when it came out that she had long had a rupture, which She had kept as an inviolable Secret, & which it was supposed nobody knew but the King & Mrs Mailborn her German nurse, Sʳ Robert said, "now I know what the Secret was of which Lady Sundon had got hold."

The Queen had a great mind to make Dʳ Sam. Clarke7 a Bishop—but he woud not subscribe the 39 articles again. Sʳ R. W. to please the Queen, endeavoured to persuade him, & urged to him that he had subscribed when he took Orders, & so enjoyed the Living of St. James's. The Doctor pleaded that he had believed them when he Subscribed, tho he did not now. Sʳ Robert said, then he ought to resign the Living to

ascendant over the Queen'" (*Reminiscences*, p. 74). The validity of Sir Robert's claim is disputed by Lady Sundon's biographer in *DNB*, who points out that the earliest symptoms of the Queen's rupture did not appear until 1724, when Lady Sundon had already been in her favor a good ten years. The Queen's German nurse is called "Mailbone" by Lord Hervey (*Memoirs*, II, 587). In the MS HW wrote "maiden names" and also "orthody" for "orthodox."

7. See the preceding note. William Whiston, *Historical Memoirs of the Life of Dr. Samuel Clarke* (London, 1730), p. 110, writes that Clarke "for some years before he died . . . perpetually refused all, even the greatest preferments, which required [that he subscribe to the thirty-nine articles]. And he let both his highest and his most intimate friends know, that he would take no sort of preferment which required it." According to Thomas Emlyn, *Memoirs of . . . the Reverend Dr. Samuel Clarke* (written 1731), in his *Works* (London, 1746), II, 491–95, "no such subscription [was] required of a bishop," but Clarke not only would not consider accepting any position lower than that of archbishop, where he would have no religious superior to answer to, but probably would not have even accepted that post because, though not subscribing himself, he would have been obliged by canon law to require newly ordained priests and deacons to do so. Clarke was rector of St. James's, Westminster, from 1709 (*DNB*).

Somebody who did believe. They disputed (it was in Kensington palace) till it was so late, that the Candles were nearly burnt out, [p. 17] & the Pages came & asked Sr Robert if he woud please to have fresh Candles! The Conference broke up without either persuading the Other.

Menage disoit que les armoiries de ces nouvelles maisons sont les enseignes de leurs anciennes boutiques.

Disc. prel. de l'histoire de Picardie[8] p. xiv. 1770.

applicable to the numb. of new Knights of Margery Nicholson. 1786.

Des qu'un Serf etoit decedè, on lui coupoit la main droite, qu'on presentoit à son Seigneur. A ce Signal il s'emparoit du peu d'effets qu'il avoit amassès. Il s'approprioit ce modique heritage à l'exclusion des Enfans du Mort. C'est ce qu'on nommoit le droit de *Mainmorte*.[9]   ib. Vol. 1. p. 218.

8. Louis-Alexandre Deverité (1743–1818), *Essai sur l'histoire générale de Picardie* (Abbeville, 1770), 2 vols., 12mo (listed Hazen, *Cat. of HW's Lib.*, No. 2050 : 20, although Hazen thinks that HW may have only borrowed the work; for Deverité, see *Dictionnaire de biographie française*, Paris, 1933–, XI, 194–95). "Menage" is Gilles Ménage (1613–92), philologist (see Elvire Samfiresco, *Ménage: polémiste, philologue, poète*, Paris, 1902); the quotation is from his *Menagiana*, first published at Paris and Amsterdam, 1693, and frequently reprinted after that. (HW owned the Paris edition of 1729, 4 vols., 12mo, where the quotation is found at III, 350; see Hazen, *Cat.*, No. 999, and also, for the editions of *Menagiana*, BM Cat., Nat. Union Cat., Bibl. Nat. Cat.) For "armoiries" HW first wrote "armoires," reproducing the typographical error in Deverité. Margaret (or Margery) Nicholson (?1750–1828), a barber's daughter, on 2 Aug. 1786 attempted to stab George III as he arrived at St. James's Palace from Windsor. Declared insane, she was sent to Bedlam, where she died *(DNB;* see also *GM* Aug. 1786, LVI, Pt. ii, 708–10). The King subsequently created numerous new knights in conjunction with the presentation of congratulatory addresses on his escape. Among those so knighted were Benjamin Hammett, alderman of London (11 Aug.), Richard Tawney, senior alderman of Oxford City (13 Aug.), Stephen Nash, sheriff of Bristol (18 Aug.), and Michael Nowell, sheriff of Cornwall (25 Aug.) (W. A. Shaw, *The Knights of England*, London, 1906, II, 299; *Daily Advertiser*, 12, 16, 24, 26 Aug. 1786). As an example of the humble origins of these men, Hammett, who rose to become an eminent banker and M.P., is said to have started his London career as a porter in a bookshop on Fish Street Hill (*GM* Aug. 1800, LXX, Pt. ii, 798; Namier and Brooke, II, 575).

9. "*Mainmorte* . . . Terme de jurisprudence. État des serfs qui, en vertu d'anciens droits féodaux, étaient privés de la faculté de tester et de disposer de leurs biens quand ils n'avaient pas d'enfants; c'était le seigneur qui était

Formerly the streets were so bad & dirty that people went on such Stilts as Children now use. The K. of Prussia in the mem. de Brandebourg says Courtiers used to go to Court on Stilts.[1] ib. vol. 2. p. 318.

Sr Horace Mann the younger[2] was so very gratefull and affectionate to his Uncle Sr Horace the Elder, the very amiable old Minister at Florence, that Mr W. said, "When human Nature is excellent, the Term *Man* ought to be spelled with a double *n*."

leur héritier" (Emile Littré, *Dictionnaire de la langue française*, Paris, 1962–63, IV, 1850). According to Voltaire, even the legitimate offspring of a serf could be dispossessed of their father's goods "s'ils n'ont pas toujours vécu avec leur père dans la même maison et à la même table" (*Œuvres complètes*, ed. L. Moland, Paris, 1877–85, XXVIII, 355–56). With regard to the origin of the term, he writes: "Ce mot . . . vient, dit-on, de ce qu'autrefois, lorsqu'un de ces serfs décédait sans laisser d'effets mobiliers que son seigneur pût s'approprier, on apportait au seigneur la main droite du mort, digne origine de cette domination" (ibid., XV, 427). Littré comments: "Cette étymologie . . . est fausse. *Manus* a déjà en droit romain et a conservé en vieux droit français le sens de puissance, domaine. Ici *main* veut dire le droit de transmettre et d'aliéner. . . . Quant au sens de *mort* en ce mot, il . . . signifie éteint, sans force" (*Dictionnaire*, IV, 1851).

1. "La plûpart des rues n'étoient point pavées: aucun allignement n'existoit. Nous voyons encore quelquefois des enfans dans leur jeux marcher montés sur de hautes échasses; on se servoit de ces facilités pour traverser les rues & en franchir la boue. Il en étoit de même d'un bout de l'Europe à l'autre, les courtisans, dit l'historien illustre de Brandebourg, se rendoient ainsi à la cour de Potzam [*sic*] à Berlin" (Deverité, II, 317–18). The reference is to Frederick II, the Great, King of Prussia, *Mémoires pour servir à l'histoire de la maison de Brandebourg*: "Les courtisans étoient obligés d'aller en échasses au château de Potzdam lorsque la cour s'y tenoit, à cause des boues qu'il falloit traverser dans les rues" (new ed., Berlin and The Hague, 1751, p. 302; HW's copy listed Hazen, *Cat.*, No. 1140).

2. Sir Horace Mann (1744–1814), Kt., 1768; 2d Bt., 1786; M.P. His uncle was Sir Horace Mann (1706–86), cr. (1755) Bt.; K.B., 1768; chargé d'affaires, resident, and envoy at Florence, 1736–86. With the elder Mann, who was a distant cousin and boyhood friend, HW kept up a steady and voluminous correspondence from their meeting at Florence in 1739–41 until the elder Mann's death over forty-five years later. (Their correspondence, consisting of over 1700 letters, fills volumes 17–25 of the Yale Walpole Edition.) The elder Mann died the night of 16–17 Nov. 1786 (*YWE* XXV, 664). The letter from the younger Mann which HW mentions is printed ibid., XXV, 662 (dated 25 Sept. 1786); HW's reply is missing, except for the fragment recorded here (printed ibid., XXV, 663).

Sr Hor. jun^r. set out directly & travelled night & day, when ever he heard his Uncle was ill, as he did in Sept. 1786—and finding his Uncle still alive, wrote Mr W. word of it. He replied, "I want another letter with a still better account. They who feel, cannot keep their minds in the equilibrium of a pair of scales: Fear & Hope have no Equiponderant weights: the moment [p. 18] the one turns the balance, it swells extravagantly, tho perhaps inflated by air."

Pitts says Matthew Paris was Pictor non vulgaris, probably an Illuminator—but quere whether he had seen any of his works.

See Dr Berkenhout's^3 Biogr. Litter. Vol. 1. p. 18.

Tho. Winter,^{4} natural Son of Card. Wolsey. ib. 118.

Rich. Taverner^5 Clerk of the Signet to Henry 8th. and an

3. John Berkenhout (ca. 1730–91), M.D.; physician and miscellaneous writer. HW's copy of his *Biographia Literaria; or a Biographical History of Literature . . . Volume I. From the Beginning of the Fifth to the End of the Sixteenth Century* (London, 1777), 4to, is listed Hazen, *Cat. of HW's Lib.*, No. 3291 (no more volumes were published). In the article on Matthew Paris (d. 1259), historian and monk, Berkenhout cites John Pits (1560–1616), *De illustribus Angliæ scriptoribus* (Paris, 1619), p. 337, as calling Paris "manuarius, scriptor, pictor non vulgaris." HW does not mention Paris as an artist in his *Anecdotes of Painting* and seems skeptical here about his having been one; however, it has since been firmly established that Paris was the illustrator of many books. See *DNB* and Richard Vaughan, *Matthew Paris* (Cambridge, 1958), pp. 205–34.

4. Thomas Wynter, product of the "uncanonical" marriage of Wolsey and "one Lark's daughter"; archdeacon of Cornwall 1537–43 (*DNB*, s.v. Wolsey; see also A. F. Pollard, *Wolsey*, London, 1929, pp. 306, 308–12). He is mentioned in Berkenhout, in the article on Thomas Lupset, as having gone to France accompanied by Lupset, who was his tutor.

5. Richard Taverner (?1505–75), religious reformer and author, clerk of the signet to Henry VIII and Edward VI; he lost his place on the accession of Queen Mary and retired to his house at Norbiton, Surrey. In 1541, after the fall of his patron Cromwell, Taverner was briefly imprisoned in the Tower for concealing from the government and communicating to others a report that Anne of Cleves was pregnant by Henry VIII; this episode is noted in Berkenhout, p. 142, n. *b*. Elizabeth Shepherd (ca. 1701–88), m. (1725) Sir John Philipps (ca. 1701–64), 6th Bt., 1743, lived at Norbiton Place, "opposite to Norbeton-hall on the other side of the road," which had been the residence of Taverner (A. Anderson, *History and Antiquities, of Kingston upon Thames,* Kingston, 1818, pp. 57–59; W. D. Biden, *The History and Antiquities of . . . Kingston-upon-Thames,* Kingston, 1852, p. 94; *GM* Oct. 1788, LVIII, Pt. ii,

Author, lived at Norbiton hall in Surry. Qu. if not the House now so called belonging to Lady Philipps close to Kingston. p. 143. Taverner was committed to the Tower for slandering Anne of Cleve. ib.

To inquire when or why the famous Countess of Carlisle was committed to the Tower before the restoration, as it is said She was, in the life of Christian Countess of Devonshire.[6] I have no where else met with that Event. As she had betrayed Charles 1st. to Pym, She probably like the Earl of Holland, had again changed Sides, & dabbled for the King.

On Dr Dee's[7] black stone in my collection.

Kelly did all his feats upon
The Devil's looking-glass a Stone.
Hudibras. pt. 2. canto 3d. 631.

936). Norbiton Hall at this time belonged to "one Greenly" (*Victoria History of the County of Surrey*, ed. H. E. Malden, London, 1902–12, III, 504).

6. Thomas Pomfret, *The Life of the Right Honourable and Religious Lady Christian Late Countess Dowager of Devonshire* (London, 1685), p. 80 (HW's copy, now *WSL*, listed Hazen, *Cat. of HW's Lib.*, No. 3900). Lady Devonshire was Christian Bruce (1595–1675), daughter of Edward, 1st Lord Kinloss, m. (1608) William Cavendish (1590–1628), 2d Earl of Devonshire, 1626. Lucy Percy (ca. 1600–60), daughter of Henry, 3d Earl of Northumberland, who m. (1617) James Hay (ca. 1580–1636), cr. (1622) Earl of Carlisle, was noted for her beauty, wit, and penchant for intrigues Long a confidante of Charles's queen, Henrietta Maria, she nevertheless in 1642 warned John Pym (1584–1643), leader of the Parliamentary opposition, of the King's march on Parliament to arrest him and four others for sedition; while in 1649 she was sent to the Tower by the Council of State for having intrigued with the Royalists, though apparently a friend of the Parliamentarians. Lord Clarendon, in his *History of the Rebellion*, ed. W. D. Macray (Oxford, 1888), I, 434, n. 2, connects her defection to Pym with that of Henry Rich (1590–1649), cr. (1624) Earl of Holland, who subsequently switched his allegiance several more times before being executed (by the Parliamentarians). Lady Carlisle was released from the Tower late in 1650, after some eighteen months' imprisonment; despite this experience, she seems to have kept up her intriguing until her death.

7. Dr. John Dee (1527–1608), mathematician and astrologer. His "black stone" was an obsidian mirror of Aztec origin through which he claimed to be able to communicate with spirits; it was given to HW by Lord Frederick Campbell in 1770 or 1771 and is now in the British Museum. HW affixed a label to the case for the stone on which he wrote Butler's lines with the comment: "Kelly was Dr Dee's associate and is mentioned with this very stone

We seldom consider the goodness of Providence in all the degrees & shades of its kindness. It not only gives us food & medicines, but furnishes us with Succedaneums. Even Palliatives are present.

[p. 19]   For Miss Burney.

Qui se donne à la Cour, se derobe aux talens.
life of Voltaire.[8]

A. is the reverse of Janus, for he has neither reflection nor foresight.

Charles Sackville Earl of Middlesex[9] seeing the beautifull Lady Ross in Ireland, who was very virtuous, said, "I wish She was Lady Ros*common*."

in *Hudibras*, Part 2. Cant. 3. v. 631." Edward Kelley (1555–95), a native of Worcestershire and reputed adept in the occult sciences, was Dee's associate from 1582 to 1589. See *DNB;* Peter J. French, *John Dee: The World of an Elizabethan Magus* (London, 1972), p. 113, n. 2, et passim; *YWE*, XXIII, 286–87 and nn. 48, 51; Hugh Tait, " 'The Devil's Looking-Glass': The Magical Speculum of Dr John Dee," in *Horace Walpole: Writer, Politician, and Connoisseur,* ed. W. H. Smith (New Haven, 1967), pp. 195–212.

8. Théophile-Imarigeon Duvernet (ca. 1734–96), *La Vie de Voltaire* (Geneva, 1786) (reviewed *GM* Nov. 1786, LVI, Pt. ii, 970; for Duvernet, see *Dictionnaire de biographie française*, Paris, 1933–, XII, 1037–38). On the subject of "Voltaire courtisan . . . Années de 1745-à-1748" (chap. xii), Duvernet writes: "Voici encore un temps de mort pour le génie de Voltaire: de plusieurs années nous ne verrons en lui le philosophe: nous ne verrons qu'un bel-esprit attaché au char de la fortune, & justifiant cette maxime de Moliere: 'Qui se donne à la Cour se dérobe à son art' " (p. 121). There is no other record of HW's having owned or read this book; his misquoting the line from Molière (as well as his failure to attribute it to that author) suggests that he may have heard it at second hand, or hastily scanned the book at a friend's. (The exact source of the line has not been found.) Fanny Burney, the novelist, had on 17 July begun service as second keeper of the Robes to Queen Charlotte (*YWE*, XXXIII, 518, n. 6); HW, in a letter to Hannah More 15 June 1787, lamented "the loss of her company and her writings" (ibid., XXXI, 247). See below, pp. 75, 93.

9. Charles Sackville (1711–69), styled Earl of Middlesex, 1720–65; 2d Duke of Dorset, 1765; a "dissolute and extravagant man of fashion" (*DNB*). The Lady Ross referred to is perhaps Olivia Edwards (ca. 1731–1820), m. 1 (1754) Richard Parsons (ca. 1718–64), 2d Earl of Rosse (in Ireland), 1741 (grandson of the Lady Ross mentioned below); m. 2 (1770) John Bateman. By "Lady Roscommon" Middlesex perhaps meant Angel Ingoldsby, m. (1719) Robert

The Duchess of Tirconnel[1] had three daughters by her first Husband George Hamilton, Lady Kingsland, Lady Dillon & Lady Ross—not the Lady mentioned above.

On Jenkinson Lord Hawksbury's[2] motto
Non sine pulvere Palma.

Dillon (d. 1722), 7th Earl of Roscommon, 1715; however, it is more likely that he was merely making a pun on the name.

1. Frances Jennings (ca. 1648–1731), elder sister of Sarah, Duchess of Marlborough (see below, p. 111), m. 1 Sir George Hamilton (d. 1676), Count Hamilton in France; m. 2 (1681) Richard Talbot (1630–91), cr. (1685) Earl and (1689) Duke of Tyrconnel (forfeited 1691); a noted beauty of the Court of Charles II. Her three daughters by Hamilton were (1) Elizabeth (d. 1724), m. (1685) Richard Parsons (ca. 1656–1703), cr. (1681) Viscount Rosse; (2) Frances (d. 1751), m. 1 (1687) Henry Dillon (d. 1714), 8th Viscount Dillon, 1691, m. 2 Patrick Bellew (d. 1720); and (3) Mary (d. 1736), m. (1688) Nicholas Barnewall (1668–1725), 3d Viscount Barnewall of Kingsland, 1688. HW was informed of the Duchess's three daughters in a letter of 31 Jan. 1784 from the Hon. Charles Hamilton (1704–86), grandnephew of Sir George Hamilton and Anthony Hamilton, who wished to correct errors about his family in Anthony Hamilton's *Mémoires du comte de Grammont* (which had been printed by HW at Strawberry Hill in 1772). See the letter, printed Toynbee, *Supplement*, III, 289–92; *YWE*, XXXIII, 527, n. 7; *The Scots Peerage*, ed. Sir James Balfour Paul (Edinburgh, 1904–14), I, 53–55, 61; Hazen, *SH Bibl.*, 96–99; *Cat. of HW's Lib.*, No. 2511.

2. Charles Jenkinson (1729–1808), politician; cr. (21 Aug. 1786) Baron Hawkesbury (about which time he was also made president of the Board of Trade and chancellor of the Duchy of Lancaster); cr. (1796) Earl of Liverpool. The motto, meaning "not without dust the palm [of victory]," is adapted from Horace, *Epistles*, I, i, 51: "Cui sit condicio dulcis sine pulvere palmae?" ("to whom may be the condition of sweet victory without dust?"). Early in his career Jenkinson attached himself to the Crown as the only stable element in the ever-shifting political scene; his closeness to the King earned him the envy and hatred of many, including HW, who, in a detached MS memorandum written ca. 1786 (now *WSL*) declared: "There is no man now living who has done so much mischief and deserved public odium, so much, as Charles Jenkinson." Accusing Jenkinson of having authored the "fatal" Stamp Act, and of having most recently plotted against the liberties of the Irish, HW asserts: "Till Jenkinson is driven from his M[ajest]y's confidence, neither country [England or Ireland] can be secure of peace or liberty. He is always machinating ag[ainst] the constitution, & tho so entirely trusted, is the most pernicious enemy the K[ing] has." Jenkinson's influence with the King was undoubtedly great, but HW's penchant for the dramatic leads him here and elsewhere to greatly exaggerate that influence (cf. *Mem. Geo. III*, IV, 89–90, n.). Similarly, HW's characterization of Jenkinson as an evil counsellor working to subject the constitution has to be dismissed as pure fancy.

Since Jenky by the dust thro which he toil'd
Either complains or brags his robes are soil'd,
Till his ambiguous meaning is adjusted,
We sure may wish his Jacket were well dusted.

Another.

Of all the new-made Peers we thought
    Jenky had fewest qualms;
Yet lo! he owns his title bought
    Not without dirty *palms.*

[p. 20]   Miss Reade[3] the Paintress had a Niece who at five years old had an extraordinary talent for drawing groupes of Children, but She did not make much progress afterwards. Miss Reade at 60, herself carried her to India to settle her, & did marry her there to Mr Oakley, since in the Government,

See *DNB;* Namier and Brooke, II, 674–78; Ninetta S. Jucker, ed., *The Jenkinson Papers 1760–1766* (London, 1949), pp. xxiv–xxvii et passim; and below, p. 148. "To dust one's jacket" is a colloquialism, dating from the late seventeenth century, meaning to thrash, to give one a beating (Partridge).

3. Catherine Read (1723–78), portrait painter (Thieme and Becker, XXVIII, 61); for mentions of her in HW's earlier books of materials, see *Anecdotes of Painting,* V, 4, 136 (the present item is printed pp. 136–37). In his copy of the catalogue of the exhibition of the Royal Society of Artists, 26 April 1771 (now *WSL*), HW has identified sketches "by a child of eight years old" (items 309 and 310) as by the "niece of Miss Reade. wonderfull": this was Helena Beatson (1762–1839), m. (1777) Charles Oakeley (1751–1826), cr. (1790) Bt.; governor of Madras, 1790–94. A portrait of her by her aunt, showing her drawing at the age of five, was engraved as a mezzotint and published in 1768 (reproduced *Connoisseur,* 88 [1931], 380). Fanny Burney wrote of her in her diary for Feb.–March 1774, when she was going on twelve, that she had "a most astounding genius for drawing, though never taught. She groupes figures of children in the most ingenious, playful, and beautiful variety of attitudes and employments, in a manner surpassing all credibility, but what the eye itself obtains" (Fanny Burney, *The Early Diary . . . 1768–1778,* ed. A. R. Ellis, London, 1889, I, 274). Miss Beatson accompanied her aunt to India in 1775, where she married Oakeley, who had been in the service of the East India Company since 1766. Miss Read in 1778 began the return voyage to England, but died before reaching her destination, on 15 Dec. See *DNB,* s.v. Charles Oakeley; *GEC, Baronetage,* V, 262–63; Lady Victoria Manners, "Catherine Read: the 'English Rosalba,'" *Connoisseur* 88 (1931), 376–86; "Catherine Read and Royal Patronage," ibid., 89 (1932), 35–40; "Catherine Read: the Last Phase," ibid., 89 (1932), 171–78.

but Miss Reade died on her return at the Cape of Good
Hope.

Motto for an Author who has a mixture of Obscurity &
Clinquant[4]

Post nubila Phebus.

Art is the filigraine of a little mind, & is twisted, and involved & curled, but woud reach farther if laid out in a strait
line.[5]

Two Clergymen disputing whether ordination woud be
valid without the imposition of both hands, the more formal
one said, "do you think the Holy Dove coud fly down with
only one Wing?"

1787.

Jan. 6. Apropos to the marriage of William new King of
Prussia[6] with Mlle Finkenstein, his Queen living, S^r W^m.

4. Literary or artistic "tinsel," false glitter (*OED*). The motto, which is a
classical proverb, means "after clouds, the sun." Pope, *Dunciad*, IV, 61 and
n., alludes to the "modern Phoebus of French extraction. . . . Of whom see
Bohours"; D. Bohours, *The Arts of Logick and Rhetorick*, trans. J. Old-
mixon (London, 1728), p. 365, defines this Phoebus as "an appearance of
light glimmering over the obscurity, a semblance of meaning without any
real sense" (cited Pope, *Dunciad*, ed. J. Sutherland, 2d ed., Twickenham Edition of the Poems of Alexander Pope, London, 1953, p. 347).

5. See HW on "cunning," above, p. 23.

6. Frederick William II (1744–97) succeeded his uncle, Frederick the Great,
as King of Prussia on the latter's death, 17 Aug. 1786 (Isenburg, *Stammtafeln*,
I, taf. 63). According to a report in the *London Chronicle* 6–9 Jan. 1787,
"Since his accession to the throne, [Frederick William] has become enamoured
of a young lady of the highest rank and of the most exquisite beauty. . . .
He has since publicly married the young lady, and allowed her to share the
honours of his former Queen." Frederick William's queen was Frederica
(1751–1805) of Hesse-Darmstadt, whom he married in 1769 (Isenburg, loc.
cit.); the *General Evening Post* 9–11 Jan. identifies the "young lady of the
highest rank" as "daughter to his minister, the Count of Finkenstein." The
report of the marriage was subsequently contradicted in the *London Chronicle* 13–16 Jan., and HW wrote to Lady Ossory 21 Jan. 1787, "Are you not
sorry, Madam, that the King of Prussia's bigamy is not true?" (*YWE*, XXXIII,
555). "Mlle Finkenstein" was Amalie Elisabeth von Voss (d. 1789), cr. (1787)
Gräfin Ingenheim; her brother Otto Karl Friedrich had married (1780) the

Musgrave[7] lent me a little book printed at Amsterdam 1697 in French called La Vie & les Amours de Charles Louis Electeur Palatin. That Prince was Son & Heir of Frederic King of Bohemia & Elizabeth Daughter of James 1st. & the same who came over during the Civil War, & was supposed to have kept too well with the Parliament.[8] It was the same

daughter of Graf Fink von Finkenstein, Frederick the Great's first minister (see sources cited ibid., n. 11). According to Mirabeau, "Le mercredi, 22 [Nov.] . . . fut le jour remarquable où Mademoiselle de Voss accepta la main du roi, et lui promit la sienne. Il fut résolu qu'on serait agréer à la reine le plan d'un mariage du côté gauche"; however, the clergy told the King "his intentions were impossible," and that there was no precedent for it (letter of 2 Dec. 1786, in Honoré-Gabriel Riquetti, Comte de Mirabeau, *Histoire secrète de la cour de Berlin,* "Londres," 1789, II, 187–88; *London Chronicle* 6–9 Jan.). The issue of this "marriage," Gustav Adolf Wilhelm, Graf Ingenheim, was born 2 Jan. 1789.

7. Sir William Musgrave (1735–1800), 6th Bt.; antiquary. The book he lent HW, of which an English translation based on an earlier edition was published at London, 1692, is noted Hazen, *Cat. of HW's Lib.,* No. 4019; a single copy, 12mo, is in the British Museum (not listed in the Nat. Union and Bibl. Nat. Cats.). Charles Louis (1617–80), Elector Palatine, son of Frederick V (1596–1632), Elector Palatine and King of Bohemia, by Elizabeth (1596–1662), daughter of James I of England, married (1650) Charlotte (1627–86), daughter of William V, Landgrave of Hesse-Cassel, by whom he had Charles II (1651–85), Elector Palatine, 1680, and Elizabeth Charlotte (1652–1721), who married (1671) Philippe (1640–1701), Duke of Orleans and brother of Louis XIV. Separating from his first wife in 1657, he married (1658) Marie Luise (1634–77), daughter of Freiherr Christof von Degenfeld, to whom he gave the title of Raugräfin (Rhinegravine). By her he had eight sons, called after her Raugrafen (Rhinegraves), five of whom survived infancy: (1) Karl Ludwig (1658–88); (2) Karl Eduard (1668–90); (3) Karl Moritz (1671–1702); (4) Karl August (1672–91); and (5) Karl Kasimir (1675–91). Charles II married (1671) Wilhelmine Ernestine (1650–1706), daughter of Frederick III of Denmark, by whom he had no children; he was succeeded by his cousin, Philipp Wilhelm (1615–90), Count Palatine of Neuburg, 1653, whose father had turned Catholic on succeeding to the Dukedom of Neuburg in 1614 (Isenburg, I, tafn. 33–34, II, taf. 18; see also below and notes following).

8. See Carola Oman, *Elizabeth of Bohemia* (London, 1938), pp. 341, 361–63, 372, 374, and Ludwig Haüsser, *Geschichte der Rheinischen Pfalz,* 2d ed. (Heidelberg, 1856), II, 564, et passim. In an address presented to both Houses of Parliament, 14 Sept. 1644 (afterwards published as *Motives and Reasons, Concerning his Highnesse the Prince Elector Palatines Comming into England,* London, 1644), Charles Louis declared that "he shall ever hold in high esteem and value the advice they shall thinke fit to give him" (p. 4); in an earlier letter to the Lords he had pledged himself "still to endeavour all means of gratitude and service towards them" (ibid., p. 7). Henri de la Tour

Prince who challenged Marshal Turenne for his barbarity in the Palatinate.

[p. 21]   The book says that Charles Louis married Charlotte Landgrave of Hesse, by whom he had Charles his Successor, & the second Wife of Philip Duke of Orleans Brother of Louis 14. But afterwards Charles Louis fell in love with Mlle Degenfelt his Wife's Maid of Honour, & the Electress finding *Latin* letters that passed between them & reproaching him with them at dinner before the Margrave and Margravine of Baden,[9] he gave his Wife a box of the Ear & made her nose bleed. At last he married his Mistress, pretending he had divorced his Wife without her knowledge, tho in a letter to him

d'Auvergne (1611–75), Vicomte de Turenne, general and Maréchal de France, devastated the Palatinate during the campaign of 1674–75, prompting Charles Louis to write him a letter in which he challenged him to single combat; Turenne returned a courteous reply in which he declined to duel on the grounds that he could not leave his post at the head of the army (Haüsser, II, 633; *La Vie et les amours de Charles Louis Electeur Palatin,* pp. 70–77).

9. "Mr. le Prince de Bade Dourlac, & Madame la Princesse sa femme" (ibid., p. 137); this would have been Frederick V (1594–1659), Margrave of Baden-Durlach, 1622, m. (as his fifth wife) (1652) Elizabeth Eusebia (d. 1676) of Fürstenberg (Isenburg, I, taf. 85). Another version of this anecdote says that the Elector boxed Charlotte's ears after she threw a dish at him during dinner (Oman, p. 394). In an alleged memorial of Charlotte to the Emperor Leopold, printed *La Vie et les amours,* pp. 112–87 (see below, p. 41, n. 2), it is asserted that one of her pages accidentally found "prés de la porte du cabinet de mon epoux, une lettre écrite en latin, qui s'addressoit à S.A. . . . c'étoit un billet doux, & que la Deguenfeld qui l'écrivoit" (p. 124; the billet-doux is printed pp. 124–26). "Je résolus de faire fouiller dans la cassette de cette friponne, où je trouvay trois lettres en latin, que mon epoux luy avoit écrite" (p. 128; the letters are printed pp. 129–35). The correspondence of Charles Louis and Mlle Degenfeld has been preserved and published in *Schreiben des Kurfürsten Karl Ludwig von der Pfalz und der Seinen,* ed. W. L. Holland (Tübingen, 1884); it includes no Latin letters, but a series of billets-doux in Italian in which the Elector and Mlle Degenfeld adopt the pseudonyms of Montecelso and Rosalinda (pp. 1–7). Also preserved is a letter of Charlotte to her brother, William VI of Hesse-Cassel, dated 11 March 1657, in which she describes her discovery in Mlle Degenfeld's cabinet, not of letters from her husband to Mlle Degenfeld, but of pledges of troth drawn up between them (pp. 16–17); these pledges are in German (printed ibid., p. 14). In the MS HW apparently started to write "*Latin* letters that expressed their love"; "expr" is crossed out before "passed between them."

She[1] had once sd She woud submit to his pleasure. By this second Wife he had four Sons, who were called Rhingraves, but they could not inherit from him.[2] his Wife presented a memorial to the Emperor Leopold stating her story & grievances, but it does not appear that anything was done about it. She outlived her Husband four years & her Son restored her to her rank. He, tho married, died without children, & was supposed, says the book, to have been made incapable of Children & at last poisoned by his Physician at the Instigation of the Jesuits, having declared his Cousin the Duke of Neugburgh a Roman Catholic his Heir.

The Book says it was not to the Elector, but to the Electress that the Physician gave drugs to prevent her having Children.

1. I.e., Mlle Degenfeld; the letter referred to is the first Latin letter mentioned above.

2. Mlle Degenfeld on 31 Dec. 1667 formally renounced for herself and for her children all claim of succession to the Palatinate (*Allgemeine Deutsche Biographie*, 1875–1912; rpt. Berlin, 1967–71, XV, 331). For five years after her separation from her husband Charlotte, who refused to give him a divorce, remained in Heidelberg in hopes of obtaining a reconciliation; only in 1662 did she return to Cassel after all her attempts, including a supposed appeal to Leopold I (1640–1705), Holy Roman Emperor, 1658, had failed (Haüsser, II, 612; Isenburg, I, taf. 18). The alleged memorial from Charlotte to the Emperor, printed in *La Vie et les amours,* pp. 112–87, as "une pièce qui a couru long temps en Allemagne" (p. 107), is almost certainly spurious. Besides the apparent discrepancies of fact mentioned above (p. 40, n. 9), it includes a number of high melodramatic and improbable scenes, such as the one where "Charlotte" describes herself as about to shoot Mlle Degenfeld, but is prevented by a Count Hohenloo, who snatches the pistol from her hand and throws it out the window (pp. 179–80). In 1680, upon her husband's death, Charlotte's son Charles sent her 40,000 gulden in payment of her debts, and she returned to Heidelberg (*Allgemeine,* XV, 325). According to *La Vie et les amours,* p. 188, "On a dit que le medecin de Charles, fit entrer quelques ingrédiens, dans les remedes de la princesse son epouse, qui rendirent inutiles toutes les caresses de cét Electeur." In any event, continues *La Vie,* after the death of Charles his physician was charged with having poisoned him, at the instigation of the Jesuits; public clamor against the physician forced the new Elector to imprison him, but he was not prosecuted (pp. 189–90). If indeed there was a poison plot, it is unlikely that the new Elector was implicated in or condoned it; his brief reign was marked by an enlightened toleration of Protestants, who made up the vast majority of his subjects (see *Allgemeine,* XXVI, 29–30). "Neugburgh" is so in the MS.

I think the Wife of Marshal Duke Schomberg[3] was Daughter of one of those Rhingraves. I remember Queen Caroline treated his granddaughter the Countess of Holderness & afterwards of Fitzwalter, as a relation from that left handed Marriage.

[p. 22] Eighteen Convicts being hanged in one day in january, a Woman was crying an account of their Execution, but called them nineteen. A Gentleman asked her why She said nineteen, when there had been but 18 hanged? She replied, "Sʳ, I did not know *you* had been reprieved."[4]

Feb. 1ˢᵗ. from Monsʳ. Dutens.[5]

When the present Prince of Piemont was 7 years old, his Preceptor instructing him in Mythology told him all the

3. HW presumably means Frederick Herman von Schönberg or de Schomberg (1615–90), Maréchal de France, 1675–85, cr. (after his naturalization as an English citizen, 1689) Duke of Schomberg; a famous soldier who died gallantly at the Battle of the Boyne. His granddaughter, Frederica (ca. 1688–1751), married first (1715) Robert Darcy (1681–1722), 3d Earl of Holdernesse, 1692, and second (1724) Benjamin Mildmay (1672–1756), cr. (1730) Earl Fitzwalter. However, it was Marshal Schomberg's *son*, Meinhard (1641–1719), Frederica's father, also a prominent soldier who succeeded as 3d Duke, 1693, who married Caroline Elizabeth (1659–96), daughter of Charles Louis and Mlle Degenfeld and therefore *sister* of the Rhinegraves. Marshal Schomberg married first (1638) Johanna Elizabeth of Schönberg auf Wesel (d. 1664), by whom he had Meinhard, and second (1669) Susanne de Haucourt (d. 1688) (*GEC*; Isenburg, I, taf. 33). In the MS HW first wrote "Landgraves," then crossed out "Land" and inserted "Rhin" above.

4. HW repeated this anecdote in a letter to Lady Ossory 1 Feb. 1787, where he mentions having heard it the night before (*YWE*, XXXIII, 558). The eighteen convicts were hanged on 9 Jan., "before the debtors-door in Newgate"; for their names and crimes, see *London Chronicle* 6–18 Jan. and *GM* 1787, LVII, Pt. i, 84–85.

5. Vincent-Louis Dutens (1730–1812), French-born antiquary and diplomat who settled at London in 1784 as historiographer to George III. Charles Emmanuel (1751–1819), Prince of Piedmont, succeeded to the throne of Sardinia as King Charles Emmanuel IV in 1796 (abdicated 1802); presumably Dutens heard these bon mots of the Prince while at the Court of Turin, where he was secretary to the English envoy, 1758–61, and English chargé d'affaires, 1761–62, 1764–65, and 1781. He included them in the third volume, entitled *Dutensiana*, of his *Mémoires d'un voyageur qui se repose* (London, 1806), pp. 50–51; there he says that the Prince "n'avoit pas encore sept ans" when he uttered the first, and identifies the preceptor as Hyacinthe-Sigismond Gerdil (1718–1802), Cardinal, 1777. He also says that the Prince was fifteen

Vices were enclosed in Pandora's box. "What! all!" said the Prince. Yes, all—"no, s^d the Prince; Curiosity must have been without." When he was about Eighteen, the King admitted him to Council. He concluded he might give his opinion, & often did—but finding It was not minded, he woud go no more. Soon after, the King & Queen talking on business, the Prince spoke his Sentiments. "Comment! s^d the King, vous voulez regler mes affaires!" Non, s^d the Prince; Je ne regle que ma montre—& Elle va bien."

In the Drawing room hung a Venus & Cupid by Michael Angelo, in which, instead of a bit of Drapery, the Painter had placed Cupid's foot between Venus's thighs. Queen Caroline asked General Guise,[6] an old Connoisseur, if it was not a very fine Piece? he replied "Madam, the Painter was a fool, for he has placed the foot where the hand should be."

[p. 23]   An account of pictures painted by Tilly Kettle[7] is in the Supplement to the Gentleman's Magazine for 1786. p. 1145.

or sixteen when first admitted to the council of his father, King Victor Amadeus III (1726–96), but this is impossible, since Victor Amadeus did not succeed to the throne until Feb. 1773, when Charles Emmanuel was twenty-one. Victor Amadeus's queen, whom he married in 1750, was Maria (1729–85), daughter of Philip V of Spain. See *Dictionnaire de biographie française*, Paris, 1933–, XII, 893–94; *NBG*, s.v. Dutens and Gerdil; Isenburg, *Stammtafeln*, II, taf. 114; D. B. Horn, ed., *British Diplomatic Representatives 1689–1789*, Camden Society, 3d ser. 46 (London, 1932), pp. 125–26.

6. Gen. John Guise (1682 or 83–1765), army officer and art collector (see *YWE*, XVII, 485, n. 6; XXXIII, 55; XXXV, 462, n. 11, et passim). The painting, actually a copy from a design by Michelangelo, was brought to England in 1734 and subsequently bought by George II for Queen Caroline; it is now part of the collection in Hampton Court Palace. Hogarth satirized it in his *Analysis of Beauty* (London, 1753), p. 4, for its lack of truth to nature. For more particulars of its history, see George Bickham, *Deliciæ Britannicæ*, 2d ed. (London, ca. 1750), p. 52; Ernest Law, *The Royal Gallery of Hampton Court Illustrated* (London, 1898), p. 110; C. H. Collins Baker, *Catalogue of the Pictures at Hampton Court* (Glasgow, 1929), p. 105; also, Salvatore Quasimodo, *L'Opera completa di Michelangelo pittore* (Milan, 1966), p. 105. This anecdote is printed in *Anecdotes of Painting*, V, 118–19, as is the next item, on Tilly Kettle, p. 51.

7. Tilly Kettle (1735–86), portrait painter, died at Aleppo while on a second expedition to India, where he had acquired a fortune in the 1770s (*DNB;*

Dr Farmer's[8] Elucidation of the Sources whence Shakespeare drew the Subjects & circumstances of many of his Plays, put an end to the fantastic discussions on his supposed Learning. But the best Comment on the marvellous powers of his Genius in drawing & discriminating Characters is contained in Mr Whateley's *remarks on some of the Characters of Shakespeare* (viz, Macbeth & Richard 3ᵈ.) printed for Payne, in a thin Octavo pamphlet, 1785. It ought to be prefixed to every Edition of Shakespeare as a preface, & will tend more to give a just Idea of that matchless Genius than all the notes & criticisms on his Works. It woud teach men to study & discover new magic in his works, instead of settling the text of many scenes that are not worth being understood. When he

Thieme and Becker, XX, 222–23). The account of his paintings in *GM, Supplement*, 1786, LVI, Pt. ii, 1145–46, describes three pictures at Busbridge, the seat of Sir Robert Barker (ca. 1732–89), cr. (1781) Bt., and also mentions various works exhibited at the Society of Artists, concluding with "the ceremony of a Gentoo woman taking leave of her friends and distributing her jewels previous to her ascending the funeral pile of her dead husband," exhibited in 1776 (see Algernon Graves, *The Society of Artists of Great Britain 1760–91*, London, 1907, pp. 135–36). In the MS HW first wrote "Supplement for."

8. Richard Farmer (1735–97), D.D., master of Emmanuel College, Cambridge, author of *An Essay on the Learning of Shakespeare* (Cambridge, 1767); HW's copy, now *WSL*, is listed Hazen, *Cat. of HW's Lib.*, No. 1609:17:1. The main thesis of the *Essay* is that Shakespeare's knowledge of classical history was gotten through English translations (see Augustus Ralli, *A History of Shakespearian Criticism*, 1932; rpt. New York, 1959, I, 63). In a letter to William Cole (27 Jan. 1782) HW called Farmer "by much the most rational of Shakespeare's commentators" (*YWE*, II, 293). Thomas Whately (ca. 1728–72), politician and writer, left unfinished at his death his *Remarks on Some of the Characters of Shakespeare*, which was published by his brother, the Rev. Joseph Whately (*DNB;* Namier and Brooke, III, 627); the printer was Thomas Payne (1719–99), bookseller "at the Mews-Gate, Castle-Street, St. Martin's" (title page) (see H. R. Plomer, G. H. Bushnell, and E. R. McD. Dix, *A Dictionary of the Printers and Booksellers . . . in England, Scotland and Ireland from 1726 to 1775*, Oxford, 1932, p. 195). Whately in the *Remarks* attempts to show how Shakespeare, in the case of Macbeth and Richard III, succeeds masterfully in distinguishing the motives of two characters whose careers are outwardly so similar; for an extended summary of his argument, see Ralli, I, 91–92. This passage is printed in HW's *Notes . . . on Several Characters of Shakespeare*, ed. W. S. Lewis (Farmington, 1940), pp. 18–19. In the final sentence HW first wrote "were their characters" but crossed out "their" and inserted "the" above.

wrote carelessly & ill & only to please the Mob, it signifies not whether he used one silly word or another. To show how perfectly he possessed the knowledge of Human Nature, might hint to future Authors that Plot, rules, nor even poetry, are not half so great beauties in Tragedy or Comedy as a just imitation of Nature, of Character, of the Passions & their Operations in diversified Situations. How inadequate woud Voltaire or Racine appear to their Office, were the Characters in their Tragedies to be scrutinized & compared like those of Macbeth & Richard!

[p. 24]   a good Charade (I dont know by whom)

My first runs at you, my second runs into you, my whole runs through you.

Buckthorn.[9]

March 10th. 1787. Saw again Lady Lucan's[1] Collection of Miniatures, all painted by Herself—there are *356*—besides those She has given away. I have four by Her.

9. A shrub whose berries were formerly used as a powerful cathartic (*OED*).

1. Margaret Smith (d. 1814), m. (1760) Sir Charles Bingham, 7th Bt., cr. (1776) Baron and (1795) Earl of Lucan. HW, commenting on her miniatures in the preface to the fourth volume of his *Anecdotes of Painting* (published 1780), pp. vii–viii, wrote that she "has arrived at copying the most exquisite works of Isaac and Peter Oliver, Hoskins and Cooper, with a genius that almost depreciates those masters, when we consider that they spent their lives in attaining perfection; and . . . soaring above their modest timidity, has transferred the vigour of Raphael to her copies in water-colours"; this exaggerated praise shows HW's characteristic lack of objectivity when assessing the work of a friend. The four works by Lady Lucan at Strawberry Hill were: (1) "John duke of Lauderdale . . . from the original by Cooper, in the possession of lady Greenwich"; (2) "William Henry duke of Gloucester . . . after Meyer"; (3) "Thomas Seymour lord Sudley, brother of the protector Somerset . . . from the original in the possession of the marquis of Buckingham"; and (4) "a young man in black . . . from a portrait by Titian, in the collection of the duke of Devonshire" ("Des. of SH," *Works*, II, 423, 435, 477). The four artists mentioned here are (1) John Hoskins (d. 1664), miniature painter at the Court of Charles I; (2) Paul Brill (or Bril) (1554–1626), Flemish landscape painter who settled at Rome; (3) Peter (or Pierre) Bordier, seventeenth-century painter in enamel; and (4) Jean Petitot the elder (1607–91), French miniature painter at the Courts of Charles I and Louis XIV (Thieme and Becker, IV, 345; V, 16–17; XVII, 545–46; XXVI, 493). HW here and in *Anecdotes of*

She showed me a capital Head by Hoskins, one of the finest of his works, of Algernon Percy Earl of Northumberland, Lord Admiral. It is a large Oval Miniature. on the back is a very fine Landscape in Enamel from Paul Brill—I suppose by Peter Bordier, brother in law of Petitot. This valuable piece belongs to Charlotte Countess dow. of Aylesford, Daughter of Charles Duke of Somerset, who married the Daughter & Heiress of Josceline Earl of Northumberland.

Some short time before the French Fleet appeared off Plimouth in the late War, the Duke of Orleans being in company with Sʳ Joseph Yorke² (I dont know whether it was not at Spa) & talking indecently before some Ladies, Sʳ Joseph did not smile, on which the Duke said to him "Vous ne riez pas!" [p. 25] Sʳ Joseph looked grave, but sᵈ nothing. the Duke

Painting (*Works*, III, 256–58) confuses Peter Bordier, who was Petitot's first teacher, with his younger cousin Jacques Bordier (1616–84), also a painter in enamel, who was Petitot's collaborator for 35 years and who married Petitot's wife's sister (Thieme and Becker, IV, 345; XXVI, 493). He is also slightly mistaken (or at least misleading) in his genealogy explaining the descent of the miniature: Algernon Percy (1602–68), 14th Earl of Northumberland, 1632, lord high admiral of England, was succeeded by his only son Joceline (1644–70), 15th Earl, 1668, who, dying without male issue, left the Percy estates to his daughter Elizabeth (1667–1722). Elizabeth, however, was the *first* wife of Charles Seymour (1662–1748), 6th Duke of Somerset, 1678, who by his *second* wife, Charlotte Finch (d. 1773), had Charlotte (1730–1805), m. (1750) Heneage Finch (1715–77), 3d Earl of Aylesford, 1757. (HW correctly distinguishes the two wives below, p. 112). This item is printed in *Anecdotes of Painting*, V, 235.

2. Sir Joseph Yorke (1724–92), K.B., 1761, cr. (1788) Baron Dover; army officer; diplomat; politician; minister and ambassador at The Hague 1751–80. Louis-Philippe-Joseph de Bourbon (1747–93), Duc de Chartres, Duc d'Orléans, 1785, later known as "Philippe Égalité," was a commander of the French fleet during the War of the American Revolution; the fleet appeared off Plymouth in Aug. 1779, and an invasion of England was actually planned, but never executed (see *YWE*, XXIV, 506, and n. 4; A. Temple Patterson, *The Other Armada*, Manchester, 1960, pp. 133, 155, et passim; Amédée Britsch, *La Jeunesse de Philippe-Égalité*, Paris, 1926, pp. 258–302 et passim). As for the Duke's indecency, HW wrote to Mason and to Mann in May 1783, during the Duke's first visit to England, that he appeared at a dinner party given by Lady Clermont with buttons on his sleeve depicting horses and dogs copulating (*YWE*, XXV, 409; XXIX, 302). HW later called him "monster" for his apostasy to the republicans during the French Revolution (ibid., XXXIV, 174).

continued "est ce que Vous ne riez jamais?" he replied, "rarement, Monseigneur." soon after the Duke talked of the intended Invasion, & said, "Si nous faisons une Descente, que direz vous?" Sʳ Joseph answered, "Alors, Monseigneur, je rirai."

The Drawings of Cosin,³ who wrote on the principles of Landscape & reduced them to a certain Number, & who taught to draw Landscape by random blots, were sold by auction in March 1787. Mrs Harcourt, who was Daughter of Mr Darby, widow of Mr Lochart, & wife of General Harcourt brother of the second Earl, was taught by Cosins & certainly drew admirably in that way, tho She did not begin to draw at all till near Thirty.

Cipriani's⁴ Drawings sold by auction by Christie April 2ᵈ. 1787.

3. Alexander Cozens (d. 1786), landscape painter in watercolors. For his various systems of composition, see A. P. Oppé, *Alexander and John Robert Cozens* (London, 1952), pp. 44–76; in 1785 he published at London *A New Method of Assisting the Invention in Drawing Original Compositions of Landscape*, in which he explained his method of using blots to assist the imagination in landscape composition. His drawings were sold at Christie's 31 March 1787 (Oppé, pp. 42–43); among the purchasers was Maj. Gen. William Harcourt (1743–1830), 3d Earl Harcourt, 1809, brother of George Simon (1736–1809), 2d Earl Harcourt, 1777. Gen. Harcourt's wife, Mary Danby (1749–1833), daughter of William Danby (not Darby) (1712–81) of Swinton, Yorkshire, and widow of Thomas Lockhart (d. 1775) of Craighouse, had been a pupil of Cozens (ibid., pp. 34–35; *GEC;* John Fisher, *The History and Antiquities of Masham and Mashamshire,* London, 1865, pp. 282–83). Mrs. Harcourt exhibited at the Royal Academy in 1785 and 1786 (Oppé, p. 35); HW mentions her in his "Book of Materials," 1771–85, p. 90, under "Ladies & Gentlemen distinguished by their Writings, Learning or Talents in 1783," as drawing "landscapes finely in chiaro scuro." The present item is printed in *Anecdotes of Painting,* V, 91–92.

4. Giovanni Battista Cipriani (1727–85), historical painter and engraver. "To be sold by auction by Mr. Christie, at his great room in Pall-Mall, this and two following days, a most capital collection of high-finished drawings, sketches, &c. in his best manner, by the late much-esteemed artist Signor J. Baptiste Cipriani, deceased" (*Daily Advertiser* 2 April 1787); other drawings, pictures, and prints had been sold at Christie's and Hutchins's in March 1786 (*DNB*). Cipriani in 1779 had appraised the great collection of pictures

May 1787.

On quarrel between K[ing] & Pr[ince] abt. paying the debts of the Latter, Wilkes⁵ quoted these lines of Virgil, changing one word,

> Improbus ille puer, crudelis Tu quoque *Pater,*
> Crudelis *Pater* magis, an Puer improbus ille.

On Charles Fox declaring in the House of Commons by order of the Prince of Wales that he is not married to Mrs Fitzherbert, Geo. Selwyn, who does [p. 26] not love Fox, s^d the Prince's Instructions to the latter were exactly the words of Othello,

> "Villain, be sure Thou prove my Love a Whore."

Many have thought the Egyptians derived from the Chinese, & others vice versa. In one respect the Two Nations had

at Houghton (formerly the seat of Sir Robert Walpole) for sale to Catherine the Great of Russia, and was in 1782 commissioned by HW's nephew George, 3d Earl of Orford, to do paintings for that seat. HW called his paintings "flimsy" and his drawings "trumpery" (*YWE*, XXIV, 441, XXV, 316; XXXVI, 237). This item is printed in *Anecdotes of Painting*, V, 91.

5. John Wilkes (1725–97), radical politician; author of the *North Briton.* George, Prince of Wales (afterwards George IV) by the summer of 1786 had accumulated debts of over £250,000. After an exchange of unpleasant letters with his father a compromise was reached whereby he was granted an additional allowance of £10,000 a year, while Parliament voted £161,000 for the payment of his debts and £60,000 for the completion of Carlton House, his residence (John Brooke, *King George III*, New York, 1972, pp. 320–21). The lines from Virgil (*Eclogue VIII*, 49–50) as adapted mean: "Shameless is that boy, hard-hearted too are you, O father; / Is the father more hard-hearted, or the boy more shameless?"; *pater* has been substituted for *mater*, and also the lines have been inverted. The Prince on 15 Dec. 1785 secretly married Mrs. Maria Fitzherbert, a twice-widowed Roman Catholic. When in April 1787 an inquiry into the relationship of the Prince and Mrs. Fitzherbert was threatened in the House, Charles James Fox, who had allied himself politically with the Prince, attempted to clear the air by declaring (on 30 April) that the marriage had not taken place. It is doubtful that the Prince had given Fox explicit instructions to do so; rather, Fox, met with repeated denials of the marriage by the Prince himself, took it upon himself to make the declaration. See Christopher Hibbert, *George IV, Prince of Wales 1762–1811* (London, 1972), pp. 47–58, 64–70; Loren Reid, *Charles James Fox* (Columbia, Mo., 1969), pp. 225–29. The line from *Othello* is from Act III, scene iii. For Selwyn's relations with Fox, see S. Parnell Kerr, *George Selwyn and the Wits* (London, 1909), pp. 279–87.

great resemblance: Each very early made great progress in the Arts of Sculpture, Painting & Architecture; but then stopped short, & never made the least improvement afterwards.[6] one wonders less at this want of Imagination in the Egyptians, when one knows that they had no poetry.

In my Opinion the three Worst books, considering the quantity of valuable material that they contain, that were ever written for bad Style, bad method, bad arrangement, anticipation & repetition, are Harte's life of Gustavus Adolphus, Adam Smith on the wealth of Nations, & Monsr. D'Ancarville's on the Progress of the Arts.[7]

6. HW wrote to William Robertson, the historian, 20 June 1791: "I have long thought, that nations who made early progress in science and arts, and stopped short, are like forward children who have quick parts at five years old, were advanced no farther at fifteen, and at thirty are blockheads. Such have been the Egyptians and the Chinese; the former, the more contemptible, for having carved most beautiful heads of statues, they never discovered that they could detach the arms and legs from the block, at least never convey any idea of motion" (*YWE*, XV, 211). HW owned several works on the Egyptians and Chinese, among them Charles Rollin, *Histoire ancienne des Égyptiens* (Paris, 1730), 7 vols., 12mo (Hazen, *Cat. of HW's Lib.*, No. 1205); Jean-Baptiste du Halde, *Description . . . de l'empire de la Chine* (Paris, 1735), 4 vols., folio (ibid., No. 874, now *WSL*); and Cornelius de Pauw, *Recherches philosophiques sur les Égyptiens et les Chinois* (Berlin), 2 vols., 12mo (ibid., No. 3134). Editions of the last work were published in 1773, 1774, and 1788; Hazen leans towards HW's having owned the latest, but the observation here suggests that he owned one of the earlier. Pauw (for whom see also below, p. 78) denies in his study any communication between the Chinese and Egyptians (Preface et passim); explores the reason why the two peoples, and all orientals in general, allegedly failed to make significant progress in painting and sculpture (Part II, section iv); and compares the architecture of the two peoples in order to emphasize the differences (Part II, section vi). HW also comments on the supposed want of poetry and imagination among the Egyptians, below, p. 55; he interpolated the sentence here in a smaller hand at some later date. This passage has been printed in *Anecdotes of Painting*, V, 16.

7. Walter Harte (1709–74), *The History of the Life of Gustavus Adolphus* (London, 1759), 2 vols., 4to; Adam Smith, *An Inquiry into the Nature and Causes of the Wealth of Nations* (London, 1776), 2 vols., 4to; and Pierre-François Hugues, called D'Hancarville (1719–1805), *Recherches sur l'origine, l'esprit et les progrès des arts de la Grèce* (London, 1785), 3 vols., 4to. HW's copies of the first two works are listed Hazen, *Cat.*, Nos. 464, 3260; he seems not to have purchased a set of the third (see ibid., No. 3536). In a letter to Henry Zouch (14 May 1759) HW described Harte's book as "sadly written,

No wonder K. was so false, considering whose Son he was & coud any good come out of two Nazareths?[8]

Difficult to know the Truth betw. K. & P. Two Liars do not, like two Negatives, make a Truth.

Charles Fox had nothing of Tomorrow in him—that is, tho the Head of a Party and tho so eager when in [p. 27] the House of Commons, yet he cared so little about Politics at all other times, & had so little policy or Schemes, that he never thought beyond the present day.[9]

yet very amusing from the matter" (*YWE*, XVI, 31), and also noted in the margin of his copy of Chesterfield's *Letters* (London, 1774), I, 499 (now *WSL*), "Harte's Gustavus is a sample of a very bad style & the method, worse." (Thomas Carlyle called the book a "wilderness"; see the article on Harte in *DNB*). Criticism of D'Hancarville's book, which was to have been continued, was generally so adverse that D'Hancarville never finished it (see Antoine-Alexandre Barbier et al., *Dictionnaire des ouvrages anonymes,* 3d ed., Paris, 1872–79, IV, 31).

8. An allusion to John i. 46: "Can there any good thing come out of Nazareth?"; HW turns this bon mot into a couplet below, p. 85. In *Mem. Geo. II,* I, 77, he states that the worst quality of George III's father, Frederick, Prince of Wales (d. 1751), was "insincerity, and indifference to truth," while his writings are full of references to the devious character and baleful influence of George's mother, the Princess Augusta (d. 1772), who with her supposed "lover," the King's favorite, Lord Bute, allegedly encouraged the King to attempt unconstitutional extensions of the royal prerogative during his reign. George III himself HW accuses of insincerity, hypocrisy, and treachery throughout *Mem. Geo. III* (see II, 235–40; III, 101; IV, 159, et passim). HW's feelings of antipathy began early with the King's persecution of HW's friend Henry Seymour Conway over general warrants in 1764 (the King acquiesced in Conway's dismissal from his regiment for voting against them in Parliament), and were augmented by what HW regarded as the King's tyrannical mishandling of the American situation, leading to the Revolution (see Bernhard Knollenberg, "Walpole: Pro-American," in *Horace Walpole: Writer, Politician, and Connoisseur,* ed. W. H. Smith, New Haven, 1967, pp. 85–90; J. C. Riely, "Horace Walpole, Friend of American Liberty," *Studies in Burke and His Time,* 16 [1974], 5–21). In a letter to Thomas Walpole 14 May 1781, HW applies the saying about Nazareth to George III and the Prince of Wales his son, mentioning the *"favourable* comparison that would be made in preference to hypocrisy over debauchery" (*YWE*, XXXVI, 198).

9. Elsewhere HW deplores the "follies, which . . . make all that is admirable and amiable in [Fox], only matter of regret to those who like him as I do" (HW to Henry Seymour Conway, 28 May 1781, *YWE,* XXXIX, 376–77). The most striking symptom of Fox's early immaturity was an addiction to gambling that caused great embarrassment to his political allies.

May. The prosecution of Hastings,[1] tho he shoud escape at last, must have good effect. It will alarm the Servants of the Company in India, that they may not always Plunder with Impunity, but that there may be a retrospect; & it will show them that Even bribes of Diamonds to the Crown, may not secure them from prosecution.

Montaigne has in few words given a system of the progress of the Mind that resembles so much that of Prior in his Alma,[2] that I think it very probable that Prior, who was a

1. Warren Hastings (1732–1818), governor general of India 1772–85. On 10 May 1787 he was impeached by the House of Commons for alleged corrupt and illegal practices during his administration; the trial, which opened in Westminster Hall before the House of Lords on 13 Feb. 1788, dragged on for seven years until he was acquitted on all counts on 23 April 1795. HW had long been a critic of the East India Company's policies of "plundering and terrorizing"; see, e.g., his letters to Sir Horace Mann of 22 March and 8 May 1771, and of 5 March, 9 April, 4 Nov. and 22 Dec. 1772 (*YWE*, XXIII, 282, 305, 387, 400, 414, 451). "Bribes of diamonds to the crown" is an allusion to a large diamond sent by the Nizam of Hyderabad to the King through Hastings, which was presented by Lord Sydney at the levee on 14 June 1786; it was rumored that the diamond was really a bribe from Hastings, against whom proceedings in the Commons had already begun (ibid., XXXIII, 568, n. 7). See Keith Feiling, *Warren Hastings* (London, 1954), pp. 343–71; P. J. Marshall, *The Impeachment of Warren Hastings* (Oxford, 1965), passim; Lucy S. Sutherland, *The East India Company in Eighteenth-Century Politics* (Oxford, 1952), pp. 296–300; below, pp. 76, 98. HW owned *Articles of Charge of High Crimes and Misdemeanours, against Warren Hastings . . . Presented to the House of Commons . . . by . . . Edmund Burke* (London, 1786), and *The Minutes of What Was Offered by Warren Hastings . . . at the Bar of the House of Commons* (London, 1786) (Hazen, *Cat. of HW's Lib.*, Nos. 1609:49:2–3, now *WSL*).

2. "Alma: or, The Progress of the Mind," a dialogue in three cantos in which Prior facetiously charts the progress of the soul upwards from the legs in childhood to the head in maturity:

> My simple *System* shall suppose,
> That ALMA enters at the Toes;
> That then She mounts by just Degrees
> Up to the Ancles, Legs, and Knees:
> Next, as the Sap of Life does rise,
> She lends her Vigor to the Thighs:
> And, all these under-Regions past,
> She nestles somewhere near the Waste:
> Gives Pain or Pleasure, Grief or Laughter;
> As we shall show at large hereafter.

great Reader & even imitator of French Authors, borrowed
the hint thence—here is Montaigne's Idea;

"La Chaleur naturelle, disent les bons Compagnons, se
prent premierement aux pieds; cellela touche l'Enfance: dela
elle monte à la moyenne region, ou Elle se plante long tems,
& y produit, selon moi, les seuls vrais plaisirs de la vie corpo-
relle: les autres voluptès dorment au prix. Sur la fin, & à la
mode d'une vapeur, qui va montant & s'exhale, elle arrive au
gozier, ou elle fait sa derniere pose." Essais liv. 2. Chap. 2. p.
213 edit. fol. 1640.

[p. 28]   Our summers are often, tho beautifull for verdure, so
cold, that they are rather *green Winters*.[3]

Cardinal Fano,[4] who hoped to be Pope after Marcellus 2[d]
by the interest of Charles 5th., yet to gain the patronage too of

> Mature, if not improv'd, by Time
> Up to the Heart She loves to climb:
> From thence, compell'd by Craft and Age,
> She makes the Head her latest Stage.
>
> (Canto I, ll. 252–65)

H. Bunker Wright and Monroe K. Spears, eds., *The Literary Works of Matthew Prior*, 2d ed. (Oxford, 1971), II, 964, credit William Jackson (1730–1803),
composer and miscellaneous writer, with having first thought of the passage
from Montaigne's "De l'Yvrognerie" as the source of Prior's "system," but
Jackson's suggestion does not appear until 1798 (in his *Four Ages*, London,
1798, pp. 254–55). Prior's "Alma" was first published in his *Poems on Several Occasions* (London, 1718), pp. 317 ff.; HW's copy, now *WSL*, is listed
Hazen, *Cat.*, No. 2047. His copy of Montaigne's *Essais* (Paris, 1640), folio, is
listed ibid., No. 880. *Au prix* means "in comparison," and *gosier*, "gullet."

3. HW includes this witticism in his letter to Lady Ossory 14 June 1787:
"*Green winter* . . . is the highest title due to this season, which in southern
climes is positive *summer*" (*YWE*, XXXIII, 561; see also ibid., I, 328; XXXIV,
143).

4. Pietro Bertano (1501–58), bishop of Fano, 1537; papal nuncio at the
Court of Charles V, 1548; cardinal, 1551 (*Enciclopedia cattolica*, Vatican,
1949–54, II, 1464). Marcellus II (1501–55), born Marcello Cervini, had been
pope for less than a month when he died on 1 May 1555. In a dispatch of
10 May, Jean de Saint-Marcel d'Avançon (ca. 1511–65), the French envoy at
Rome (see *Dictionnaire de biographie française*, Paris, 1933–, IV, 812–13),
informed Henri II of the intrigues of Bertano, who was supported by the
Imperialists: "M'a mandé . . . le Cardinal Fano par un nommé Jean-Antoine
Rusra, qu'il se tient asseuré d'estre Pape, s'il plaist au Roy de l'asseurer des
voeux des Cardinaux François, & qu'il passera, pourveu que lesdits Cardinaux

Henry 2ᵈ of France, offered the Latter's Embassador to make
a League with his master for driving Charles out of Italy—
"promet encore, says the Embassador to the King, de faire
entrer son Frere, *qu'il dit etre meilleur Francois* que Chretien,
au service de sa Majestè."
v. Collect. universelle des Memories partic. relatifs à
l'hist. de France. Tome xxiii. p. 444.
In the Mem. de Tavannes⁵ in same coll. it is said that
the University of Paris declared in favour of the divorce of

lui donnent leurs voeux, les articles qui ensuivent, à sçavoir une ligue offen-
sive pour chasser l'Empereur d'Italie, & remettre le Roy du Duché de Milan
. . . [il] promet encore de faire entrer son frère [not further identified] qu'il
dit estre meilleur François que Chrestien, au service de Sa Majesté" ("Observations des editeurs sur le troisième livre des mémoires de messire Blaise de
Montluc, maréchal de France," in *Collection universelle des mémoires par-
ticuliers relatifs à l'histoire de France*, ed. J.-A. Roucher, A.-C. Bellier-
Duchesnay, and A. Perrin, London and Paris, 1785–91, XXIII, 444, citing
Guillaume Ribier, *Lettres et memoires d'estat, des roys, princes, ambassadeurs
et autres ministres, sous les regnes de François premier, Henri II. & François II*, ed. M. Belot, Paris, 1666, II, 611; HW's set of the *Collection universelle* is listed Hazen, *Cat. of HW's Lib.*, No. 3084). The King was not
receptive to Bertano's overture, and Bertano was not elected. Cf. Ludwig,
Freiherr von Pastor, *History of the Popes*, ed. F. I. Antrobus et al. (London,
1891–1953), XV, 2–3, 62.

5. Gaspard de Saulx (1509–73), seigneur de Tavannes, maréchal de France;
his *Mémoires* were first published posthumously by his son, Jean, Vicomte de
Tavannes (*NBG*). "Henri Roy d'angleterre preste partie de l'argent donné à
l'Empereur par le Roy François, & par ce moyen gagne l'Université de Paris
qui favorise le divorce de l'Anglois contre Catherine d'Autriche tante de
l'Empereur . . . " (*Mémoires de messire Gaspard de Tavannes, maréchal de
France, commençant en 1522, & finissant en 1573*, in *Collection universelle*,
XXVI, 26). The request for the loan is contained in a paper submitted by the
French ambassadors to Henry VIII, 19 Feb. 1530, calendered in *Letters and
Papers . . . of the Reign of Henry VIII*, ed. J. S. Brewer, J. Gairdner, and
R. H. Brodie (1864–1920; rpt. Vaduz, 1965), IV, Pt. iii, 2799. The loan was
to be used in payment of a ransom for the release of Francis I's two sons,
the Dauphin and the Duke of Orleans, who had been given as hostages in
his place after his capture by Charles V's forces at the battle of Pavia in
Lombardy in Feb. 1525. By means of this loan and other concessions Henry
induced Francis to use his influence to obtain a decree from the University
of Paris favorable to his divorce from Catherine of Aragon; the decree, dated
2 July 1530, was subsequently read (with the favorable opinions of other foreign universities) in the House of Commons on 30 March 1531 (ibid., pp. 2753,
2780, 2794–95, 2814, 2821, 2834, 2854, 2876, 2892–93, 2903–04, 2923, 2927, 2940,
2971; *DNB*, s.v. Henry VIII).

Hen. 8. because he had lent Francis 1st money to discharge his ransom to Charles 5th.

Epigram by John Lord Hervey[6] on Henrietta Duchess of Newcastle, Daughter of Henrietta Dss of Marlborough, being in love with James Earl of Berkeley, who was very gouty:

6. John Hervey (1696–1743), summoned to the Lords in his father's barony as Lord Hervey of Ickworth, 1733; author of *Memoirs of the Reign of King George the Second* (first published in an edition by John Wilson Croker, London, 1848); the Sporus of Pope's *Epistle to Dr. Arbuthnot*. His epigram and verses here have not been previously published, nor are they among the Hervey MSS in the Bury St. Edmunds and West Suffolk Record Office (information courtesy of Prof. Robert Halsband, Univ. of Illinois at Urbana-Champaign). Henrietta Godolphin (d. 1776) was daughter of Francis, 2d Earl of Godolphin by Henrietta Churchill (1681–1733), daughter of the famous John, 1st Duke of Marlborough (the victor at Blenheim) and *suo jure* Duchess of Marlborough, 1722; she married (1717) Thomas Pelham Holles, cr. (1715) Duke of Newcastle-upon-Tyne and (1756) Duke of Newcastle-under-Line. HW makes frequent jokes about her "beard" and mad appearance (see, e.g., *YWE*, IX, 128, 199; XXXI, 10; XXXV, 271). James Berkeley (1680–1736), 3d Earl of Berkeley, 1710, was a distinguished naval officer; the Duchess's unrequited love for him may have been kindled at the time of the death of his wife, the former Lady Louisa Lennox, in 1717, several months prior to the Duchess's marriage to the Duke. Felton Hervey (1712–73), tenth son of John, 1st Earl of Bristol by his second wife, Elizabeth (John, Lord Hervey was the first), was groom of the Bedchamber to the Duke of Cumberland, 1737–56 (Sedgwick, II, 132–33); HW wrote of him in a letter to Sir Horace Mann, 8 Oct. 1742 OS, that he proposed attending George II on an expedition to Flanders on a "warhorse . . . having richer caparisons than any of the expedition," besides "a gold net to keep off the flies—in winter" (*YWE*, XVIII, 69–70). "The tenth is he, the Parson's fee" presumably refers to a niggardly but widespread practice of giving the parson as his tithe the poorest part of one's produce, if anything (see "Parson's side, pinching on the" in Partridge); i.e., Felton Hervey is the poorest part of his father's offspring (with perhaps the added implication that his father would have liked to have given him away to the parson). The portrait here is belied (at least with respect to Felton's relations with his father) by Lord Bristol's *Letter-Books* (Wells, 1894), I, 365–66; II, 2, et passim, which show Felton, as a child, to have been spoiled by his doting parents, and, as a grown man, to have been regarded with affection by Lord Bristol as "the only son of all those it pleased God to give me, who never yet had disobliged me" (ibid., III, 312). Lord Hervey probably wrote these lines out of jealousy, exacerbated by the fact that after falling out of his mother's graces, he was replaced by Felton as his mother's heir. See Robert Halsband, *Lord Hervey: Eighteenth-Century Courtier* (New York, 1974), pp. 53, 275, et passim.

Thou loving Soul with that unlovely face,
Thou foulest Offspring of the fairest race,
Cease to lament: had Nature meant him kind,
She'd not have made him lame, but struck him blind.

[p. 29]
    Ld Hervey's verses on his Brother Felton Hervey.

Of Ickworth's Boys, their Father's joys,
    There is but one a bad one;
The tenth is he, the Parson's fee,
    And indeed he is a sad one.
No love of fame, no sense of shame,
    And a bad heart, let me tell ye:
Without, all brass; within, all Ass,
    And the Puppy's name is Felly.

Many barbarous Nations have had early poetry. Perhaps the ancient Egyptians had, tho Imagination does not seem ever to have abounded amongst them. That no Writings of that people, either in verse or prose, have come down to us,[7] may be accounted for by their absurd & clumsey Invention of, and adherence to, Hieroglyphics. In fact any Nation that loves to wrap up its knowledge in mystery, was not likely to be ambitious of acquiring fame & immortality by preserving & transmitting its writings to posterity.

L'aristocratie est moins favorable aux lettres que la Democratie et le Gouvernement Monarchique &c
    Tableau des Revolutions de la litterature. 1786.[8] p. 23.

7. HW's remarks, of course, antedate the discovery of the Rosetta Stone in 1799, which made possible the deciphering of the ancient Egyptian language. His condemnation of hieroglyphics, reflecting a typically Augustan distaste for mystery and needless obfuscation, is predicated on the mistaken notion, stemming from the ancient Greeks and assumed down through his own time, that the hieroglyphs were symbolic or allegorical, whereas in fact they were phonetic.

8. Carlo Giovanni Maria Denina (1731–1813), *Tableau des révolutions de la littérature* (Paris, 1786), 12mo, translated from the Italian; HW's copy is listed Hazen, *Cat. of HW's Lib.*, No. 3008. Denina's book was first published

Les Romains disoient avec simplicitè, ce qu'ils faisoient avec grandeur. 141.

L'on vous donne toujours un Rival, lors meme que vos talens ne vous en laissent aucun. 184. the case of Shakespeare & Ben. Johnson.

[p. 30] Ramus sentoit trop les beautès des Anciens pour en admirer les defauts. 190.—so ought we to judge of Shakespeare.

at Turin, 1760, as *Discorso sopra le vicende della letteratura;* it subsequently went through several editions and was translated into many languages (*Enciclopedia italiana,* ed. G. Gentile and C. Tumminelli, Rome, 1929–39, XII, 617). The translation HW owned was presumably an unauthorized one, as there appeared at Berlin, 1786–90, a two-volume version entitled *Discours sur les vicissitudes de la littérature . . . traduit de l'italien sous les yeux de l'auteur* (Bibl. Nat. Cat.); no other record or copy of HW's translation has been found. The extract on Ramus with the comment on Shakespeare and the long passage on Shakespeare and the French following have been printed in HW's *Notes . . . on Several Characters of Shakespeare,* ed. W. S. Lewis (Farmington, 1940), pp. 19–21. With regard to the first quotation, HW dismissed aristocracy as "a republic of tyrants," believed that a "mere democratic government" could never subsist for long, and regarded absolute monarchy as the ultimate in tyranny (see *YWE,* XXXIII, 342, and n. 8; below, pp. 63–64) but felt that a balance of democracy and monarchy, as epitomized in the constitutional monarchy of England, provided the ideal climate for the flourishing of individual liberty, and therefore of the arts. With respect to the rivalry of Shakespeare and Ben Jonson, he wrote in his "Book of Materials," 1771–85, p. 63, "Compare Ben Johnson's Catiline with Hamlet. The former is all pedantry and bombast" (printed *Notes on Shakespeare,* p. 13). Pierre de la Ramée (1515–72), the French humanist philosopher better known as Petrus Ramus, included in the large body of his works commentaries on various classic authors, including Cicero and Virgil (see *NBG*). HW met the naturalist Georges-Louis Le Clerc (1707–88), Comte de Buffon, at Paris in 1766, and described him as "an excellent old man, humane, gentle, well-bred" (*YWE,* XXXIX, 191, and n. 15); his copy of Buffon's *Histoire naturelle* is listed Hazen, *Cat.,* No. 2152 (see also *Dictionnaire de biographie française,* Paris, 1933–, VII, 629–31). "Correction" (for "correctness") in the long passage on Shakespeare and the French is so in the MS and is a rare Gallicism (*OED*). Although HW's admiration for the character of Falstaff was boundless (see the Introduction and below, p. 152), he surprisingly neither owned nor mentions anywhere Maurice Morgann's celebrated *Essay on the Dramatic Character of Sir John Falstaff* (London, 1777), a brilliant tour de force in which Morgann pays tribute to Shakespeare's genius and skill in rendering credible such a many-facetted creation. Perhaps HW was put off by the ostensible aim of the work, which is to prove that Falstaff is no coward.

On those who quote much, cette fureur de vouloir paroitre savant de la science d'autrui. 198.

He says of the Writers in reign of Louis 14. L'excellent meme etoit devenu commun. 209.

Il faut distinguer les negligences & la negligence. 220. A great Writer may have the former, & they may even be beauties: the latter produces a bad Writer.

He says, Buffon has made une historie excellente des memes Sujets (animals) dont la Fontaine avoit fait des Drames si interessans. 224.

There are gleams of Sense in that book that make one wonder the Author did not make a better book on so fruitfull a Subject.

He gives the French the Superiority in Eloquence, in which they are vastly inferior to our orators: and in Taste— but their Taste is too timid to be true Taste—or is but half Taste. Their Authors are more afraid of offending Delicacy & rules, than ambitious of Sublimity. Shakespeare, with an improved Education & in a more enlightened Age might easily have attained the purity and correction of Racine; but nothing leads one to suppose that Racine in a barbarous age w^d have attained the grandeur, force & nature of Shakespeare. Racine had been taught by Corneille to avoid all the faults of their Predecessors, & was taught by his own judgement & by that of his Friend Boileau, to avoid the faults of Corneille. The Latter was inspired with Majesty by Roman Authors & Roman [p. 31] Spirit; Racine with delicacy by the polished Court of Louis 14. Shakespeare had no Tutors but Nature and Genius. he caught his faults from the bad taste of his Cotemporaries. In an age still less civilized Shakespeare might have been wilder, but woud not have been vulgar. Had he drawn absolute Savages, instead of Clowns, perhaps we shoud have had as beautifull delineations of a State of Nature, as he has given in his pictures of the passions in a corrupted State of Society, I mean, in his Macbeth, Othello, Richard 3^d—in short, in all his best Scenes. He who invented such a

Compound as Falstaffe, & coud make every feature of such a
fictitious character perfectly natural, coud not have failed in
painting simple Natures.

Nothing has shown more fully the prodigious Ignorance of
human Ideas & their littleness, than the Discovery of Mr Her-
schell,[9] that what used to be called *the Milky way* is a portion
of perhaps an infinite Multitude of Worlds!

Henry Bunbury,[1] the 2[d]. Hogarth, was in 1787 appointed
Groom of the bedchamber to Frederic Duke of York.

This passage is remarkably applicable to God's supposed
predilection for the Jews,

————steriles nec legit arenas
Ut caneret paucis, mersitque hoc pulvere Verum.
Lucan's Pharsal.[2] 9. 576.

9. Sir William Herschel (1738–1822), Kt., 1816, the noted astronomer. HW,
in a facetious mood, wrote to Lady Ossory 4 July 1785 that Herschel "has
discovered that the Milky Way is not only a mob of stars, but that there is
another dairy of them still farther off" (*YWE*, XXXIII, 475). In a paper read
before the Royal Society 17 June 1784, Herschel reported that "on applying
the telescope to a part of the *via lactea*, I found that it completely resolved
the whole whitish appearance into small stars," and also that he discovered
"in the time of only 36 minutes . . . no less than 31 nebulæ" (*Scientific
Papers*, London, 1912, I, 158, 160).

1. Henry William Bunbury (1750–1811), amateur artist and caricaturist,
was extravagantly admired by HW, who in the advertisement to the fourth
volume of his *Anecdotes of Painting* (Strawberry Hill, 1780), refers to "the
living etchings of Mr. H. Bunbury, the second Hogarth, and first imitator
who ever fully equalled his original." His appointment as groom of the Bedchamber to Frederick (1763–1827), Bishop of Osnaburgh 1764–1802, cr. (1784)
Duke of York, second son of George III, is recorded in the *Royal Calendar*,
1788, p. 279. See J. C. Riely, "Horace Walpole and 'the Second Hogarth,'"
Eighteenth-Century Studies, 9 (1975), 28–44.

2. HW, who thought that Lucan "often says more in half a line than
Virgil in a whole book," but "was lost in bombast if he talked for thirty
lines together" (HW to William Mason, 25 June 1782, *YWE*, XXIX, 256), in
1760 brought out an edition of the *Pharsalia* at the Strawberry Hill Press
(see Hazen, *SH Bibl.*, 46–50). The lines quoted mean, "Did he choose barren
sands that he might prophesy to a few? Did he bury truth in this dust?"
HW in 1746 wrote an imitation of the first book of Lucan, verses 32–66; the
MS is now *WSL* (see *YWE*, XIII, 16, and n. 107).

Pigmalion, King of the Pigmies, as Oberon of the Fairies.[3]

[p. 32] In Nichols's Bibl. Topogr. Brit.[4] No. 42. p. 525. is a Dialogue between Q. Elizabeth & Lambarde. Her ⟨Majesty⟩ calls her avaricious Grandsire, "her good grandfather Henry 7th.

3. HW elaborates this pun in his letter to Henry Seymour Conway 11 Nov. 1787, where he calls the druidic temple erected by Conway at Park Place "the *chorea* of the pigmies" and goes on to paraphrase Virgil, *Aeneid*, I, 363–64: "As I forget too what is Latin for Lilliputians, I will make a bad pun, and say—

—*portantur avari*
Pygmalionis *opes*—

Pygmalion is as well-sounding a name for such a monarch as Oberon" (*YWE*, XXXIX, 460–61). The quotation means "the treasures of greedy Pygmalion are carried away"; "carried away" refers to the fact that Conway's temple was transported to Park Place from its original location on the island of Jersey (of which Conway was governor) as a gift to him from the inhabitants of Jersey.

4. John Nichols's *Bibliotheca Topographica Britannica*, with contributions by numerous antiquarians, was published in parts at London starting in 1780; HW owned an eight-volume set of the numbers published through 1790 (Hazen, *Cat. of HW's Lib.*, No. 3348). No. 42, which came out in 1787, contains, *inter alia*, "Memoirs of William Lambarde, Esq. [1536–1601]; the eminent Lawyer and Antiquary"; Appendix 7 to the "Memoirs" (pp. 525–26) consists of Lambarde's account of his conversation with Queen Elizabeth in her privy chamber at East Greenwich, 4 Aug. 1601, in which the Queen alludes to her "good grandfather King Henry VII" lending monies to his subjects "for their good," but "with assurance of good bond for repayment," so as not to "dissipate his treasure or lands." For HW on Henry VII's avarice, see below, p. 136. No. 45 of the *Bibliotheca Topographica Britannica* was also published in 1787. On p. 198 is recorded, from the parish registers of Maidstone, the burial on 3 May 1655 of "a crisome, son of Susan Owen, widow; the reputed father Thomas Matthew, Hair-dresser, base." This occurrence of the term *hairdresser* precedes the earliest example in the *OED* by 116 years (from *Humphrey Clinker*, 1771); however, in the seventeenth century it presumably did not denote the kind of highly specialized professional (of whom HW is evidently thinking) who later appeared in France and by the end of the eighteenth century had given rise to such outlandish fashions in both France and England (see Richard Corson, *Fashions in Hair. The First Five Thousand Years*, New York, 1965, pp. 19, 360, et passim). HW is likewise probably mistaken about the child's having been christened; the term *chrisom* was apparently used at times to denote an infant that had died without the rite of baptism, though it more usually meant a child who

In No. 45 of the same Work p. 198 is mentioned so early as 1655, & consequently even before the Restoration *a Hair-Dresser,* one Thomas Matthew; & it adds to the drollery of the circumstance that in those pious times he had a bastard Child Christened.

Dignus imperandi, si non imperasset,[5] is an admired Sentence of Tacitus on Galba, and sounds prettily; but if weighed, only proves that Men were mistaken, and had formed too high an opinion of that Emperor, before he was tried.

If Paris lived now, & preferred Beauty to Power, & Riches, it woud not be called his *Judgment,* but his *want of Judgment.*[6]

Temptations are more tempting than Self denial.

Syrop of Sweethearts, distilled in the honeymoon.

Riddle on Scarlet.

> They oft a livery of my name assume,
> Who only find in my first half their doom.[7]

[p. 33]   Bon mot in a late newspaper[8] versified.

had died shortly after being baptized (see *OED* and *Bibliotheca Topographica Britannica,* loc. cit.).

5. "Worthy of ruling, if he had not ruled." HW's quotation is faulty; the original, found in Tacitus, *Histories,* I, 49, reads: "Omnium consensu capax imperii, nisi imperasset" ("by the consensus of all capable of rule—had he not ruled"). Servius Sulpicius Galba (3 B.C.–69 A.D.), an able military commander and administrator, was proclaimed emperor by his soldiers in opposition to Nero, whom he succeeded upon the latter's death (68 A.D.), but he proved an ineffective ruler and was assassinated the following year. HW owned two editions of Tacitus's *Opera* published at Amsterdam, 1685 (2 vols., 8vo) and 1701 (1 vol., 24mo), and also an English translation by Thomas Gordon, published at London, 1728–31, 2 vols., folio (Hazen, *Cat.,* Nos. 1103, 2093, 2133).

6. Paris, selected by the gods to adjudge the prize of beauty among Hera, Aphrodite, and Pallas Athena, awarded the prize to Aphrodite, who had offered him as an inducement the hand of the fairest woman in the world.

7. The riddle probably refers to the scarlet livery of the soldier, who finds his doom in the scars of battle.

8. Not found.

How much on outward Show does all depend,
If Virtues from within no lustre lend!
Strip off th'externals *M* and *Y*, the rest
Proves *M*ajesty itself is but *a Jest*.

Motto for ridiculous Tragedies.

Vix retinet lacrymas, quia nil lacrymabile cernit.[9]

M[r] Sparman[1] in his voyage round the World with Capt.
Cook (v. L'esprit des journaux for Nov. 1787) thinks that
Skeletons of Elephants being found in Siberia might be occasioned by their having multiplied so greatly in their native
soil, that they had been forced to migrate into other Countries in search of provender—but is it likely that Animals
produced in the hottest climates wd have wandered into the

9. "With difficulty one holds back tears [of laughter], because one discerns
nothing worthy of tears," after Ovid, *Metamorphoses*, II, 796: "Vixque tenet
lacrimas," etc. In the original passage the hag Envy can scarce restrain tears
of chagrin because she sees no cause for others' tears in Tritonia's city, which
is basking in wealth and splendor. HW owned several copies of the *Metamorphoses;* Hazen, *Cat.*, No. 2286, suggests that he may have turned to the
Petrus Burmannus edition of the *Opera* (Amsterdam, 1713–14) when he
quoted from Book II in his letter to George Montagu, 10 Aug. 1762 (*YWE*,
X, 38). See HW's lines "to Ponderosus," below, p. 95.

1. Anders Sparrman (1748–1820), Swedish physician, naturalist, and ex-
plorer, accompanied Capt. Cook on his second voyage around the world
(1772–75) and wrote up an account of his travels entitled *Resa till Goda
Hopps- Udden, Södra Pol-Kretsen och omkring Jordklotet,* etc.; the first
volume was published at Stockholm, 1783, and translated into German,
Dutch, French, and English (the last as *A Voyage to the Cape of Good Hope,
towards the Antarctic Polar Circle, and round the World,* London, 1785).
Excerpts from the French translation (published at Paris, 1787, in 2- and
3-vol. editions) were printed in the Nov. 1787 issue of *L'Esprit des journaux
françois et étrangers* (HW's copies listed Hazen, *Cat.*, Nos. 3011, 3314); they
include Sparrman's conjecture, based on the discovery of the bones and
teeth of "éléphans" in Siberia, that excessive numbers forced "des troupes
d'éléphans . . . à quitter leurs habitations natales; qu'insensiblement, ou par
une suite soudaine et précipitée, ils se sont trouvés dans des latitudes plus
rigoureuses; que là, surpris par un froid d'automne ou d'hiver, ils se sont
enfoncés encore plus avant dans le nord, dispersés dans la Sibérie et les
contrées voisines . . ." (French translation, 2 vol. ed., I, 366–67, 368–70, summarized and cited *L'Esprit des journaux,* Nov. 1787, p. 10). See Nils Bohman
et al., eds., *Svenska Män och Kvinnor: Biografisk Uppslagsbok* (Stockholm,
1942–55), VII, 147; BM Cat.; Bibl. Nat. Cat.; Nat. Union Cat.

coldest, while so many congenial regions were open to them? and if expelled by too numerous a population, numerous hosts wd have gone, & numerous Skeletons have been found— If a dozen Skeletons had even been found in Siberia, it woud not support such an Hypothesis. Were the Cause and the Consequences true, no doubt, the Wolves & Foxes of the North, coud they have been Authors, woud have told us lamentable Stories of the inundations of barbarous Elephants that had poured on Siberia from the South, & massacred or expelled the poor native Wolves & Foxes!

[p. 34]   The Passions seldom give good Advice but to the Interested & Mercenary. Resentment generally suggests bad measures. Second Thoughts & good nature will rarely, very rarely, approve the first hints of Anger. We often repent of our first thoughts, & scarce ever of our Second. The sure way of judging whether our first thoughts are judicious, is to sleep on them. If they appear of the same force the next morning as they did over night, & if good nature ratifies what good Sense approves, we may be pretty sure we are in the right.

Justice is rather the activity of Truth, than a Virtue in it-self: Truth tells us what is due to Others, & Justice renders that Due. Injustice is acting a Lie.

A new-married Husband sitting by his Wife, took her feet into his lap, saying, "give me your pretty little footsies." Not very long after, being in the same position, the Lady, recollecting the former douceur, was so obliging as to lay her pretty little footsies again on her Husband's knee, when He, roughly shoving them off, cried, "take away your damned great hocks!"

[p. 35]   Account of John Astley[2] the Painter in European Magazine for Dec. 1787. p. 467.

2. John Astley (ca. 1730–14 Nov. 1787), portrait painter. He "studied chiefly at Florence" (HW's "Book of Materials," 1759–70, p. 154), where about 1751 he executed a portrait of Sir Horace Mann which Mann subsequently sent to HW; this portrait hung in the Refectory at Strawberry Hill and is now

New notices on Engravers in gentl. mag. for D⁰. p. 1089.[3]
Academy of painting at Liverpool. ib. 1101.

Silly people are apt to say, I had rather be governed by an absolute Monarch than by the Mob.—but no country is governed by the Mob.[4] In a meer Democratic Government, a sort of Government that never can exist long, the Multitude may

WSL (YWE, XX, 309–10 and illustration; "Des. of SH," *Works,* II, 401). Other works by Astley at Strawberry Hill included portraits of Mann's twin brother, Galfridus, and of Lord Hertford, HW's cousin (after Liotard) (ibid., II, 401, 444; *YWE,* XXI, 34, illustration; XXXVII, 6, illustration). The account of Astley in the *European Magazine,* loc. cit., is heavily moralistic in tenor, and concentrates on the follies and excesses of Astley's life. (He gave up painting after marrying a rich widow, and lived extravagantly on the inheritances he accumulated by the opportune deaths of two wives, his stepdaughter, and his brother.) See *DNB* and Thieme and Becker, II, 206. This item is printed in *Anecdotes of Painting,* V, 18, along with the item from HW's "Book of Materials" cited above, and two newspaper cuttings about Astley pasted by HW in his "Book of Materials," 1771–85, pp. 71 and 117.

3. These notices consist of additions and corrections to the second volume of Joseph Strutt's *Biographical Dictionary: Containing an Historical Account of All the Engravers* (London, 1785–86), 2 vols., 4to, in a review of that volume "by a correspondent at Dublin." HW's copy of this work, now *WSL,* is listed Hazen, *Cat. of HW's Lib.,* No. 254; in the first volume, on the verso of the half title, he wrote: "This author makes many mistakes both in proper names & languages, probably from being little versed in the latter; but the book is usefull." The reviewer in the *GM* is more critical, dismissing the work as "a very ordinary performance" full of errors. In the course of his remarks he chides the author for quoting, in the article on Nicholas Lanier, "Basan in preference to that useful and agreeable work, *The Anecdotes of Painting,* where there is a considerable article relative to this Lanier, to which, at least, he ought to have referred." For all its faults, however, Strutt's *Biographical Dictionary* became "the basis of all later works of the kind" (*DNB*). On p. 1101 of the *GM* is a review of *The Exhibition of the Society for Promoting Painting and Design in Liverpool,* 2d ed. (Liverpool, 1787), 4to, containing an account of that Society, which was formed in 1783, and a list of the current exhibitors, who included Gainsborough, Reynolds, Fuseli, and Stubbs. HW's notation of the "academy" is printed in *Anecdotes of Painting,* V, 15.

4. This passage was perhaps inspired by a discussion of the current popular unrest in France; HW noted in his "Journal 1783–91," ed. G. P. Judd IV, Diss. Yale 1947, s.v. December 1787 (MS now *WSL*), "Great dissatisfactions in France, even in provinces. . . . Queen did not dare to go to the opera." For studies of the mob in eighteenth-century France and England, see George Rudé, *The Crowd in History: A Study of Popular Disturbances in France and England 1730–1848* (New York, 1964), pp. 19–65 et passim; *Paris and*

do many absurd & many unjust things—but what is called the Mob in any regal Country, however limited the Crown, is an accidental, & a very transient tumult, & never did last above a few days—whereas the Power of an absolute Monarch is permanent, & can exercise injustice & tyranny at all seasons & at all times—nor is there any remedy, but when the Tyranny is so frequent & so outrageous, that it occasions the murder of the Tyrant—without preventing the Succession of another as bad.

Heap coals of fire on the head of yr Enemy[5]—this most uncharitable advice is found in a book, of which Charity is reckoned the Standard Principle. Were the Text in Hebrew, Divines woud no doubt tell us that It means the contrary of what it says—the poverty of that tongue obliging it to express opposite & contradictory ideas by the same term, a confusion from which all other languages have luckily escaped, & which seems very ill chosen for delivering positive Precepts. How can a Positive Command be given in a language that implies both, "Do this, or do the Reverse."

[p. 36] Pedants make a great rout about Criticism, as if it were a Science of great Depth, & required much pains & knowledge—Criticism however is only the result of good Sense, Taste & Judgment—three Qualities that indeed sel-

London in the Eighteenth Century: Studies in Popular Protest (New York, 1971), pp. 268–318 et passim. Of contemporary absolute monarchs HW was harshest in his criticism of Catherine the Great, whom he called the "Tisiphone of the North," and whom he suspected of having murdered her husband, Peter III, to gain the throne; see YWE, XXXIV, 144, and below, p. 142.

5. This "advice" is found in the New Testament at Romans xii.20. This passage is interesting mainly for its underscoring of HW's skeptical attitude toward the Bible as a repository of divine wisdom and authority; it also reveals his scorn of biblical exegetes who were wont to interpret ambiguous passages in the light of their own prejudices and preconceptions (see YWE, XI, 3, n. 2). For the characteristics and development of the Hebrew language, see William Chomsky, Hebrew: The Eternal Language (Philadelphia, 1957), p. 98 et passim.

dom are found together, & extremely seldom in a Pedant, which most Critics are.[6]

1788.

When the Prince of Wales & the Duke of York went to visit their brother Prince William[7] at Plymouth, and all Three being very loose in their manners, & coarse in their language, Pr. William said to his Ship's Crew, "now I hope you see that I am not the greatest Blackguard of my family."

When S[r] Rob. Walpole had quitted the Administration in 1742, & had retired to Houghton, he went to dine with Mr Lee Warner[8] at Walsingham. After dinner a very aged

6. HW, in a letter to George Colman the elder (10 May 1783) complimenting the dramatist on his translation of Horace's *Ars Poetica* (HW's copy listed Hazen, *Cat. of HW's Lib.*, No. 3222:19:7), praises his commentary on the grounds that in it he has followed the dictates of common sense, rather than "the profound laws of criticism" (Toynbee, XII, 444–45, MS now Harvard College Library). HW also jokes about the theories of literary critics in his letter to Henry Fox 24 July 1746 and in a note to his tale of 'Patapan" (*YWE*, XXX, 105, 290, n. 16), and calls pedantry "the sublime of vulgarism," below, p. 151.

7. Prince William Henry (1765–1837), third son of George III, created (1789) Duke of Clarence, King of England as William IV, 1830–37. His father having chosen a naval career for him, he was at this time post captain of the *Pegasus*, which on 27 Dec. 1787 arrived at Plymouth from Cork after a tour of the Americas. On 8 Jan. his brothers the Prince of Wales and the Duke of York came to pay him a visit, staying till the 11th; the various ceremonies and reviews attendant on their visit are described *GM* 1788, LVIII, Pt. i, 77. HW also alludes to the coarseness of George's sons (and of princes in general) below, p. 131, and he repeats an indelicate jest of the Prince of Wales, p. 153. In his "Journal 1783–91," ed. G. P. Judd IV, Diss. Yale 1947, he writes that Prince William (now Duke of Clarence) called Madame Schwellenberg "you damned old bitch" for failing to curtsy to him.

8. Henry Lee Warner (1681–1760) of Walsingham Abbey, Norfolk; M.P. for Hindon 1711–13 (*Burke's . . . Landed Gentry*, London, 1972, III, 934). Though Sir Robert was indeed first sent away to school "sixty years before," i.e., in 1682, when he was six, and his first schoolmaster, Richard Ransome, was in fact a clergyman who would have been ninety-five in 1742, the veracity of this anecdote (and hence its value as a moral exemplum) is doubtful on two counts: first, Richard Ransome's school was not at Walsingham, but at Great Dunham, some twenty miles south; second (and more seriously), according to the Norwich register of wills, Ransome died in 1694, which would make the

Clergyman, who had kept a little School in that town sixty years before, desired to be presented to him, & then told Sr Robert that he had been his first School Master in his Infancy (which Sr R. recollected) & had then from his early parts foretold his future greatness—This did not proceed from any flattery in the good man, tho it might from partiality & a little pardonable Self love—but what an Instance of beautifull Disinterestedness! Sr Robert had not only been partial to Norfolk- [p. 37] men, & called too partial by his Enemies, but most favorable to his Masters & fellow Scholars. He had made Dr Weston, who had been his Under Master at Eton School, Bishop of Exeter, & his Friend & fellow collegian Dr Bland, Provost of Eton & Dean of Durham—yet in twenty years that his Administration lasted, the honest Minister of Walsingham, tho so near a neighbour, had never claimed his Scholar, nor let him know of his own existence, till Sr Robert had lost all power of serving him!

Another singular Adventure happened to Sr Robert after his retirement. One day just before dinner he found in the arcade at Houghton three persons, who looked like Substantial Merchants, who had been seeing his house, & as he always loved to converse with people of business, or trade or farmers, he fell into conversation with them, & finding them sensible, invited them to dine with him, which they accepted. Liking them still better on farther conversation, he pressed them to pass the Evening with him and lodge there that night, which they also accepted, & the Liking seemed mutual. Next morning they left Houghton.

About a month afterwards Sr Robert coming to town, and

"very aged clergyman" at best an impostor (Venn, *Alumni Cantab.*; see also J. H. Plumb, *Sir Robert Walpole: The Making of a Statesman,* Boston, 1956, p. 87). Stephen Weston (1665–1742), D.D. 1711, assistant master at Eton ca. 1690 and lower master 1693–1707 (Sir Robert was at Eton 1690–96), was made bishop of Exeter through Sir Robert's interest in 1724; Henry Bland (ca. 1677–1746), D.D. 1717, Sir Robert's "closest friend" at Eton, through his patronage became dean of Durham, 1728, and provost of Eton, 1733 (ibid., p. 88; Sir Wasey Sterry, *The Eton College Register 1441–1698,* Eton, 1943, pp. 37–38, 348, 360).

stopping at Brandon, when standing at the window till dinner was ready, he observed the initials of three Christian and three surnames with a date of the Month & year (which proved to be the Day in which the three Merchants had been at Houghton) and underneath Words to this Effect, that

the above three Persons (whose initials only were specified) had passed that Day at Houghton; & yet, tho they confessed they had [p. 38] been received & treated with the greatest civility, condescension and humanity, they owned they had never passed a more Unhappy Day in their lives.

So Strange a Declaration gave occasion to various conjectures & expositions, but seemed resolved only into one of these Two—

Either, that the Persons in question were such inveterate & prejudiced Enemies of Sᵣ Robert, that all his good humor & affability coud not surmount their mortification at seeing him so contented with retirement, & enjoying happiness, affluence & honour after all his unjust persecutions—but this Interpretation woud betray such Malignity in the Writers, that one woud not only hope but think that coud not be the spirit of the Inscription—& as it was obvious that the Writing was left with the hope of its meeting Sᵣ Robert's eye, or of its being reported to him, it is not only more good natured & charitable, but more probable that the second Solution was the genuine one; viz.

that the Three Persons in question had been poisoned against Sᵣ Rob. by the malicious Writings & reports of his bitter opponents, & had even acted against him on those grounds; but that finding his goodness, good nature & great sense conformable to the character uniformly given of him by his friends (& since his death universally acknowledged) & being conscious that they had, or had endeavoured to hurt him, they were ashamed of having been so kindly treated by him, which they had deserved so little at [p. 39] his hands, & were therefore desirous of marking their repentance, tho they had not resolution enough to confess more openly their recognition of their errors—had they had frankness & spirit enough to have done so, I think they woud have passed a happy day, not a miserable one.[9]

I have sometimes seen Women, who woud have been sensible enough, if they woud have been content not to be called *Women of sense*—but by aiming at what they had not, they only proved absurd—for Sense cannot be counterfeited.

Nolo Episcopari is Latin for, I lye.[1]

It amazes me when I hear any Person prefer Blindness to deafness.[2] Such a person must have a terrible dread of being Alone. Blindness makes one totally dependent on Others, & deprives us of every Satisfaction that results from Light. By Deafness one gains in one respect more than One loses; one misses more nonsense than Sense.

When Sr Robert Walpole was dying, he told Ranby[3] his Chirurgeon that he desired his Body might be opened. Ranby

9. The portrait which HW presents here is an example of his increasing tendency in later years to idealize his father's memory (see the Introduction). Brandon, where Sir Robert saw the declaration and initials inscribed, is a town in Suffolk on one of the main routes from Norfolk to London.

1. *Nolo episcopari*, "I do not wish to be made a bishop," was a phrase in the liturgy voiced as a matter of form by a newly appointed bishop during his ordination; it soon became a proverbial expression indicating false modesty.

2. HW in a letter to Sir Horace Mann (11 Jan. 1758) mentions his dipping his head in a pail of cold water to remedy an eye malady: "This I am told may affect my hearing, but I have too constant a passion for my eyes to throw away a thought on any rival" (*YWE*, XXI, 168). To this Mann replied (11 Feb. 1758): "Don't risk the loss of so precious a faculty," but "Sir William Stanhope assured me when he was here that if he could only recover from his deafness or rather thickness of hearing, that he would that instant willingly become blind. No one, I think, can understand this, but the fact is that deaf people are always melancholy, and the blind commonly gay" (ibid., XXI, 177). HW in 1779 also complained of being blind in one eye from the gout (ibid., XXX, 268). His preference of deafness to blindness is especially understandable because of his devotion to reading and the visual arts and his insensitivity to music. He appears to have first written "unsense" for "nonsense" in the MS; the first syllable has been crossed out and "non" substituted above the line.

3. John Ranby (1703–73), principal sergeant surgeon to George II. After Sir Robert's death he published a *Narrative of the Last Illness of . . . the Earl of Orford* (London, 1745); HW's copies are listed Hazen, *Cat. of HW's*

acting great horror, cried, "Good God, my Lord, dont talk of that!" "nay, said S[r] Robert, it will not be till I am dead, & that I shall not feel it—nor you neither."

Ld Bath[4] used to say of Women, who are apt to say that they will follow their own judgment, that They coud not follow a worse Guide.

[p. 40]   When Prince William was at Cork in 1787,[5] *an old Officer (Gen. Paterson)* dined with him, & happened to say he had been forty years in the Service: the Prince with a sneer asked what he had learnt in those forty years. The old gentleman justly offended, said, "S[r], I have learnt, when I am no longer fit to fight, to make as good a retreat as I can"—& walked out of the room.

King Renè of Anjou[6] (father of Margaret Queen of Henry 6th.) was a strange Compound of amiable, great and trifling

Lib., Nos. 1608:51:1, 2492:3, 2493:1 (the first two are now *WSL*). This item has been printed, together with another transcript by HW of Sir Robert's last words, in *YWE*, XXVI, 12.

4. See above, p. 20; for another sample of his wit, see also *YWE*, XXXVII, 474.

5. See above, p. 65 and n. 7. In the MS "*Gen. Paterson*" has been inserted (without parentheses) above the line; HW probably underscored "an old officer" at the same time. James Paterson (d. 1789), Maj. Gen. in the Army, 1782, was named colonel of the 28th Foot, stationed in Ireland, in July 1787 (*Army Lists*, 1788, p. 104); his obituary in *GM* 1789, LIX, Pt. ii. 670, notes his gallantry at the battle of Belleisle in 1761, where "he was the first man who mounted the rock with his company," and "had to sustain a dreadful conflict," etc. Philip Ziegler, *King William IV* (London, 1971), p. 59, reports another rude remark of Prince William, made to a fellow naval officer, Capt. Newcombe. Upon the Prince's jeering at his being the son of a schoolmaster and asking why he had not followed the same career, Newcombe is said to have retorted: "Why, sir . . . I was such a stupid, good-for-nothing fellow, that my father could make nothing of me, so he sent me to sea."

6. See above, p. 10; René's daughter, Margaret of Anjou (1429–82), married (1445) Henry VI, King of England (*Burke's Peerage*, p. lv). An early panegyric on René is in Jean de Bourdigné's *Chronique d'Anjou et du Maine* (first published 1529), ed. Comte de Quatrebarbes and Victor Godard-Faultrier (Angers, 1842), II, 229–31 (see also *NBG*). His *Traité des tournois* was completed ca. 1452 (Jacques Levron, *La Vie et les mœurs du bon roi René*, Paris, 1953, p. 218); for an account of his processions, see Edgcumbe Staley, *King René d'Anjou and his Seven Queens* (New York, 1912), pp. 337–38. René married

qualities. He was so excellent a Sovereign as to acquire the Surnom of the Good. He was brave in war, delighted in tournaments & wrote on them, instituted festivals & processions, partly religious partly burlesque, was a fond Husband, a romantic Lover, a good Painter for that age, & a true Philosopher, or if the reader pleases, as insensible, as if he had none of the Sensibilities I have mentioned. His Mistress dying in his absence, he ordered her Tomb to be opened that he might contemplate her dead body; and he woud not listen to the news of his Son having lost the Kingdom of Naples, because he w^d not be disturbed when painting a picture of a Partridge.

[p. 41]   How is it possible for A to know that B is inspired, unless A is inspired too?

If A is not inspired, ought he not to conclude that it is more probable that B lies, than that he has received a Supernatural gift? and ought not A to think so the more, as Men of all Religions almost have pretended to Inspiration!

If A, without being inspired himself, believes that B is inspired, & reports so, what is A's authority worth?

If a Man were now to say that he is Inspired, he woud

twice: first (1420) Isabelle de Lorraine (1410–53) and second (1454) Jeanne de Laval (1433–98) (*YWE*, XIV, 69, nn. 4, 6). A version of the anecdote of his painting a partridge when learning of the loss of Naples is in the article on Jane II, Queen of Naples, in Pierre Bayle's *General Dictionary, Historical and Critical* (London, 1734–41), VII, 720 (HW's copy listed Hazen, *Cat. of HW's Lib.*, No. 2039): "He was drawing a partridge, when news was brought him of the loss of the kingdom of Naples, nor would he for all that leave his work, so much did his mind delight in it" (from Pierre Matthieu's *History of Lewis the Eleventh*, London, 1614). René lost Naples in 1442; however, other sources (see M. A. Hookham, *The Life and Times of Margaret of Anjou*, London, 1872, II, 334–35) say that he reacted thus to the news of his loss of Anjou, which occurred in 1474. This is a more likely story, since René was actively engaged in the struggle for Naples, whereas in 1474 he had been retired to Provence for several years (see Levron, pp. 91–96, 269, 272). René's son (presumably his eldest, Jean, Duc de Calabre, is meant) was not in command at the loss of Naples, and died four years before the loss of Anjou (see *YWE*, XIV, 69, n. 8); but in 1462 he was at the head of an expedition to Naples which ended in defeat (Levron, p. 129). HW's version of the story seems to be a confused conflation of all the foregoing circumstances.

not be believed—Inspiration is therefore like Witchcraft, which ceased[7] to be pretended as soon as it ceased to be believed.

One of the great mischiefs of our Possessions in India is the vast Distance. At the End of the last War with France, two novel Engagements by Land, & one by Sea, In which four score Officers & 2000 Soldiers were slain, happened, before an account of the peace coud reach India.[8]

So low a Sum as one Halfpenny has been put into our Stocks, as a Broker on his own knowledge told Mr Churchill[9] —It was probably on a wager that so small a Sum wd be received.

The Beggars in England have an Estate of two millions a year settled on them by Law (poor's rates) & yet are little the better for it.[1]

7. In the MS "the" is crossed out after "ceased."

8. Though the preliminary articles of peace between Great Britain and France were signed at Versailles in Jan. 1783, news of the signing did not reach the opposing forces in India until the end of June; by that time a major land battle had been fought before Cuddalore (13 June) followed by a minor engagement (24 June), and a naval action had also taken place (20 June). For accounts of the battles and estimates of the casualties, which were heavy on both sides, see S. P. Sen, *The French in India 1763–1816* (Calcutta, 1958), pp. 356–59, 367–74, and H. W. Richmond, *The Navy in India 1763–1783* (London, 1931), pp. 339–79; also *GM* 1783, LIII, Pt. ii, 1050; 1784, LIV, Pt. i, 64–65, 137–38. In the MS HW wrote "naval" for "novel," an obvious slip which has been emended.

9. Charles Churchill (?1720–1812), M.P.; HW's brother-in-law. (He married HW's half sister, Lady Mary Walpole, illegitimate daughter of Sir Robert Walpole by Maria Skerrett.)

1. According to statistics compiled in compliance with 26 George III, c. 56 (1786), the average annual sum raised by the Poor Rate for the years 1783–85 amounted to £2,167,760, while the average expenditure in relief of the poor was £2,004,238. In view of the chronic inefficiency and corruption of those charged with managing relief, it is a moot point just how much of this sum was actually "settled on" those for whom it was intended. See Sidney and Beatrice Webb, *English Poor Law History. Part I: The Old Poor Law* (1927; rpt. Hamden, 1963), pp. 153–54 et passim. Besides giving sums to individuals in distress through his agent, Grosvenor Bedford, HW was an active supporter in the 1780s of David Porter's efforts to improve the lot of chimney sweepers (see *YWE*, XVI, 217; XXXIX, 428) and an outspoken critic of the

[p. 42]   In the American War the Ladies wore caps which They called *Washington Caps*. An English Lady asking what They were, Mrs Anne Pitt,[2] Sister of the great Lord Chatham, but of a contrary Party, replied, "Washington caps are made out of an old English *Mob*." A *Mob* was an old fashioned cap that used to be worn by Servant-maids & wives of the common People.

In 1788 when Abolition of the Slave Trade was in agitation, D[r] Porteous[3] Bp of London, & the humane Miss Hannah More the Poetess were amongst the Warmest Advocates for

slave trade (see below). "Poor's rates" is so in the MS, a usage of the eighteenth and nineteenth centuries (*OED*).

2. Anne Pitt (1712–81), sister of William Pitt the elder, afterwards Lord Chatham; HW's correspondent. Chatham was of course the great defender of the Americans against the repressive measures of the North ministry, both before and during the Revolution. No other mention of "Washington caps" has been found. For other examples of Anne Pitt's wit, see *YWE*, X, 39; XXIV, 6, 430–31.

3. Beilby Porteus (1731–1809), bishop of Chester, 1776–87, and of London, 1787–1809. In 1788 both he and Hannah More (who in Feb. of that year published a popular poem against the slave trade, entitled *Slavery*; see ibid., XXXI, 260, n. 7) were among the most zealous supporters of Sir William Dolben's efforts to get a bill through Parliament designed to ameliorate the lot of negro slaves being shipped to the West Indies, where their chief employment was in the planting, harvesting, and distilling of sugar cane. The report HW heard of the Bishop having "grown less zealous" was without foundation; in 1789, upon the introduction by William Wilberforce of his bill to abolish the slave traffic itself, Porteus wrote to the Rev. W. Mason (13 May 1789): "It is with heart-felt satisfaction I acquaint you that Mr. Wilberforce yesterday opened the important subject of the slave trade in the House of Commons. . . . He was supported in the noblest manner by Mr. Pitt, Mr. Burke, and Mr. Fox, who all agreed that the slave trade was the disgrace and opprobrium of this country, and that nothing but entire abolition could cure so monstrous an evil. It was a glorious night for this country" (R. I. and S. Wilberforce, *The Life of William Wilberforce*, London, 1838, I, 219–20, cited by Frank J. Klingberg, *The Anti-Slavery Movement in England*, 1926; rpt. Hamden, 1968, p. 85). In a letter to Hannah More (ca. 10 Sept. 1789) HW suggested the substitution of machines for men in the sugar fields as a practical solution to the labor shortage which the abolition of slavery would produce (*YWE*, XXXI, 324–25); for his opposition to the slave trade, see also below, p. 84. *Candid* and *candied* were homonyms in the eighteenth century (and indeed are so today in Great Britain; the standard long *e* pronunciation of the second syllable of *candied* is a twentieth-century American development). After the seventeenth century the term *sugar-candied,* in its figurative sense of "sweet, sugared, honeyed, flattering"

the destruction of that execrable traffic. Mr W. one evening told Miss More that he heard the Bishop was much softened & grown less zealous. She said, "the Bishop is very candid." Mr W. replied, "I suppose he is *Sugar-candied.*" The cultivation of Sugar was the chief use of Negros.

Miss More besides writing a poem in behalf of the abolition, wrote a pamphlet at the same time recommending the strict observance of Sunday, called an Essay on the manners of the great. & She was so rigid herself in that practice, that except to Church, She never stirred out of her house on that day. Having staid one Saturday evening at a Lady's house till near twelve, without thinking it was so late, & looking at her Watch, [she] was frightened at seeing the hour—"what, s^d Mr W. are you afraid you have tapped Sunday?"

Excellent Motto to N°. 406 of the Spectator.

et quæ

Ispe sibi tradit Spectator. Hor.[4]

[p. 43]   In the new Edit. of the Spectator,[5] which pretends to gives notes & illustrations, there is one note that is a heap of

(with a connotation of falseness), came increasingly to be used only in conjunction with a pun on *candid* (meaning "just, sincere"), so that by the time of the publication of the *OED* article on *sugar-candied* (in 1919) that term is said to be used only in that manner. HW is of course making a double pun, with reference to the sugar industry, suggesting perhaps that the Bishop has been bribed to soften his stance. For background on the abolition movement in England, see Klingberg, Dale H. Porter, *The Abolition of the Slave Trade in England, 1784–1807* (Hamden, 1970); and Roger Anstey, *The Atlantic Slave Trade and British Abolition 1760–1810* (Atlantic Highlands, N.J., 1975); for Hannah More's involvement in that movement, see Annette M. B. Meakin, *Hannah More* (London, 1911), pp. 234, 247, 250, 257, 260–61, et passim, and M. G. Jones, *Hannah More* (Cambridge, 1952), pp. 83–86, et passim. Hannah More's *Thoughts on the Importance of the Manners of the Great to General Society* was published at the beginning of 1788, while she was still writing *Slavery* (*YWE*, XXXI, 260); HW was fond of teasing her about her Sabbatarianism, and wrote a jocular essay entitled "Thoughts on Keeping Holy the Sabbath" (printed ibid., XXXI, 433–37; see also ibid., XXXI, 260–61, 300, 363, 365).

4. "And which the spectator sends to himself" (Horace, *Art of Poetry*, ll. 181–82). This is the motto to the *Spectator* No. 402, not 406.

5. The first annotated edition of the *Spectator*, published in eight volumes at London, 1788 (the advertisement in Vol. I is dated 23 April 1788), begun

blunders, tho the Persons so well known. The famous Lady Mary Wortley Montagu who was daughter of a Duke of Kingston, & who only married a Mr Wortley Montagu, a very distant relation of the Duke of Montagu, is made Daughter of the latter, who was the Person, who assembled a Company of Long Chins.

Motto for the Bulse.[6]

Did ever Diamond cost a Man so dear?

Dr Young.

D° for Dr Johnson.

—Pensions can excite

To make a Patriot black, a Courtier white.

by Bishop Percy and completed by Dr. John Calder (see above, p. 18 and n. 7; also, Boswell's *Life of Johnson*, ed. G. B. Hill and L. F. Powell, Oxford, 1934–50, II, 501–03). Lady Mary Wortley Montagu (see above, p. 6, n. 6) was the eldest daughter of Evelyn Pierrepont (ca. 1665–1726), 5th Earl of Kingston-upon-Hull, 1690, cr. (1715) Duke of Kingston-upon-Hull; she married (1712) Edward Wortley Montagu (1678–1761), M.P., ambassador to Turkey, 1716–17 (Namier and Brooke, III, 661). The *Spectator* No. 371 describes a party of men with long chins assembled at Bath as a jest by "one of the wits of the last age, who was a man of a good estate," and who himself "was very much distinguished" by a long chin. The Percy-Calder edition (V, 231) very dubiously identifies this wit, not as the Duke of Montague (see below), but as "Villars, the last Duke of Buckingham, and father of the late Lady Mary Wortley Montagu," i.e., George Villiers (1628–87), 2d Duke of Buckingham, 1628, poet, dramatist, and rake, author of *The Rehearsal* (for a mention of a "foot of chin" in a poem by Buckingham, which may have given rise to an oral tradition of the "wit" being Buckingham, see Donald F. Bond, ed., *The Spectator*, Oxford, 1965, III, 397, n. 1). Since HW, in a letter to Lady Ossory 21 Jan. 1787 (*YWE*, XXXIII, 554), mentions a company of stammerers assembled at Bath by "the late Duke of Montagu," i.e., John Montagu (1690–1749), 2d Duke of Montagu, 1709, it appears that he is confusing Buckingham either with this Duke or with his father, Ralph (1638–1709), 1st Duke of Montagu, 1705, who was at one time committed to the Tower for attempting to force a duel on Buckingham; Edward Wortley Montagu was second cousin once removed of the first Duke and third cousin of the second.

6. A reference to the package containing a large diamond sent by the Nizam of Hyderabad to the King through Warren Hastings in 1786 (see above, p. 51, n. 1). The quotation is from Edward Young, *Love of Fame, the Universal Passion*, Satire I, l. 94 (HW's copies of this poem are listed Hazen, *Cat. of*

Arthur More[7] & the Elder Craggs, who both were considerable Men in the reign of Queen Anne, had both been originally Footmen. The Former was very insolent, the Latter
humble. One day More had given himself great airs just as
he was going to carry Craggs somewhere in his Coach. As
Craggs got into it, he turned to A. More & said, "faith, I
am often going to get up behind; are not you?" On telling
this Story to D[r] Burney, he said, "So one may say in the
plural number, what one must not say in the Singular."

In the Catalogue of 500 living Authors published in 1788,[8]
there is a very neat & just satire on the Queen for taking Miss
Burney, the authoress of those excellent Novels Evelina &
Cecilia into her service, & yet employing her only in menial

HW's Lib., Nos. 3934–35). The second quotation has not been found; HW
was among those who castigated Samuel Johnson for accepting a pension (in
1762) after being so critical of pensioners in his dictionary (see HW to William Cole 27 April 1773, to William Mason 19 Feb. 1781, *YWE*, I, 310;
XXIX, 111).

7. Arthur Moore (ca. 1666–1730), economist and politician. According to
Bishop Burnet's *History of His Own Time* (London, 1724–34), II, 622 (HW's
copy listed Hazen, *Cat.*, No. 1092), Moore "had risen up from being a footman without any education to be a great dealer in trade." The "elder
Craggs" was James Craggs (1657–1721), postmaster general, 1715; his son, also
named James (1686–1721), was secretary of state, 1718. HW includes this
story also in his letter to Sir Horace Mann 1 Sept. 1750 OS: "This old
Craggs, who was angry with Arthur More, who had worn a livery too, and
who was getting into a coach with him, turned about and said, 'God! Arthur,
I am always going to get up behind; are not you?" (*YWE*, XX, 181). "Dr.
Burney" was Charles Burney (1726–1814), Mus. D., the music historian and
father of Fanny Burney, the novelist.

8. *Catalogue of Five Hundred Celebrated Authors of Great Britain, Now
Living* (London, 1788), 8vo, by ——— Marshall (not further identified; HW's
copy is listed Hazen, *Cat.*, No. 3819). For Fanny Burney's service at Court,
see above, p. 35, n. 8, and below, p. 93; HW mentions this "satire" to
Hannah More in his letter of 12 July 1788 (*YWE*, XXXI, 271). The gold
muslins presented by the Hastings would of course be regarded by their
enemies as a further attempt by them to ingratiate themselves with the King
and Queen and thus help bring about a favorable verdict in Hasting's trial
before the Lords. Mrs. Hastings (the former Baroness von Imhoff) was a
favorite of the Queen from her arrival in England in 1784, when she presented Charlotte with an ivory bed allegedly inlaid with gold (see HW's
"Journal 1783–91," ed. G. P. Judd IV, Diss. Yale 1947, s.v. September 1784;
also, *YWE*, XI, 295, and below, Appendix A).

offices, in these words; "since that time the hours of this celebrated Genius are said to have been chiefly occupied in the folding of muslins."—(gold Muslins presented by Mr & Mrs Hastings.)

[p. 44]   Satiric Inscription on Joseph 2ᵈ.⁹
          Written on the walls of a Madhouse at Vienna;

Josephus ubique Secundus,
hic Primus.

A prudish Lady being told by a married Lady that She had a Major in the House with her when her Husband was absent, showed great surprize, tho She said nothing. The Other then asked the Prude leave to bring the Major into her pew at Church. New Surprize! but the same Silence. When Sunday arrived, & the Lady brought her friend the Major, the astonished Prude coud not resist instantly whispering the other Lady, "you did not tell me he had grey hairs!"¹

A Gamester, who was very clever, being accused of having a Child by his Aunt, Judge P. said, "he is the last Man who I shoud have thought woud have *cousin'd* himself.
                              cozen'd

A devout Gentlewoman, who thought it wicked to play at cards on Sundays, tho She played on all the other days, a

9. Joseph II (1741–90), Holy Roman Emperor 1765–90. The inscription means "Joseph—everywhere second, / Here first." Joseph's foreign policy was largely a failure; his last setback was a disastrous campaign against the Turks in 1787–89, the lack of success of which was due in no small measure to his insistence on leading his troops himself, despite his mediocre abilities as a field commander (see S. K. Padover, *The Revolutionary Emperor: Joseph the Second 1741–1790*, London, 1934, pp. 358–70; Paul P. Bernard, *Joseph II*, New York, 1968, pp. 133, 135–38). HW depicts the Emperor in his writings as a scheming tyrant whose policies have been responsible for the wholesale shedding of human blood (see, e.g., *YWE*, XXV, 566–67; XXXIII, 503–04, 524; XXXV, 392).

1. HW includes this anecdote in his letter to Lady Ossory 6 Sept. 1788 (ibid., XXXIV, 18), where he identifies the "married lady" as Lady Onslow, i.e., Henrietta Shelley (1731–1809), m. (1753) George Onslow, 4th Baron Onslow, 1776, cr. (1801) Earl of Onslow.

Gentleman asked her if She thought the other six days of the week had no Souls to be saved!

[p. 45] Princes who make War from Ambition, are the most detestable Sort of Gamesters, for in the Game of War, unfortunately, the Cards, fishes & counters (the Soldiers) suffer by an ill run more than the Gamesters.[2]

Pope Paul 4th.[3] affected to rate the dignity of Cardinal so high, that he woud with difficulty allow the Chancellor of France, Bertrand, under Henry 2[d], to be a Cardinal, saying,

---

2. HW includes this figure in his letter to Lord Beauchamp, 13 July 1788 (*YWE*, XXXIX, 463). "Fishes" were small flat pieces of bone or ivory used instead of money or for keeping account in games of chance; sometimes they were made in the form of a fish (*OED*).

3. Giovanni Pietro Caraffa (1476–1559), pope as Paul IV, 1555–59, noted for his strong stand against secularism in the Church, "eut beaucoup de peine à nommer cardinal ["Le Chancelier Bertrand"]," i.e., Jean de Bertrand (d. 1560), keeper of the seals under Henry II of France, 1551–59, archbishop of Sens, 1557, cardinal, 1557. "Le Pontife prétendoit 'que la dignité de cardinal est si grande, qu'elle n'admet en compagnie aucun office séculier, et qu'un cardinal ne devroit pas accepter un royaume, à cause que c'est une dignité temporelle & séculière & ne pouvoit ni devoit estimer autre dignité plus grande que la sienne, ni en accepter, si ce n'étoit le pontificat' . . . " ("Observations des éditeurs sur le neuvième livre des mémoires de François de Rabutin," in *Collection universelle*, XXXIX, 296–97, n. *a*, citing a dispatch of Jean-Paul de Selve, the French ambassador at Rome, in Guillaume Ribier, *Lettres et mémoires*, II, 682 [full citations of these works given above, p. 52, n. 4]; for Bertrand, Rabutin, and Selve, see *Dictionnaire de biographie française*, Paris, 1933–, VI, 274–75, and *NBG*). In Nov. 1584 Pope Gregory XIII gave his support in general terms to the Holy League in France, formed to prevent the spread of Protestantism in that country; shortly after the League declared Charles de Bourbon (1523–90), cardinal, 1548, to be heir presumptive in preference to the Protestant Henry of Navarre (afterwards Henry IV). When Henry III had the head of the League, Henri de Guise, assassinated (in 1588), the League proclaimed that he had forfeited the Crown and declared the Cardinal King as Charles X; after Henry was himself assassinated the following year, Pope Sixtus V "was inclined to give his support and help to the League," though "he saw very little real solution of the problem of the succession in the proclamation of Cardinal Bourbon as King Charles X, since . . . [Bourbon] was in the power of his rival" (Ludwig, Freiherr von Pastor, *History of the Popes*, ed. F. I. Antrobus et al., London, 1891–1953, XXI, 325; see also ibid., XIX, 541–46, and *Dictionnaire*, VI, 1394). Following the death of Bourbon in May 1590, there was a rapprochement of the Pope

that That rank did not admit of a secular companion; & that a Cardinal ought not even to accept a kingdom, as being a secular & temporal Office.—yet some of his Successors were ready to set up the Cardinal of Bourbon, who was called Charles 10th, as King of France, against the true King Henry 4th.

v. observations on the memoires de Rabutin in the 39th. Vol. of Collection univers. des Memoires partic. relatifs à l'hist. de France, p. 297.

Paul 4. called the Loss of Calais the jointure that Philip 2[d]. settled on Q. Mary in the return for the fortune She brought him of the kingd. of England.   ib. p. 519.

On Nobility

Ils pensoient toujours à leur noblesse & jamais à leur Ignorance.

Disc. prelim. to Pauw's Recherches sur les Grecs.[4]

and Navarre, culminating in Henry's abjuration of Protestantism in 1593. In Jan. 1558 Queen Mary I of England, who had married Philip II of Spain in 1554, lost Calais to the French; Pope Paul's sarcastic comment, that this loss was "le douaire que le roy Philippe luy avoit assigné au lieu du dot qu'elle luy avoit porté en mariage," alludes to the fact that it was Philip who had drawn Mary into the war with France, and reflects in particular his enmity towards Mary, who had defied him over the recall of Cardinal Pole to Rome (see *DNB;* the Pope's remark is recorded in a dispatch of Selve to Henry II of France, 1 Feb. 1558, in Ribier, II, 725, cited *Collection universelle,* XXXIX, 318–20). "In the return" and "p. 519" are so in the MS.

4. Cornelius de Pauw (1739–99), *Recherches philosophiques sur les Grecs* (Berlin, 1787–88), I, p. iii, with reference to the Thessalians (for Pauw, see *NBG*). HW's copy is listed Hazen, *Cat. of HW's Lib.,* No. 3135. He wrote to Lady Ossory 10 Feb. 1789 that "the Abbé [Barthélemy] is . . . a little too partial to the Grecian accounts of their own virtues; and . . . M. Pauw and Dr. Gillies [author of *The History of Ancient Greece,* London, 1786] have lately unhinged their scale of merits" (*YWE*, XXXIV, 40). For Pauw's researches on the Egyptians and Chinese, see above, p. 49, n. 6; HW animadverts on Lycurgus and the Lacedaemonians, below, p. 94. With regard to the ignorance of the nobility, HW wrote to Sir Horace Mann 20 April 1766 that "thinking . . . is equivalent to the headache in a man of quality," and noted in his "Paris Journals, Anecdotes 1765": "It is said that learning polishes a nation: it certainly does not polish the possessors. Who are so polished as the French nobility, yet who are so ignorant?" (*YWE*, VII, 354; XXII, 415).

Everybody has two pairs of eyes, one for himself, the other for others.

[p. 46]　good Puns of T. Warton,[5] Poet Laureate.

A Physician's Daughter of Oxford being called a Venus, he said, yes, She is the Venus de Medicis.

Being told the King wore a Watch in a ring, he s^d, Time coud not hang heavy on his hands.

A Person building a Privy in his garden like a fortification,
bombs
Warton s^d, It was an Arsenal for bums.

An excellent definition of Allegory told me by Miss Berry,[6] She did not know by whom;

Allegory is either a gauze that hides nothing, or a blanket that nobody can see through.

An Epigram (from the same) on Ld Spencer's picture by

---

5. Thomas Warton (1728–90), poet and literary historian, currently Camden professor of history at Oxford, was made poet laureate in 1785 upon the death of William Whitehead. HW had known him since 1762, when Warton presented him with the second edition of his *Observations on the Fairy Queen of Spenser* (see Hazen, *Cat.*, No. 1840). "Medicis" is so in the MS (cf. *YWE*, XXVIII, 97; XXXII, 29; XXXV, 54); "Medici," surname of the famous Tuscan ruling family, also means "physicians" in Italian. For an example of a ring watch see G. H. Baillie, *Watches* (London, 1929), Pl. 53. "Bombs" and "bums" were evidently homonyms in the eighteenth century; the first volume of *OED*, published in 1888, still gives "bŭm" as a second pronunciation of "bomb."

6. Probably Mary Berry (1763–1852), authoress, who along with her sister Agnes (1764–1852) was HW's correspondent and intimate friend in his old age; HW usually designates Agnes by her first name to distinguish her from Mary. HW writes in *Anecdotes of Painting*: "Allegorical personages are a poor decomposition of human nature, whence a single quality is separated and erected into a kind of half deity, and then, to be rendered intelligible, is forced to have its name written by the accompaniment of symbols. You must be a natural philosopher before you can decypher [*sic*] the vocation of one of these simplified divinities. . . . How much more genius is there in expressing the passions of the soul in the lineaments of the countenance!" (*Works*, III, 48). The current Lord Spencer was George John Spencer (1758–1834), 2d Earl Spencer, 1783. In 1758 his father John, 1st Earl Spencer (1734–83) purchased the painting by Sacchi (1599–1661) from the collection of Henry Furnese; HW, in his "Book of Materials," 1759–70, p. 19, calls it "capital" and says that his father, Sir Robert, once offered £700 for it (see

Andrea Sacchi of a naked Apollo crowning Merit in the Person of a Musician cloathed;

> Dear Merit, if you're blest with riches,
> For God's sake buy a pair of breeches,
> And give them to your naked Brother,
> For one good turn deserves another.

The Origine of Lord Bute's[7] favour with Frederic Prince of Wales came from an odd accident. He & Lady Bute lived at Egham, & were so poor that they kept no carriage. One day the Apothecary of the place told my Lord that the Prince & Prss were to be at Maiden races where a Tent [p. 47] was prepared for them, & offered to carry him thither in his chaise, which Ld B. accepted. After dinner the Prince & Prss had a mind to play at Whisk, but wanted a Fourth. Being told Bute was in the Village, they sent for him; but they played till it was so late, that the Apothecary had been forced to return home to attend his business; & left Ld Bute not knowing how to get home as it was a very rainy night. The Prince happened to ask how he was to go back, or learnt his distress, & offerred to carry him with them to Cliefden; and did. The next morning Lord Bute, who then was studying

also *YWE*, XXI, 172–73; Thieme and Becker, XXIX, 289–91). The painting in 1928 was at Spencer House, St. James's Place (*YWE*, XXI, 173, n. 17).

7. John Stuart (1713–92), 3d Earl of Bute, 1723; lord of the Bedchamber to Frederick, Prince of Wales (d. 1751), 1750–51; first lord of the Treasury and prime minister, 1762–63; he married (1736) Mary Wortley Montagu (1718–94), cr. (1761) Baroness Mount Stuart, daughter of Lady Mary Wortley Montagu, the letter writer (see above, pp. 6, n. 6, 73, n. 5). This anecdote, with some variations, is reported in Sir Nathaniel W. Wraxall's *Historical and . . . Posthumous Memoirs . . . 1772–1784*, ed. H. B. Wheatley (London, 1884), I, 319–20 (first published 1815), with Mrs. Piozzi's comment, "Curious, and I believe quite true" (ibid., I, 319, n. 2). Wraxall dates the meeting as taking place about 1747. Cliefden or Cliveden was a seat of the Prince of Wales in Buckinghamshire, 3 miles northeast of Maidenhead, where the races allegedly took place (HW's "Maiden" is so in the MS); *Baily's Racing Register* (London, 1845) lists no races at Maidenhead until 1751, after the Prince's death (I, 98). Bute is said by HW to have later become the Princess of Wales's lover and a dark influence over George III (see above, p. 50, n. 8); these charges are dismissed by John Brooke as "a Gothic romance with no foundation in fact" (Namier and Brooke, III, 597).

botany, walking in the garden, discovered that he knew every plant, which pleased his R. H. so much, that he kept the Earl two or three days; & not long after, appointed him a Lord of his bedchamber.

Garrick[8] once going into a Chaise with Mrs Kennicot, wife of the Hebrew D[r], & a very learned & clever woman, said to her in jest, "What! if we shoud go off together!" She replied, It woud be the only time that *you* woud *go* off without applause."

S[r] Rob. Walpole the last year of his life hearing Monticelli[9] sing, said to an old Lady by whom he was sitting, "Why shoud not I sing ⟨Madam⟩? I am one of God Almighty's Eunuchs.

Epigram 1788.

In politics and farming George surpasses
All Kings, for selling Sheep, & buying Asses.[1]

8. David Garrick (1717–79), the famous actor and dramatist. Ann Chamberlayne (d. 1830), sister of Edward Chamberlayne, secretary of the Treasury in the second Rockingham administration (*YWE*, II, 310, n. 3), married (1771) Benjamin Kennicott (1718–83), D.D., 1761, biblical scholar. Fanny Burney wrote in 1786 that she "has rendered herself famous . . . by having studied [Hebrew] after marriage, in order to assist her husband in his edition of the Bible; she learnt it so well as to enable herself to aid him very essentially in copying, examining, and revising" (*Diary and Letters*, ed. C. Barrett and Austin Dobson, London, 1904–05, III, 122). HW owned Kennicott's *Letter to Dr. King, Occasion'd by His Late Apology* (London, 1755), 8vo (Hazen, *Cat. of HW's Lib.*, No. 1608:77:4, HW's copy now *WSL*). Kennicott's great work was his *Vetus Testamentum Hebraicum, cum Variis Lectionibus* (Oxford, 1776–80), 2 vols., folio.

9. Angelo Maria Monticelli (1710–64), Italian male soprano (castrato) singer; active at London 1741–46 (*Grove's Dictionary of Music and Musicians*, 5th ed., ed. E. Blom, London, 1954, V, 859). Sir Robert's remark was made in 1742, three years before his death; HW wrote to Sir Horace Mann 7 Jan. 1742 OS: "Last night I had a good deal of company to hear Monticelli and Amorevoli. . . . Sir R[obert] liked the singers extremely; he had not heard them before. In the middle of the concert, he cried out, (you know his style) 'Faith, I don't see why I should not sing, I am God Almighty's eunuch now!' " (*YWE*, XVII, 274).

1. The epigram alludes to the King's profitable farming and stock breeding activities; he was satirized in numerous prints and caricatures as "Farmer

[p. 48] Mottoes which I have written under some prints
in my Collection of English portraits.[2]

Under that of Quin the Actor, after he had left the Stage,

Quin ubi se à Scenâ et vulgo in secreta remorat.

Under Ld Ch. Justice Hale ——— & Chancellor Jefferies
in opposite pages,

Quantum vertice in auras atherias—tantum radice
in Tartara tendit.

George" (see John Brooke, *King George III*, New York, 1792, pp. 211–12;
M. D. George, *Catalogue of Political and Personal Satires . . . in the British
Museum. Vol. VI. 1784–1792*, London, 1938, Nos. 6918, 6934, 7131, 7355, et
passim). In a character of George III written about this time, HW asserts
that "though every now and then forced to take well-intentioned ministers,
he never kept them long enough for the nation to reap much benefit from
their services" (MS draft on the blank portions of Mrs. Dickenson's letter to
HW, 22 Sept. 1788, printed *YWE*, XXXI, 285–86).

2. HW's collection of English portraits consisted of nineteen portfolios
containing over 5,000 prints. The portfolios were broken up into lots and
sold at London in 1842; some fifty prints are now in the British Museum, and
another score at Farmington (Hazen, *Cat.*, No. 3636). James Quin (1693–1766),
actor, retired from the London stage in 1751 but occasionally played the role
of Falstaff in benefits thereafter; HW's portrait of him was presumably the
one advertised in the London sale, 4th day, lot 556, as "Mr. Quin as Falstaff,
by McArdell, *extra fine*" (*A Catalogue of . . . Engraved Portraits . . . Collected by Horace Walpole, Earl of Orford; Which Will be Sold by Auction,
by Mr. George Robins* [13–22 June 1842], London, 1842, p. 64). HW's motto,
adapted from Horace, *Satires*, II, i, 71, means: "Quin, when he had removed
himself from the stage and public into retirement"; the motto puns on
"Quin," which in the original is a particle meaning "nay, rather." Sir Matthew Hale (1609–76), lord chief justice of the King's Bench, 1671–76, was
noted for his great charity and integrity, while George Jeffreys (ca. 1648–89),
Kt., 1677, cr. (1681) Bt. and (1685) Baron Jeffreys of Wem, lord chancellor
of England, 1685–88, was notorious for his brutality and lack of principle.
The catalogue of the London sale, p. 44, mentions a print of "the right
honble. George Lord Jeffreys, Baron of Wem, Lord High Chancellor of England . . . G. Kneller pinxit, R. White sculpsit . . . *extra fine and rare*"
(3d day, lot 381), but none of Hale. The quotation is from Virgil, *Georgics*,
II, 291–92 and *Aeneid*, IV, 445–46, and refers in the original to the oak tree
("in auras atheras" should be "ad auras aetherias"): "So much as it reaches
with its top to the ethereal airs [heaven], so it extends with its root into
Tartarus [hell]."

When Lord Foley & his Brother applied to the House of Lords to set aside their Father's[3] Will, & make a new one for him, that they might discharge the vast Sums they had borrowed of Jews, Mr Geo. Selwyn said, "the Jews will now prefer the New Testament to the Old."

One may well believe the historic part of the Old Testament, for most of the Kings are represented as bad as Those of any other Country. In that respect the Roman history might as well be a religious book.

Oct. 4. 1788. Mrs Dickenson,[4] Niece of Sr W. Hamilton Envoy to Naples, told me that Lord Mansfield told her Pope made this Epigram, which I have heard before, on Embalming Queen Caroline;

Here lies wrapt up in twenty thousand towels
The only proof that Caroline had bowels.

3. Thomas Foley (1716–77), cr. (1776) Baron Foley. HW wrote to Sir Horace Mann (11 Aug. 1776) that Foley's sons, Thomas (1742–93) 2d Baron Foley, 1777, and Edward (1747–1803), to discharge gambling and racing debts had borrowed enormous sums at such extravagant rates that the interest amounted to £18,000 a year (*YWE*, XXIV, 231). After Lord Foley's death his sons petitioned the House of Lords (5 March 1778) for a private bill for "a jointure upon . . . Harriot Lady Foley . . . and to enable the trustees and executors named in the last will and testament of Thomas Lord Foley, lately deceased, to raise money by sale of . . . real estates . . . for payment of certain debts"; the bill was rejected, largely for fear it would set a dangerous precedent (*Journals of the House of Lords*, XXXV, 341–44, 495, cited *YWE*, XXXIII, 10, n. 21; see also other sources there cited).

4. Mary Hamilton (1756–1816), m. (1785) John Dickenson; HW's correspondent (*YWE*, XXXI, 205 et passim). Her uncle, Sir William Hamilton (1730–1803), K.B., British envoy to Naples, 1764–1800, was the noted vulcanologist and collector of antiquities whose second wife, Emma, had the famous affair with Lord Nelson. For Mansfield, see above, p. 21, n. 3. HW pasted the following newspaper cutting, ca. 1786, in his "Book of Materials," 1771–85, p. 115: "Queen Caroline died of what the physicians call a navel rupture [see above, pp. 29–30 and n. 6]; and for a long time before that event, had refused to see her eldest son [the Prince of Wales]. With allusion to both these circumstances, Mr. Pope produced the following virulent couplet, by way of epitaph on her Majesty: 'Here lies [etc.] . . . ' " The couplet was first included in the collected works of Pope in Joseph Warton's edition (London, 1797), IV, 308, where Warton has "forty thousand" for "twenty

[p. 49]   Madame du Deffand⁵ said of the dark ages of Superstition and Chivalry, "alors On croyoit tout, & On ne craignoit rien."

Passages from a work of mine⁶ written in 1769 on the Troubles in America, & now (1788) very applicable on the question of abolishing the Slave trade;

"Authority never measures Liberty downwards. Rarely is Liberty supposed to mean the Independence of those below us. It is our own freedom from the Yoke of Superiors. The Peer dreads the King; the Commoner the Peer; the Americans the Parliament. Each American Trader that resisted, thought himself a Brutus, a Hampden, while he wrestled with the House of Commons—yet his poor Negroes felt that their Master Brutus was a worse Tyrant than Nero, or Muley Ishmael. Had the Parliament of England presumed by one Godlike Act to declare all the Slaves in our Colonies free men, not a Patriot in America but woud have Clamoured against the violation of Property, & protested that to abolish the power of imposing chains, was to impose them." H. W.

thousand" (see Alexander Pope, *Minor Poems,* ed. N. Ault and J. Butt, Twickenham Edition of the Poems of Alexander Pope, London, 1954, pp. 390, 392–93).

5. Marie de Vichy-Champrond (1696–1780), m. (1718) Jean-Baptiste-Jacques-Charles du Deffand de la Lande, Marquis de Chastres; HW's intimate friend and correspondent and hostess of a famous salon at Paris (see also above, p. 23, n. 7). For other examples of her wit, see *YWE,* XXVIII, 468, XXX, 264; XXXII, 282, et passim.

6. HW's *Memoirs of the Reign of King George the Third,* not published until 1845; the passages cited refer to events in America in 1767 but were written in 1769 (see Hazen, *Bibl. of HW,* 93–96; *Mem. Geo. III,* III, 24–25). The "prophet" of the second quotation is George Grenville, who had predicted that repeal of the Stamp Act would encourage the Americans to further resist the actions of Parliament (ibid., III, 25–26). John Hampden (1594–1643), statesman, was a staunch opponent of Charles I who died heroically fighting the royalists, while Muley Ismail (1646–1727), Sultan of Morocco, 1672–1727, by his wholesale executions earned the sobriquet of "the Bloodthirsty" (*YWE,* XXXIV, 163 and n. 11). For HW's opposition to slavery, see also above, p. 72 and n. 3.

from the same work.

It is a Prophet's Holyday when Woes accomplish his Prediction.

Account of paper by Earl Stanhope[7] on a remarkable Thunderstorm in Scotland, in the Gentl. Mag. for Oct. 1788, taken from Philos. Trans. for 1787.

Edward Duke of York[8] hearing the Prince & Prss condole with Persons of the Drawing room who had been ill or had had some misfortune, said, when a Boy, very civilly to the old Lady [p. 50] Abercorn, "Papa, and Mama, and I, are very sorry that you have such a red face."

That Lady Abercorn, who was a Plummer, had a great deal of wit. Having at Tunbridge invited a Clergyman to Dinner, & he eating voraciously, She said, "pray, Sr, what brought you to Tunbridge?" he replied, "Loss of appetite, Mdm." "Lord, Sr, replied Lady A. I hope no poor Man has found it."

On the Son of F. & A.[9]

G—— to be bad was destin'd from the Womb;
Out of *Two* Nazareths what Good coud come?

7. Charles Stanhope (1753–1816), 3d Earl Stanhope, 1786; scientist and politician. A summary of his *Remarks on Mr. Brydone's Account of a Remarkable Thunderstorm in Scotland* is included in a review of the Royal Society's *Philosophical Transactions . . . Vol. LXXVII. For the Year 1787. Part I* (London, 1787) in *GM* Oct. 1788, LVIII, Pt. ii. 908. The thunderstorm was remarkable in that it caused the death by lightning of a carrier and his horses, though there was no discharge of thunder for some miles distance; Stanhope contends that Brydone's account corroborates the theory propounded in his *Principles of Electricity*, published in 1779. During the French Revolution Stanhope's ardent republicanism earned him the nickname of "Citizen Stanhope"; see below, p. 115, and also p. 138.

8. Edward Augustus (1739–67), cr. (1760) Duke of York and Albany; second son of Frederick, Prince of Wales and the Princess Augusta. The Lady Abercorn of the anecdotes was Anne Plumer (1690–1776), daughter of Col. John Plumer of Blakesware, m. (1711) James Hamilton, 7th Earl of Abercorn, 1734; HW, in a letter to Sir Horace Mann of 30 June 1742 OS, called her "a most *frightful* gentlewoman," in allusion to her great ugliness (*YWE*, XVII, 478). "Tunbridge" in the second anecdote is Tunbridge Wells, the popular resort in Kent where people still go to drink the mineral waters.

9. I.e., Frederick, Prince of Wales and the Princess Augusta; "G——" is of course their son, George III. See above, p. 50 and n. 8. "Womb" and "come"

When Lord Talbot[1] was Chancellor & Ld Hardwicke Chief Justice, Q. Caroline one day at the Drawing room said to the Latter, "my Ld, I hear Ld Talbot is gone into the Country to hunt, which you never do." Lord Hardwicke replied, "Madam, Equity may leap over hedges & ditches, but Law is bound down to rules."

Nov. 1788. On the King being in great danger, Mr G. Selwyn said "if he dies, People will no longer be able to say that the Prince is a *mauvais Sujet*."[2]

Mr Selwyn supping often with a Lady who had constantly a hare, made excuses & said they were given to her by a Friend, He said, "Madam, you are the reverse of Gay's fable; you are the Friend with many Hares."[3]

presumably rhymed in eighteenth-century London; *come* is still pronounced "kōōm" in certain dialects.

1. Charles Talbot (1685–1737), cr. (1733) Baron Talbot of Hensol, lord chancellor of England, 1733–37. Philip Yorke (1690–1764), cr. (1733) Baron Hardwicke and (1754) Earl of Hardwicke, was chief justice of the King's Bench, 1733–37, and succeeded Talbot as chancellor upon the latter's death. His bon mot refers to the fact that the practice of equity in English law, which was the special province of the Court of Chancery, involved a recourse to general principles of justice in cases not covered by the provisions of common law, or where the application of common law would be unfair (see *OED*). Hardwicke's remark may also reveal a dissatisfaction with the "chaos of precedents" which equity itself had become; as lord chancellor he set himself the task of transforming this chaos into a scientific system (see *DNB*).

2. For the hostility between George III and the Prince of Wales, see above, p. 48 and n. 5, and below, p. 152. In Oct. 1788 the King suffered his second attack of "madness" (the first was in 1765), which did not relent until Feb. 1789. Modern authorities have recently determined that his illness was probably physiological rather than mental; Ida Macalpine and Richard Hunter suggest that he suffered from "acute intermittent porphyria" (see Macalpine and Hunter, *George III and the Mad-Business*, London, 1969, pp. 177–91 et passim; John Brooke, *King George III*, New York, 1972, pp. 322–41). The King's illness plunged the nation into a regency crisis, with the Prince of Wales's supporters wanting to set him up as regent with unrestricted powers. The prime minister, Pitt, and his followers countered with a bill designed to limit the authority of the Prince; this bill had passed the Commons and was in the Lords at the time of the King's recovery. See John W. Derry, *The Regency Crisis and the Whigs 1788–9* (Cambridge, 1963).

3. The reference is to "The Hare and Many Friends," No. 50 of the first volume (published 1727) of Gay's *Fables*, which went through over sixty editions by the end of the century.

Mr Hare[4] dealing at Faro to Admiral Pigot, who lost a vast Sum of money & insisting on sitting & playing on, [p. 51] for a great Number of hours, Mr Hare tired, said at last, "Admiral, you must be copper bottomed." This Mr Hare was the famous Wit. The Prince of Wales owing him a large Sum of money lost at play & not paying him for some time, Hare wrote to ask for it. The Prince payed, & to show he did not resent the Demand, gave a place of 300£ a yr to Hare's natural son.

On the talk of appointing the Prince Regent during the King's lunacy, Mr F.[5] said, "then we shall be governed by the *Son* and Moon."

In the Morning Herald of Nov. 20. 1788 was printed a Song beginning,
        As the Mole's silent stream crept pensive along &c
                by Mr H. Walpole[6]

4. James Hare (1747–1804), politician and wit, who held a faro bank at Brooks's with Charles James Fox and Richard Fitzpatrick (Namier and Brooke, II, 584–85); for another example of his wit, see below, p. 147. Hugh Pigot (1722–92), admiral, 1782, was also one of Fox's gaming set (Namier and Brooke, III, 281); Hare's bon mot alludes to the practice of sheathing the bottom of ships with copper as a protection against shipworm and the accumulation of weeds and barnacles (first applied to ships of the British navy in 1761; see *OED*). Hare's natural son has not been further identified; Namier and Brooke, II, 584, mentions Hare's having "several children by subsequent liaisons" after separating from his wife soon after their marriage in 1774.
    5. Perhaps Charles James Fox, the Prince's chief follower, who would not be averse to making a joke about his patron. For the proposed regency, see above, p. 86, n. 2.
    6. This song, in five stanzas, was also printed in the *London Evening Post* 19 Nov. 1787, the *London Chronicle* 20–22 Nov. 1788, and *A Collection of Poems Mostly Original by Several Hands*, ed. Joshua Edkins (Dublin, 1789), p. 87; from the last it was reprinted in HW's *Fugitive Verses*, ed. W. S. Lewis (New York, 1931), p. 187. HW's first cousin once removed, the Hon. Horatio Walpole (1752–1822), eldest son of Horatio Walpole (1723–1809), 2d Baron Walpole of Wolterton, 1757, was styled Lord Walpole, 1806–09, and succeeded his father as 2d Earl of Orford (n.c.), 1809. He married (1781) Sophia Churchill (d. 1797), daughter of HW's half sister Lady Mary Churchill (see above, p. 71, n. 9); the third stanza of the song begins, "In vain my Sophia has graces to move / The fairest to envy, the wisest to love."

It was not written by me, nor did I ever see it before. It might be written by my Cousin of the same names, Eldest son of the second Lord Walpole, who married my Neice Sophia Churchill. The Song does call the Author's Mistress, Sophia.   it was not.

The Story of the Country Gentleman[7] who was going out with his Hounds as Charles 1st. was going to fight the battle of Naseby, is in no history, but was related by Daniel Earl of Nottingham who had it from a Gentleman present. If true, it was one of the strangest Instances of Insensibility ever recorded. I have heard that on the King's reproof, the Gentleman entered into & was killed in his Service.

[p. 52]   A Person wondering at the Expression of a Man being out of his *Seven* Senses, asked Dr Hinchliffe[8] Bp of Peterborough which are the two additional Senses? he replied "Common Sense & Nonsense."

---

7. Sir Richard Shuckburgh (1596–1656), Royalist. HW was fond of recounting this anecdote as an example of either "insensibility" or philosophical indifference (see *YWE*, II, 75, and n. 4). He here departs from earlier tellings in placing the incident at the battle of Naseby (in 1645), whereas it actually took place just prior to the battle of Edgehill (in 1642). Whether due to confusion on HW's part or to his having heard a new version of the story, this change of date has the effect of heightening the apparent insensitivity of Sir Richard to the civil turmoils around him. In fact, far from being uncommitted, Sir Richard had the month before Edgehill been taken into custody by the Parliamentarians for his openly professed loyalty to the King, and had withdrawn to his Warwickshire estates to avoid imprisonment. Enlisted by the King on the latter's march to Edgehill, Shuckburgh fought bravely in that battle, and after the King's retreat, withdrew to Shuckburgh Hill, where he was severely wounded by the pursuing enemy but not killed. Daniel Finch (1647–1730), 2d Earl of Nottingham, 1682, and 7th Earl of Winchilsea, 1729, was a Tory lord who in 1688 refused to come over to the Whigs in their conspiracy against James II; the "gentleman present" from whom he allegedly heard the anecdote has not been identified.

8. John Hinchliffe (1731–94), D.D., 1764, bishop of Peterborough, 1769–94; admired and befriended by HW for his liberal stands in the House of Lords (see *YWE*, III, 156, n. 1). For other instances of the expression, "to be out of one's seven senses," see *OED*, s.v. Sense, sb. 10. According to ancient lore, the two additional senses were animation and speech (*Brewer's Dictionary of Phrase and Fable*, New York, 1970, s.v. Seven Senses).

1789.

The King of Prussia in his posthumous history of his Campaigns,[9] has shown himself more ignorant of our Affairs, than I shoud have thought he coud have been. He imputes our war with France in 1757 to the Duke of Cumberland; but the Duke of Newcastle & Lord Hardwicke were certainly the Authors.

9. Frederick II, the Great, *Histoire de la guerre de sept ans*, Vols. III–IV of his *Œuvres posthumes* (Berlin, 1788); HW evidently borrowed the volumes from his cousin, Gen. Henry Seymour Conway (see *YWE*, XXXIV, 33). For the Duke of Cumberland and Lord Hardwicke, see above, p. 27, n. 4 and p. 86, n. 1; Thomas Pelham Holles (1693–1768), cr. (1715) Duke of Newcastle-upon-Tyne and (1756) Duke of Newcastle-under-Line, was first lord of the Treasury, 1754–56, 1757–62. In chap. iii, "Cause de la rupture entre la France & l'Angleterre [etc.]," Frederick asserts that Cumberland destined his follower Henry Fox "à la place de chef de la trésorie, & à tous les emplois dont le duc de Newcastle étoit revêtu. . . . Le duc de Cumberland imagina que le meilleur moyen pour faire abandonner au duc de Newcastle ses grands emplois, seroit d'engager la nation dans une guerre avec la France, par où il mettroit le ministre dans la necessité d'ajouter de nouvelles dettes à celles dont le gouvernement étoit déjà surchargé; ce qui fourniroit des griefs à l'opposition: ou bien il se flattoit de profiter des mauvais succès possibles au commencement d'une guerre, pour en rejeter la faute sur le ministre, & le déterminer à force d'inquiétude & de persécutions à renoncer de lui-même à ses emplois" (*Œuvres posthumes*, III, 62–63). HW, on the other hand, writes in *Mem. Geo. II*, I, 400, that Newcastle welcomed the outbreak of hostilities in America (in 1754) as giving "a reverberation to the stagnated politics of the ministry: in a moment, the Duke of Newcastle assumed the hero, and breathed nothing but military preparations: he and the chancellor [Hardwicke] held councils of war; none of the ministers, except Lord Holderness, were admitted within their tent." In fact, neither Cumberland nor Newcastle wanted war, at least not when it came; but when it seemed inevitable, Cumberland was for taking at once vigorous measures against the French both in America and in European waters, while Newcastle hesitated to undertake operations in Europe until Britain had completed a system of continental alliances designed to contain France and protect Hanover. HW's eagerness to place the blame for the Seven Years' War on Newcastle reflects his intense dislike for the Duke, stemming from the Duke's political "betrayal" of his father, Sir Robert. See I. S. Leadam, *The History of England . . . 1702–1760* (London, 1909), p. 441; Basil Williams, *The Whig Supremacy 1714–1760*, 2d edn. (Oxford, 1962), pp. 334, 347–53; Evan Charteris, *William Augustus Duke of Cumberland and the Seven Years' War* (London, 1925), pp. 119–63, passim; Reed Browning, *The Duke of Newcastle* (New Haven, 1975), pp. 206–13 et passim.

He says Ld Bute made Mr Grenville,[1] Ld Halifax & Lord Egremont Ministers, & governed them. The Contrary is true, They declared against him, & he advised the King to recall Ld Chatham to get rid of them. Ld Chatham cd not agree with the King; Grenville remained Minister, remained Enemy of Ld Bute, & was again expelled by his concurrence.

I believe his Pr Majesty was not more correct in saying the Card. de Bernis[2] was disgraced for trying to make Peace ag.

1. George Grenville (1712–70), statesman; first lord of the Treasury (prime minister), 1763–65. George Montague Dunk (1716–71), 2d Earl of Halifax, 1739, and Charles Wyndham (1710–63), 2d Earl of Egremont, 1750, were secretaries of state during the early months of Grenville's administration; together the three attempted to monopolize the powers of government to the exclusion of the other ministers, and were known as the Triumvirate. Of them Frederick writes: "Bute . . . forma une nouvelle administration, composée des Lords Hallifax, Egremont, & Greenville, qui fut nommé le triumvirat; mais Bute en étoit l'âme" (*Œuvres posthumes*, IV, 283–84). While it is true that Grenville owed much to Bute for his advancement to the front rank of politics, once in office as prime minister he and his secretaries of state became violently jealous of Bute's influence with the King, even threatening to quit if Bute did not resign his role of "minister behind the curtain." Following the death of Egremont in Aug. 1763 Bute was the King's prime mover in an attempt to bring Pitt back into office; the failure of this effort strengthened Grenville's position, and Bute asked leave of the King to retire from the scene. Grenville's final expulsion from power in 1765 need not be explained as the result of covert pressure from Bute; by that time Grenville had made himself totally obnoxious and unacceptable to the King, and would have been expelled with or without Bute's concurrence. See Namier and Brooke, II, 537–43; *Mem. Geo. III*, I, 214–16, 225–34.

2. François-Joachim de Pierre de Bernis (1715–94), French secretary of state for foreign affairs, 1757; cardinal, 1758; disgraced and sent into exile 13 Dec. 1758. Frederick writes of Bernis: "Ses vues se tournèrent toutes du côté de la paix, afin de terminer . . . une guerre dont il ne prévoyoit que des désavantages. . . . S'adressant à l'Angleterre par des voies sourdes et secrètes, il y entama une négociation pour la paix; mais la marquise de Pompadour étoit d'une sentiment contraire, & aussitot il se vit arrêté dans ses mesures. . . . Il fut disgracié pour avoir parlé de paix, & envoyé en exil dans l'évêché d'Aix" (*Œuvres posthumes*, III, 347). Frederick is correct in assigning differences with Madame de Pompadour over the conduct of the war as the principal cause of Bernis's downfall; after his disgrace he was replaced as foreign minister by the Duc de Choiseul, who was as vigorously for the war as Bernis had been against it. It is undoubtedly true that Madame de Pompadour, who was responsible for Bernis's rise to power, resented his increasing independence from her, but this was at most a secondary factor in his downfall; HW's story in *Mem. Geo. II*, III, 158, that he was peremptorily dismissed as punishment for refusing to consort with her after becoming cardinal, is certainly without foundation. See Jacques Levron, *Pompadour*,

the inclination of Madame de Pompadour. She had made him Minister, & soon removed him for thinking himself independent of Her.

From the translation of Dupaty's[3] letters on Italy.

The fine Arts were with them [the Greeks] but the different dialects of the same Language—the sacred language of the beautifull. Lett. 46. p. 168.

[p. 53] The Court sees but Naples: great Capitals are at the feet of Thrones like high mountains before the Provinces. ib. Lett. 105.

Modern Poets seem to forget that Pope, without neglecting Poetry, introduced good Sense into Verse; & that when a Nation has been used to the alliance of both, the mere mechanism of words will make no impression. We have Poets & Poetesses now, who seem to aim at nothing but arranging poetic phrases without a plan & almost without a Subject. They are like the Parson of Gretna green in Scotland,[4] &

trans. C. E. Engel (New York, 1963), pp. 219–37; Marcus Cheke, *The Cardinal de Bernis* (New York, 1959), pp. 153–81; Serge Dahoui, *Le Cardinal de Bernis* (Aubenas, 1972), pp. 235–62.

3. Charles-Marguerite-Jean-Baptiste Mercier Dupaty (1746–88), French lawyer and man of letters; author of *Lettres sur l'Italie, en 1785* (Rome and Paris, 1788), translated into English by J. Povolerie as *Sentimental Letters on Italy* (London, 1789), 2 vols. This work enjoyed great popularity because of its "sensibility" and revolutionary fervor, but is now dismissed as bombastic and pretentious (*NGB; Dictionnaire de biographie française*, Paris, 1933–, XII, 318–20). Dupaty's observation on the fine arts in Greece (I, 168) reflects that broad movement in seventeenth- and eighteenth-century aesthetic theory which strove to separate the various arts from their social and functional contexts and relate them instead to one another in a higher realm of pure contemplation. The second quotation is actually found in Letter 108 (misnumbered 105), II, 187; Dupaty means that the monarch's view of the provinces is obscured by the presence of the metropolis, and he criticizes the Court of Naples for seeing Sicily as nothing but "an overgrown troublesome kingdom." The insertion in brackets in the first quotation is HW's.

4. Gretna Green, Dumfriesshire, was long famous for runaway marriages; in Scotland it was possible to be married simply by a mutual declaration of the contracting parties before witnesses (see *Brewer's Dictionary of Phrase and Fable*, New York, 1970, s.v. Gretna Green Marriages; also, HW to Mary Berry 23 April 1791, *YWE*, XI, 253, where he mentions the elopement to Gretna Green of a Miss Clementina Clerke). HW's emphasis on sense in poetry and on poetry's social role is preeminently Augustan; see the Introduction, and also HW's verses on modern poets, below, p. 93.

marry every Couplet that presents itself, without inquiring whether good Sense consents to the Union, or whether the thoughtless Candidates have any means of living & subsisting in Society.

Dr James[5] attended an affected Lady who was remarkably robust & strong, but acted delicacy, ill health, & want of appetite. She told him She cd never touch her dinner, & shd certainly be starved; might not She eat whenever She shd find she coud!—to be sure—what might She eat?—what She pleased—might She eat a few oysters?—no doubt—how many? might She eat two?—the Doctor provoked & impatient, replied—aye, two dozen, & the Shells too, & he w^d answer they wd not hurt her.

Noble Author.

The Law of a Justice of Peace & Parish Officer &c by John Lord Visc. Dudley & Ward & T. Cunningham Esq.[6] Qu^o. Lond. 1769. 4 vol^s.

[p. 54]   Canidius[7] has all the Vices that a Man of Virtue piques himself on having, as Pride & Obstinacy & Unforgivingness.

Jeremiah Meyer,[8] Enam. & Miniat. Painter, died at Kew green, Jan. 20. 1789.

5. Robert James (1705–76), M.D., inventor of a famous medicinal powder that was HW's favorite cure-all.

6. John Ward (ca. 1700–74), cr. (1763) Viscount Dudley and Ward, and Timothy Cunningham (d. 1789), *The Law of a Justice of Peace and Parish Officer: Containing All the Acts of Parliament at Large Concerning Them, and the Cases Determined on those Acts in the Court of King's Bench* (London, 1769), 4 vols., 4to. As the heading suggests, HW was interested in Lord Dudley as an addendum to his *Catalogue of the Royal and Noble Authors*, first published in 1758; he lists other works by noble authors above, p. 85, below, p. 100, et passim (see also the Introduction).

7. The Canidii were a Roman family mentioned in Plutarch and elsewhere, but the name may have been suggested by "Canidia," an old sorceress in Horace (*Epode* V; *Satires* I, viii).

8. Jeremiah Meyer (1735–89), R.A., miniature painter to the Queen and enamel painter to the King (Thieme and Becker, XXIV, 480); his death

add to preceding page of *modern Poets* &c[9]

Ye Versifiers, cease yr gleaning
Of words, all sound without a meaning,
Nor poems heap, that to our store
Add not a new Idea more;
Pindaric Odes that keep the peace,
Unlike the lawless Bards of Greece,
Who ravish'd Beauties worth possessing,
Nor staid to ask the Critic's blessing——

I was saying to Miss Agnes Berry,[1] that I wondered with her great intuition into Characters they had ventured to let Miss Burney into Court, & that they must have a perfectly good opinion of Her—yes, replied She, or a perfectly good opinion of themselves.

20 Jan. "at Kew-green, in his 54th year," is recorded in *GM* 1789, LIX, Pt. i, 90. HW mentions the auction of his drawings and prints in March 1790 below, p. 116. Both items have been printed in *Anecdotes of Painting*, V, 133.
9. See above, p. 91. HW elsewhere refers to the "sudden" and "libertine" transitions of Pindar, and to his "eccentic flights" (*YWE*, XV, 61; XVI, 297), echoing as here the Cowley-inspired stereotype of Pindar as "lawless bard." By "Pindaric odes that keep the peace" he presumably refers to the more regular Pindarics of poets like Mark Akenside (see ibid., IX, 215, XIX, 28; XXVIII, 278); at the same time he makes these a type of the frigidly formal versifying of contemporary bad poets. (Although Thomas Gray also made the Pindaric ode more regular, as HW's friend he was immune to criticism on that score; in any case, his *Elegy* for HW as for most other Englishmen placed him securely in the front rank of poets.)
1. See above, p. 79, n. 6. For Fanny Burney's service at Court, see pp. 35, 75; increasingly poor health due to the confinement and rigid etiquette led to her resignation in 1791. While at Court she continued to keep the famous diary for which she is best remembered today; in it she treats the royal family with the greatest of respect, but otherwise reveals the pettiness and intrigues endemic to Court life. HW wrote to her, 20 Oct. 1790: "You have retired from the world into a closet at court—where indeed you will still discover mankind . . . for if you could penetrate its character on the earliest glimpse of its superficies, will it escape your piercing eye, when it shrinks from your inspection, knowing that you have the mirror of truth in your pocket!" (Toynbee, *Supplement*, II, 44). Three days after her resignation he wrote to her father, Dr. Burney, congratulating him on the event (HW to Dr. Burney 10 July 1791, ibid., II, 52–53); see also HW to Hannah More 29 Sept. 1791 (*YWE*, XXXI, 360–61).

When the famous Con Philips[2] had her lawsuit with Muilman, S[r] John Strange was her Council. one day having been
long at his chambers, as She was going away, She turned back
& said to him, "you have [p. 55] asked me many questions,
pray allow me to ask you a few. How old are you? he told
her. are you married? yes. Do you love yr Wife? yes; why do
you ask?—because I never before was alone with a Man for
an hour that did not ask to lie with me.

One day Con Philips went to the Drawing-room. Queen
Caroline bid her Ld Chamberlain to send her away. He
whispered his message; She held up her finger to her nose, &
said aloud, "at twelve, my Lord," as if he had been making
an Assignation with her. On the great Stairs She met some
Ladies coming to the Drawing room; She cried out, "Ladies,
there is no Court today; the Queen says She will see no
whores today.

The Laws of Lycurgus[3] were most narrow & abominable
Institutions; & in reality, were refinements on natural bar-

2. Teresia Constantia Phillips (1709–65), courtesan. She married (1723)
Henry Muilman, a Dutch merchant (perhaps the Henry Muilman whose
death in 1772 is recorded in *GM* 1772, XLII, 247); after a year of marriage
he obtained an annulment from the Court of Arches (see *DNB; YWE,* XXIV,
35, n. 5). Sir John Strange (ca. 1696–1754), Kt., 1740, was master of the Rolls,
1750–54; he married Susan Strong (ca. 1702–47) of Greenwich (*DNB;* Namier
and Brooke, III, 491). HW records both anecdotes in his MS "Commonplace
Book of Verses," p. 4, and the second one also in a MS note to his copy
(now *WSL*) of Thomas Davies, *Dramatic Miscellanies* (London, 1784), III,
434–35 (see above, p. 11, n. 2). He there identifies the chamberlain as Lord
Grantham, i.e., Henry d'Auverquerque (ca. 1672–1754), cr. (1698) Earl of
Grantham, chamberlain to Caroline both as Princess of Wales and as Queen
Consort, 1716–37.
3. Lycurgus (fl. ?825 B.C.) was the legendary lawgiver of Lacedaemon
(Sparta). The constitution of Sparta, which he allegedly devised, divided the
power of the state among the kings, the senate, and the assembly of the
people, thus uniting the monarchical, aristocratic, and democratic principles. In
fact, the relatively few Spartans formed an aristocracy which ruled over
the remaining inhabitants of the Peloponnesus; the goods of the Spartans
were shared in common in order to free them for martial exercises, by which
they kept up their ascendancy over their neighbors. HW's observations here
were inspired by his reading of the Abbé Barthélemy's *Voyage de jeune
Anacharsis en Grèce* (Paris, 1788), 4 vols. (his copy, now *WSL,* is listed Hazen,

barism, tending to unite one Set of men in Society for the purpose of annoying all other Societies, and consequently were totally incompatible with Justice.

Lycurgus allowed the Lacedœmonians to steal—where was the use of stealing where every thing was in common!

One may believe a Person that tells an extraordinary Story *for the first time,* because extraordinary things do happen; but when that person repeats the Story, we may doubt, as the person's self is apt to add to the Story, especially if questioned, & even to believe what has been added.

To Ponderosus.[4]

**from Envy &c.

Ponder, your Comedies are woefull chaff:
Write Tragedies, when you w^d. make us laugh.

**Or bid Calypso when She wants to please,
give her Telemachus Cantharides.

The late Mr George Montagu,[5] being at a representation of Tamerlane by some young gentlemen where some of those who acted the Attendant had drunk the wine alloted for the

---

Cat. of HW's Lib., No. 262; see also below, p. 113. He wrote to Lady Ossory 24 Feb. 1789 that Lycurgus "only refined savages into greater barbarism. I will tell your Ladyship an additional observation that I made just as I broke off with *Anacharsis*—we are told that Lycurgus allowed theft and enjoined community of goods—I beg to know where was the use of stealing where there was no individual property? Does stealth consist in filching what is your own as much as any other man's?" (*YWE,* XXXIV, 42). Barthélemy writes on the Lacedaemonians and the laws of Lycurgus, II, 481–602, 624–46; III, 1–26; his assertions about Lycurgus permitting theft and the lack of individual property are found at II, 511, 516. See also *Harper's Dictionary of Classical Literature and Antiquities,* ed. H. Thurston Peck (New York, 1923), s.v. Lycurgus and Sparta; above, p. 78, n. 4.

4. See HW's "motto for ridiculous tragedies" (after Ovid), above, p. 61.

5. George Montagu (ca. 1713–80), M.P.; HW's correspondent. Presumably the *Tamerlane* of Nicholas Rowe is meant; Marlowe's play had fallen into obscurity in the eighteenth century, and was not revived until the nineteenth. Montagu's bon mot consists of a double pun: "Mutes" means actors without a speaking part, but is also a term in phonetics for one of two commonly distinguished classes of consonants, the other being the "liquids" (*OED*).

whole Set after the Play, said, "So the Mutes have drunk up the Liquids!"

Ld Weymouth[6] had two led Captains, very dull, who generally sat drinking with him at Whites till morning, but listening to him & scarce ever speaking. Mr G. Selwyn said, Ld Weymouth will some day or other be found Strangled between his two Mutes.

The Dss of Bedford[7] saying it was odd that She had played at whisk, with 3 other Duchesses, & all Four were Bs—viz. Beaufort, Bolton, Buccleugh, & herself. "yes, said Mrs Robinson Montagu, & half were D-B[s]. viz. Dowagers or -d—— B——[s].

Ld Petre[8] & his Son married each a Miss Howard, who were Sisters, & his Daughter married their Brother—so the families were Dovetailed.

6. Thomas Thynne (1734–96), 3d Viscount Weymouth, 1751, cr. (1789) Marquess of Bath. *Led-captain* was a common term for a hanger-on or parasite, while White's was of course the celebrated club at Nos. 37 and 38 St. James's Street (see Peter Cunningham and H. B. Wheatley, *London Past and Present*, London, 1891, III, 491–96). HW records another bon mot of Selwyn on Lord Weymouth (who was notorious for drinking) in a letter to Montagu 16 May 1759 (*YWE*, IX, 236). Selwyn's bon mot here alludes to the use of mutes by oriental monarchs to strangle their enemies.

7. Gertrude Leveson Gower (1715–94), daughter of John, 1st Earl Gower, married (1737) John Russell (1710–71), 4th Duke of Bedford, 1732 (*GEC; Burke's Peerage*, p. 2585). The other duchesses were Elizabeth Berkeley (ca. 1719–99), m. (1740) Charles Noel Somerset (1709–56), 4th Duke of Beaufort, 1745; Katharine Lowther (ca. 1736–1809), m. (1765) Harry Powlett (1720–94), 6th Duke of Bolton, 1765; and Elizabeth Montagu (1743–1827), m. (1767) Henry Scott (1746–1812), 3d Duke of Buccleuch, 1751, 5th Duke of Queensbury, 1810 ("Buccleugh" is so in the MS); the dowagers were Bedford and Beaufort. "Mrs Robinson Montagu," i.e., Elizabeth Robinson (1720–1800), m. (1742) Edward Montagu, was the famous "bluestocking"; "D—— B——s" of course means "damned bitches."

8. Robert Edward Petre (ca. 1742–1801), 9th Baron Petre, 1742, married (as his second wife, 1788) Juliana Barbara Howard (1769–1833); his son by his first wife, also Robert Edward Petre (1763–1809), 10th Baron Petre, 1801, married (1786) Mary Bridget Howard (1767–1843), sister of Juliana Howard. HW seems to be mistaken about Lord Petre's daughter marrying the Howard sisters' brother: according to Collins, *Peerage*, VII, 13, and *GM* 1798, LXVIII, Pt. ii, 908, his "only" daughter Anne (1769–98) married (1796) Dan. Onslow,

Churchill[9] being omitted by Dr Johnson in the lives of the Poets, puts me in mind of that passage of Tacitus, where he says, "Præfulgebant Cassius & Brutus eo ipso, [p. 57] quod Imagines eorum non Visebantur. End of Ann. 2ᵈ.

**Dalton head of Popes[1]

Loyalty is a word I do not find either in the Bible or the Statute book. It is a French word & conveys a French Idea: but ought to have a reciprocal Signification. It comes from Loy, the Law, but is now confounded with Royautè:[2] but

while Bernard Edward Howard (1765–1842), 12th Duke of Norfolk, 1815, elder brother of the Howard sisters, married (24 April 1789) Elizabeth Belasye (1770–1819), daughter of Henry, Earl Fauconberg (*GEC*). HW may have heard an incorrect report of this brother's marriage. For Lord Petre, see also below, p. 117.

9. Charles Churchill (1731–64), satiric poet, author of the *Rosciad*. He was not among the poets chosen by the booksellers of London to be included in Johnson's *Lives* (first published 1779–81) and Johnson did not volunteer to add him, though he did volunteer several others (see Boswell's *Life of Johnson*, ed. G. B. Hill and L. F. Powell, Oxford, 1934–50, III, 370 and n. 8). Boswell reports that Johnson "talked very contemptuously of Churchill's poetry, observing, that 'it had temporary currency, only from its audacity of abuse, and being filled with living names, and that it would sink into oblivion'" (ibid., I, 418). The passage from Tacitus is from the *Annals*, III, 76 (*imagines*, "images," should read *effigies*, "effigies"): "Cassius and Brutus shone forth by the very fact that the effigies of them were not beheld." In the original passage Tacitus notes the omission of Cassius and Brutus's effigies from the images of illustrious families displayed at the funeral of Junia, sister of Brutus and wife of Cassius.

1. This is all that is legible of a passage in pencil in the MS which has been written over by the three lines beginning "quod imagines" and ending "conveys a French idea." The reference is perhaps to Richard Dalton (1715–91), engraver and antiquary, surveyor of the King's pictures, 1778–91 (Thieme and Becker, VIII, 309–10); in a passage dated ca. 1788 in his "Book of Visitors," HW wrote that the King "found at Kensington the fine book of Leonardo da Vinci that had been Charles I's. Dalton persuaded him most absurdly to cut out all the heads and paste them into two volumes. Mr Lysons" (*YWE*, XII, 263). See also below, p. 125, and Appendix A.

2. The ultimate derivation of *loyalty* is from the Latin *lex*, "law," through its adjectival form *legalis*, which in Old French became *loial, leial*, which gave rise to Old French *loialté* (Modern French *loyauté*) (*OED; Oxford Dictionary of English Etymology*, ed. C. T. Onions, Oxford, 1966, s.v. Loyal). This exercise in etymology reflects HW's belief in the supremacy of the English constitution over king and subject alike, entailing mutual obligations of each

ought to imply only Attachment to the Laws, & then *Loyalty* wd be as much a Duty from the King to the People as from the People to the King.

A person commending the famous Nancy Parsons (since Lady Maynard)[3] said, She was very tender. A gentleman replied, it was no wonder She was *tender,* when She had been so long *kept.*

There may be an essential difference between the genitive 's & his; thus Attila was called Flagellum Dei, which shoud be rendered, not *God's Scourge,* but, God his Scourge; the Latter implies, a Scourge employed by God; but God's Scourge sounds as if he scourged God, as pilate did.[4]

A Lady saying, She really believed Mr Hastings innocent, Mrs Cholmondeley[5] sd, "then you have not redde his own defence."

---

toward the other within a framework of law. He thus speaks out against those reactionaries in England who would return to the medieval concept of kingship as the fount and embodiment of all authority, a concept which reached its culmination in modern times at the Courts of Louis XIV and XV; or against those who would place reverence for the person and family of the king over reverence for the law which he ideally represents.

3. Anne ("Nancy") Parsons (ca. 1735–ca. 1814), married (1776) Charles Maynard (1752–1824), 2d Viscount Maynard, 1775. Wedded early to one Horton, a West India merchant (not further identified), she became successively the mistress of the Duke of Grafton, 1763–69, and of the Duke of Dorset, 1770–73 (*YWE,* XXXII, 293, n. 2; *GEC,* VIII, 603, n. *d*).

4. HW's observation is of course highly subjective, and has no historical basis: the *his*-genitive arose in the thirteenth century from a mistaken notion that the *s* ending of the possessive case represented a contraction of the pronoun (see Albert C. Baugh, *A History of the English Language,* 2d edn., New York, 1957, pp. 290–91).

5. Mary Woffington (ca. 1729–1811), m. (1746) the Rev. Robert Cholmondeley (1727–1804), HW's nephew. HW owned *The Minutes of What Was Offered by Warren Hastings . . . at the Bar of the House of Commons* (London, 1786), also published as *The Defence of Warren Hastings* [etc.] (see above, p. 51, n. 1); this work is usually coupled with *The Answer of Warren Hastings . . . Delivered at the Bar of the House of Peers . . . November 28th, 1787* (London, 1788). "Redde" is so in the MS; *OED* notes that from the seventeenth century individual writers occasionally indicated the different pronunciation of *read* in the past tense and past participle by

Epigram 1789. (author unknown)[6]

See the Vengeance of Heaven! America cries,
George loses his reason, North loses his Eyes!
But when They attack'd us, all Europe coud find,
That the Monarch was mad, & the Minister blind.

It is memorable that my matchless collection of Miniatures of the Digby Family,[7] & my singular golden enamelled heart with variety of [p. 58] devices, bespoken by Margaret Countess of Lenox on the death of the Earl of Lenox (ancestors by Ld Darnley of the Royal Family) were offerred for sale to Queen Charlotte, who is so fond of diamonds, & who hoards

spelling it *red* or *redd* (HW does so himself below, p. 105), but the *e* ending here suggests a momentary surfacing of HW's antiquarian bent, rather than a concern for phonetics. (*Redde* was a variant form of the preterite from the thirteenth through sixteenth centuries.)

6. It is possible that HW wrote this epigram himself, was proud enough of it to include it in the *Miscellany,* but wished to disavow actual authorship of it because of its extreme virulence. Frederick North (1732–92), styled Lord North, 2d Earl of Guilford, 1790, was of course George III's prime minister and spokesman during the War of the American Revolution. HW's writings are full of invectives against North for his harsh measures on the one hand and subservience on the other, though he was not unappreciative of his wit and amiable disposition. North went blind in 1787; for a bon mot by him on his condition, see below, p. 110.

7. The family of Sir Kenelm Digby (1603–65), author, naval commander, and diplomat. The miniatures, which HW purchased in 1771 and 1775, are described in "Des. of SH," *Works,* II, 421–23, 426; he paid 300 guineas for the first set, and lauded the "superb piece of Sir Kenelm, his wife, and two sons, by Peter Oliver, after Vandyck," as "the capital miniature of the world" (*YWE,* XXVIII, 180; see also nn. 11–16). The "golden enamelled heart" is described in *Works,* II, 477, as "a golden heart set with jewels, and ornamented with emblematic figures enamelled, and Scottish mottos." It was made by order of Lady Margaret Douglas (1515–78) mother of Henry Stuart (1545–67), styled Lord Darnley, husband of Mary Queen of Scots, in memory of her husband Matthew Stuart (1516–71), 13th Earl of Lennox, killed at Stirling while a prisoner of Queen Mary. Both George III and Queen Charlotte were satirized in numerous prints of the day for their supposed miserliness and avarice; see, e.g., M. D. George, *Catalogue of Political and Personal Satires . . . in the British Museum. Vol. VI. 1784–1792* (London, 1938), No. 7836. The golden heart at least did eventually find its way into the royal collections; it was bought for Queen Victoria at the Strawberry Hill Sale in 1842 and is now in the collection of jewels at Windsor Castle (*YWE,* XV, 233, n. 1).

and locks up so carefully all rarities that are given to her—&
She refused to buy them.—She loves presents—not purchases.

Zuccarelli[8] d. at Florence in 1789.

Ld North being at the first representation of Mr St John's[9]
play of the Queen of Scots, in which the part of Queen
Elizabeth was wretchedly performed, said, "I fear Queen
Elizabeth will a second time be the death of the Queen of
Scots.

In the fourth act of the same play was a tedious dull account of the Massacre of Paris; a person in the Pitt called out
in the words that begin Pope's Essay on Man,

"Awake, my St John!"

Priscilla Lady Willoughby,[1] D[r] of Dss dow. of Ancastor,
wrote several pretty Stanzas to Lord Mansfield on his birthday. 1788. She has written other poems.

Of a Dramatic Poet who is incessantly writing indifferent
plays, may justly be said—

8. Francesco Zuccarelli (1702–88), landscape painter. He died at Florence
30 Dec. 1788 (Thieme and Becker, XXXVI, 570); HW probably read an un-
dated report of his death, such as the one in *GM* 1789, Pt. i, 276: "1789.
Lately, at Florence, Zuccarelli, the celebrated painter, whose works are well
known and much esteemed in England." This item has been printed in
Anecdotes of Painting, V, 123.

9. Hon. John St. John (?1746–93), M. P. and author. His *Mary Queen of
Scots,* a tragedy in five acts, was produced at Drury Lane on 21 March 1789
and acted nine times; the role of Queen Elizabeth was played by Mrs. Ward,
and that of Mary by the celebrated Mrs. Siddons. The "tedious dull account"
of the "Massacre of Paris" (the St. Bartholomew's Day Massacre of 1572) is in
Act IV, scene iv; the St. John of the quotation from Pope, viz., Henry St. John
(1678–1751), 1st Viscount Bolingbroke, was John St. John's uncle. See Namier
and Brooke, III, 400; *The London Stage 1660–1800 . . . Part 5: 1776–1800,*
ed. C. B. Hogan (Carbondale, 1968), II, 1139, "Index," p. cxiv; Hazen, *Cat.
of HW's Lib.,* No. 1810:47:6.

1. Priscilla Barbara Elizabeth Bertie (1761–1828), m. (1779) Peter Burrell,
cr. (1796) Baron Gwydir, *suo jure* Baroness Willoughby of Eresby, 1780;
daughter of Mary Panton (d. 1793), m. (1750) Peregrine Bertie (1714–78), 3d
Duke of Ancaster, Mistress of the Robes to Queen Charlotte. No copies of her
poems have been found.

"Dicitur et plaustris vexisse Poemata, or that he brings cartloads of his productions.[2]

It was well said, that a Man's Will is the last time in which he has an Opportunity of playing the fool.[3] **v. C⟨hatter⟩tons

Miss Mary Berry said, it was a natural Death for a Theatre to be burnt—it is so filled with combustibles.[4]

[p. 59]   Ld Camelford[5] in june 1798 sent to Geo. Hardinge Esq. from Paris six letters, supposed, five of them to a young

2. More literally translated, "And he is said to have conveyed his poems in carts" (Horace, *Art of Poetry*, l. 276).

3. The saying has not been traced; compare "But thousands die, without or this or that, / Die, and endow a College, or a Cat" (Pope, *Epistle to Bathurst*, ll. 97–98). The pencil notation is perhaps a reference to Chatterton's will, a bitter and satirical document, first printed in *A Supplement to the Miscellanies of Thomas Chatterton* (London, 1784), pp. 60–71 (*YWE*, XVI, 179, n. 6; see also above, p. 23, n. 8); for a copy and discussion of the will, see E. H. W. Meyerstein, *A Life of Thomas Chatterton* (London, 1930), pp. 334–44.

4. The Opera House, or King's Theatre in the Haymarket, burned down the night of 18 June 1789 (*YWE*, XI, 14, n. 15). Miss Berry's bon mot probably alludes to the chronic rowdiness and excitability of the London audience, particularly the pit; the Licensing Act of 1737 had effectively smothered any "combustibles" (i.e., politically inflammatory passages) in the plays themselves, unless a topical significance could be read into passages in standard works of the repertoire, as was often done.

5. Thomas Pitt (1737–93), cr. (1784) Baron Camelford, was at Paris from about the end of May to the end of August 1789 (*YWE*, XI, 53, n. 7). On 5 July he wrote to George Hardinge (1743–1816), HW's friend and correspondent, that he was sending him "a little pamphlet . . . that will give you some idea of the style of our society." This was *Lettres de la comtesse de ——— au chevalier de ———* (Paris, 1789) by Jean Devaines (d. 1803), but falsely attributed for a time to Camelford (see John Nichols, *Illustrations of the Literary History of the Eighteenth Century*, London, 1817–58, VI, 115; *YWE*, XI, 53 and nn. 8, 11; *Dictionnaire de biographie française*, Paris, 1933–, XI, 168–69). The pamphlet was described to HW by Richard Owen Cambridge (see below, p. 105), who had borrowed it from Hardinge. According to a review in Friedrich Melchior, Freiherr von Grimm et al., *Correspondance littéraire, philosophique et critique*, ed. M. Tourneux (Paris, 1877–82), XV, 479, "Ces Lettres [there are actually nine all told] . . . peignent avec autant de malice que de légèreté la nouvelle espèce de ridicules que l'effervescence actuelle des esprits vient de mettre à la mode." With regard to

Patriot Officer, & the 6th. from her Father to her on the unfitness of a young officer to judge of political Commotions. This was occasioned by the great Revolution in France.

A way to force[6] a whole company to make an Epigram, whether they will or not, & all to make the same.

Tell them, that there is a Lady who quarrels with every body alive, & cries for every body that dies: & then repeat this line as addressed to her,

The more you scold, the less you'll kiss—

all the Company will instantly repeat to themselves,

The more you cry, the less you'll p——.

Mr Barrett's[7] Hist. of Bristol published in quarto 1789. He gives a particular detail of the ravage committed in the

the current upheaval in France, Camelford wrote to Hardinge: "In England we go on slowly; but here I have seen, in less than a week, the transition made from the situation of the beginning of our Long Parliament to its Rump. Before the Assemblée des Etats, we were living in an absolute monarchy, under every abuse of monarchial power; we are now under a democracy, the most complete that exists, without a king, without a nobility or clergy, without an army, a government, or police" (Nichols, loc. cit.). The storming of the Bastille took place of course on 14 July. For HW's reaction to the Revolution, see below, pp. 115, n. 1, 123, 127, et passim.

6. HW appears to have first written "make," then "force" over "make," and finally "force" above the line. In the first line of the epigram he initially wrote "cry" for "scold," then scored it over and wrote "scold" above.

7. William Barrett (1733–89), surgeon and antiquary; author of *The History and Antiquities of the City of Bristol* (Bristol, 1789), 4to (HW's copy listed Hazen, *Cat. of HW's Lib.*, No. 539). Barrett is remembered today chiefly as the dupe of Chatterton, whose pretended poems and documents by Thomas Rowley he accepted as authentic and used in his *History*; Chatterton claimed to have found them preserved in a chest of manuscripts deposited in St. Mary Redcliffe Church by William Canynges (?1399–1474), a prominent Bristol merchant. (HW mentions Canynges's "chests" out of a mistaken notion that there were several; see *YWE*, II, 289, and Meyerstein, *Life of Chatterton*, p. 112.) On p. 589 Barrett mentions "the great ravage then committed [during the Commonwealth], and loss of deeds embezzled during that anarchy. . . . Not only the church estates but the structure itself did not escape the ravage," etc. On p. 576, n., he says that "many very valuable [parchments in Canynges's chest] there is reason to believe were taken away before, and since dispersed into private hands." Thomas Broughton (1704–74), divine, biographer, and miscellaneous writer, vicar of St. Mary Redcliffe, 1744–72, wrote the libretto for Handel's musical drama *Hercules* (1745); this is presumably the "tragedy"

Civil War in St Mary Redcliffe Church, & yet wd have you believe that Rowley's poems &c were preserved there in Canning's Chest[s]. v. page 589—nay, tho he owns he believes many were purloined by private hands, v. p. 576. note. It is to be observed that T. Broughton, an Author & Writer of a Tragedy, was Vicar of St Mary Redcliffe from 1744 to 1772, [yet] never seems to have seen or heard of Rowley's poems, tho Chatterton produced so many before 1770.

[p. 60]   Gratitude is like the Watergall,[8] which seldom attends the Rainbow, & when it does, is much fainter than what occasioned it.

In the year 1072 there was a Town in Sicily called Schera, which was taken by the Sarazins. It was afterwards called *Corleone*, I conclude, in honour of our Richard *Coeur de Lion*, who was for some time in Sicily in the year 1190.[9]   v. Esprit des journaux for the month of july 1789. p. 193.

HW refers to. HW makes the same point about Broughton with regard to Rowley in his letter to Edmond Malone, 4 Feb. 1782 (Toynbee, XII, 154). In a letter to Michael Lort, 27 July 1789, he angrily refuted Barrett's assertion (pp. 639–45) that Chatterton had sent him two letters with an account of the rise of painting in England. HW's memory was at fault, however, for Chatterton had indeed sent him these letters (printed *YWE*, XVI, 101–105 107–12), and his denial brought him into further disrepute with those who claimed that his rebuff of Chatterton helped bring about the poet's suicide (ibid., XVI, 219–20, and nn. 3, 5–7). See above, p. 23, n. 8.

8. "A secondary or imperfectly formed rainbow" (*OED*). HW uses a similar figure in his letter to Sir Horace Mann 29 June 1744 OS: "False good news are always produced by true good, like the water gall by the rainbow" (*YWE*, XVIII, 466).

9. HW's conjecture is reasonable but wrong. Though Richard I Lion Heart did visit Sicily in 1190–91, Corleone was already known as "Castrum Qurliyun" in the ninth century; the Italian Corleone was evidently derived from the Arabic *Qurliyun* by assonance (see James A. Brundage, *Richard Lion Heart*, New York, 1974, pp. 78–99; Francis M. Guercio, *Sicily*, London, 1938, p. 111 and n. 1; George Dennis, *A Handbook for Travellers in Sicily*, London, 1864, p. 242). The notion that Corleone was originally called Schera presumably stems from an old conjecture of certain geographers that it stood near the site of the ancient city of that name mentioned in Homer (see Arcangiolo Leanti, *Lo stato presente della Sicilia*, Palermo, 1761, I, 92). HW takes the date 1072 from the title of the work being reviewed in the *Esprit*

In De Sade's[1] life of Petrarch Vol. 3. p. 603. it is said that
in the year 1361 a Carthusian monk threatened Boccace that
he shoud die soon, if he did not amend his life; and to con-
firm the prediction, told Bocacce something that the Latter
thought nobody cd know but himself.

This Story is exactly like that of Ld Clarendon of Sir George
Villiers, & shows that the trick was 300 years old when practiced on the Duke of Buckingham. It was revived in France
in the reign of Louis XV, a low Artisan going to him with a
similar Secret.

An author of no celebrity wrote an Epitaph on his wife
and had it inscribed on her Monument in *red* letters. Mr

---

des journaux, loc. cit., viz., *Codex Diplomaticus Siciliæ sub Saracenorum Im-*
perio, ab Anno 827, ad 1072 (Panormi, 1788). Summarizing this work (a spurious production professing to be a translation from the Arabic), the reviewer
notes the alleged taking of "Schera (actuellement Corleone)" by a Saracen
named Muhammed in the year 214 (Islamic calendar).

1. Jacques-François-Paul-Aldonce de Sade (1705–78), abbé, and uncle of the
notorious Marquis de Sade; author of *Mémoires pour la vie de François*
Pétrarque (Amsterdam, 1764–67), 3 vols., 4to (HW's copy listed Hazen, *Cat.,*
No. 932; for De Sade, see *NBG*). According to De Sade, III, 601–03, in the
year 1362 (not 1361) Boccaccio wrote to Petrarch of his being approached by
"un Chartreux de Sienne qu'il ne connoissoit pas," named Joachim Ciani;
Ciani conveyed to him the deathbed warning of "le bienheureux Petroni
homme célèbre par la sainteté de sa vie & par ses miracles," that if he did
not "renoncer à la poésie & à ces lectures profanes," he could be certain
that he would die "bientôt." To convince Boccaccio of the truth of what he
said, "le pere Ciani lui releva un secret qu'il croyoit n'être su que de lui
seul." The story of Sir George Villiers (d. 1606), father of George Villiers
(1592–1628), cr. (1623) Duke of Buckingham, is in Clarendon's *History of the*
Rebellion and Civil Wars in England. According to the tale, about six months
before the assassination of Buckingham the ghost of Sir George appeared to
a man who had known him in his youth, and told him to go "to his son
. . . and tell him, if he did not somewhat to ingratiate himself to the people,
or, at least, to abate the extreme malice they had against him, he would be
suffer'd to live but a short time." In delivering the warning, the messenger
mentioned "those particulars, which were to gain him credit. . . . the Duke's
colour changed, and he swore he could come to that knowledge only by the
Devil" (Oxford edition, 1707–17, I, 33–36; HW's copy listed Hazen, *Cat.,*
No. 41). The anecdote of Louis XV has not been traced. HW's two spellings
of Boccaccio's name are so in the MS; the first is the usual French spelling.

Cambridge[2] said, "he was determined to have at least one of his works *redd*.

from Mr Dan. Lysons[3]

Why is a man who buys four apples for a penny and gives one away, like a Telescope?—because he makes a far-thing present.

[p. 61]   from D°.

If a pair of spectacles could speak, the name of what Ecclesiastic Writer wd they be Entitled to pronounce? answr. Eusebius—i.e. You see by Us.

In Collect. universelle of the Memoires part. relatives à l'hist. de France, in Vol. 52ᵈ. in the memoires of the Chancellor de Chiverny[4] is a Character of that Monster Philip 2d of

---

2. Richard Owen Cambridge (1717–1802), poet and wit; HW's neighbor at Twickenham.

3. Daniel Lysons (1762–1834), divine and topographer (see below, p. 154); HW made him his chaplain in 1792 (*YWE*, XV, 200, n. 1, et passim). Eusebius (ca. 260–ca. 340), bishop of Caesarea, is known as the "Father of Church History" (*Oxford Dictionary of Church History*, 2d ed., ed. F. L. Cross and E. A. Livingstone, London, 1974, s.v. Eusebius). In the first conundrum HW seems to have written and crossed out "apples from" or "apples for" before "four apples"; a farthing is of course a quarter of a penny.

4. Philippe Hurault (1528–99), Comte de Cheverny, chancellor of France; his *Mémoires* were first published in 1636 (*NBG*). "Philippes II . . . fut de forte petite stature, & neantmoins de rencontre agreable . . . & eut une complexion si bonne & si saine pendant tout le cours de sa vie, qu'il n'eut jamais de maladie que celle de sa mort, excepté qu'il estoit quelquefois sujet à des évanoüissemens . . . Il estoit grandement devotieux & Chatholique [sic], & ennemy juré & declaré de toutes héresies . . . avec cela il estoit ferme & d'un courage relevé, qui recoignoissoit incontinent & prévoyoit la fin des choses, par une sagesse & prudence admirable, [etc., etc.] . . . " ("Suite des mémoires de messire Philippe Hurault, comte de Cheverny, chancelier de France," in *Collection universelle*, LII, 26–27 [full citation above, p. 52, n. 4]; "relatives" is so in the MS). On this panegyric the editor comments: "Le lecteur jugera, en lisant ce précis de la vie de Philippe II, s'il mérite les louanges que Cheverny lui prodigue" (*Collection*, LII, 26). Philip was at war with France, 1557–59, abetted the Holy League in the wars of religion in that country (see above, p. 77, n. 3), and sent Farnese to oppose the success of the Protestant forces in France in 1590 and 1592. The "horror" perpetrated by Philip

Spain, so false, so flattering & partial p. 26. that it shows how deeply the Spirit of the Ligue had sunk, even in a Man that ought to have been more enlightened. What an abomination is a panegyric on that Odious Man from One who knew all the horrors Philip had occasioned in France, & who saw on the Throne such an excellent Prince as Henry 4th.!

But if that wretched Chancellor flattered Philip grosly, he has been more fair on his own Character, for he betrays his own dirty and mean interestedness. Having married one of his Sons to a near relation of the favorite Mistress the Dss of Beaufort, & learning the sudden death of the Dss he talks of his malheur particulier de s'etre trop promptement & trop attachè à ses alliances, par la persuasion d'autrui. p. 80.

He says that Philip 2^d. made every body speak to him kneeling, & pretended it was because he was so short, that they wd be above him.

He ⟨asserts⟩ that Henri 4. *entretenoit* sous main tous ses voisins en brouillerie & guerre. p. 84.

The Bishops of Liege used to be called *Votre Grace.* p. 276.

---

to which HW most often reverts is his ruthless suppression of the revolt in the Netherlands, where about 18,000 patriots were put to death between 1567 and 1573 (see, e.g., *YWE*, XXXII, 339–40 and n. 11). The Comte de Cheverny's son, Louis, Comte de Limours (d. 1639) married Isabelle d'Escoubleau de Sourdis, daughter of Isabeau Babou de la Bourdaisière, Marquise de Sourdis, with whom Cheverny had an affair in his old age; the Marguise was aunt of Gabrielle d'Estrées (d. 1599), Duchesse de Beaufort, mistress of Henry IV (*Dictionnaire de biographie française*, Paris, 1933–, XIII, 151–53; F.-A. Aubert de la Chenaye-Desbois and ——— Badier, *Dictionnaire de la noblesse*, 3d edn., Paris, 1863–76, VII, 345–46, X, 895). Of Philip's forcing everyone to speak to him kneeling, Cheverny writes: "Personne vivante ne parloit à luy qu'à genoux, & disoit pour son excuse à cela, qu'estant petit de corps, chacun eust paru plus eslevé que luy, outre qu'il sçavoit que les Espagnols estoient d'humeur si altiere & hautaine, qu'il estoit besoin qu'il les traittast de cette façon" (*Collection*, LII, 28–29). HW admired Henry IV for sheathing his sword "the moment he had conquered in a just cause" (*YWE*, XXXI, 438); there seems to be no support for Cheverny's allegation that, although at peace himself, the King encouraged dissension and war among his neighbors. The items on the bishops of Liège occurs in "Mémoires de Marguerite de Valois, reine de France et de Navarre," *Collection*, LII, 276: "Sa Grace (ainsi appelle-t-on l'evesque de Liege, comme un appelle un roy sa Majesté, & un prince son Altesse)."

There is a curious Account of Plays & Mysteries so late as in 1552 in Brand's⁵ hist. of Newcastle, quᵒ. 1789. Vol. 2. p:371.

5. John Brand (1774–1806), antiquary and topographer; author of *The History and Antiquities of . . . Newcastle upon Tyne* (London, 1789), 2 vols., 4to (HW's copy listed Hazen, *Cat. of HW's Lib.*, No. 3160). Under "Particulars Concerning the Corpus Christi Plays, or Miracle Plays . . . of Newcastle upon Tyne," Brand notes that "A.D. 1552, mention occurs of the merchant-adventurers, as being concerned in the exhibition of five plays. . . 'Hogmagog' was the title of one." Further on he observes, "By the ordinary of the millers, dated 1578, we may infer that the Corpus Christi plays were at that time on the decline, and never acted but by a special command of the magistrates of Newcastle" (II, 369–72). Hugh de Neville (d. 1234) holder of various offices under King John, married (ca. 1200) Joan de Cornhill (d. ?1245). Brand writes of them: "Among the fines in the 6th year of the reign of King John [1205], I found a singular entry concerning the wife of Hugh de Nevill, who gave the King two hundred hens to lie one night with the said Hugh, at that time probably a state prisoner" (II, 390, n. g). *GEC*, IX, 480, n. g, calls this entry "still unexplained," although it is cited by Edmund Burke, *Thoughts on the Cause of the Present Discontents* (London, 1770), p. 6, as a curious instance of medieval tyranny. The execution of witches noted by Brand took place in 1650, not 1670: "One wizard and fourteen reputed witches belonging to Newcastle, in company with nine thieves and a witch of the county of Northumberland, were executed upon the Town-Moor, near Newcastle upon Tyne, August 21st" (II, 478). The names of the condemned, beginning with "Mathew Boumer" and ending with "Jane Martin . . . the myllers wif of Chattim" are given, ibid., n. *i*, from the register of the parochial chapelry of St. Andrew (see HW's observation on witchcraft, above, p. 71). Of the abortive attempt to erect a college (at Durham in 1657) Brand writes: "May 15th this year, a writ of privy seal for founding an university at Durham, was signed by Oliver Cromwell, lord protector. This university . . . was soon suppressed. It is a singular fact, that George Fox [1624–91], the founder of the Quakers . . . has assumed to himself the consequence, and what he thought the merit, of having been the means of suppressing this laudable institution" (II, 485). Fox's account of his reason for opposing the university is given, ibid., II, 486, n. Ambrose Barnes (1627–1710), nonconformist, was alderman of Newcastle, 1658, and mayor, 1660–61. Brand, II, 491, n., cites the following passage from a MS life of Barnes by "M. R.": "Mr. Barnes, on his return home (from London), presaged, from the saturnine aspect of the King, that as his Majesty resembled Tiberius Caesar, so should his reign, i.e., our Lord should be crucified in it!" HW, in a letter to Henry Zouch, 20 March 1762, notes Bishop Burnet's discussion (in his *History of His Own Time*, London, 1724–34, I, 613) of the supposed physical and spiritual resemblance of Charles II and Tiberius (which seems to have been a contemporary commonplace), but disputes the physical resemblance (*YWE*, XVI, 52). For "Burnet" HW seems to have written "Hernet" in the MS, but this has been emended as an obvious slip.

Wife of Hugh de Nevil gives K. John 200 hens to be one night with her Husband who was a prisoner. ib. 390.

Fifteen Witches burnt there in 1670 by the Presbyterians. 478.

G. Fox prevents erecting a College there, as it w^d teach Pagan learning. 486.

Barnes, a Dissenter, observed, before Burnet did, that Charles 2d was like Tiberius—which I do not think he was. 491.

[p. 62]   Epigram.[6]

> Patty was a modest Maid;
> Patty was of Men afraid:
> Patty grew her fears to lose,
> And grew so brave, She lost her nose.

In Dodsley's[7] London & Environs, vol. 6. p:51. it is sd that History (but he does not quote his Author) says, that in 1052, Earl Goodwin came up the Thames to Westminster, passing London bridge, with a *powerfull* fleet, to engage the royal navy, which lay there, consisting of fifty *ships of war*.

6. HW sent this epigram to Lady Ossory in his letter of 20 June 1785 (*YWE*, XXXIII, 465); the version there has "pretty" for "modest" in the first line. Losing one's nose was a common result of tertiary syphilis, and as such the object of much ribaldry. The epigram is included in HW's *Fugitive Verses*, ed. W. S. Lewis (New York, 1931), p. 180, where the text is taken from the letter.

7. Robert Dodsley (1703–64), poet, dramatist, and bookseller; publisher (and perhaps editor) of *London and Its Environs Described* (London, 1761), 6 vols., 8vo (HW's copy listed Hazen, *Cat.*, No. 697), he is best remembered for his *Collection of Poems by Several Hands* (see below, p. 126). Godwin or Godwine (d. 1053) was earl of the West Saxons. In the passage which HW cites, it is further noted that "matters being accommodated between the King [Edward the Confessor] and Earl Godwin, the latter returned, and repassed the bridge." The sources for this episode are the Abingdon, Worcester, and Peterborough Chronicles, and the Vita Eadwardi (see E. A. Freeman, *The History of the Norman Conquest of England*, Oxford, 1873–79, II, 213–24, 421–25). The ships of the eleventh century were of course tiny in comparison with those of the eighteenth. There is no record of the width of the arches of the wooden bridge Godwin had to pass, though a passage in the *Heimskringla* of Snorri Sturluson claims that the bridge was so broad that two wagons could pass each other on it (see Gordon Home, *Old London Bridge*, New York, 1931, p. 11).

It is plain, that these *powerfull* fleets could not have consisted of Ships larger than a coal-lighter. The bridge is said to have been only of wood:—how wide were the Arches?

Old persons complain of loss of Memory, yet never forget their own old Stories; tho they do forget how often they have told them.

Thoughts in the form of Maxims, addressed to young Ladies on their first Establishment in the World. By the Countess Dow. of Carlisle.[8] small duod[mo]. 1789.

Account of James Paine[9] Architect, in Obituary to Gentlem[s]. Magazine for December, 1789.   & Francis Hierons of Warwick Archit. died in Dec. 1789.

W[m]. Edward, Archit. who built the remarkable Bridge at Pont y Pridd in Wales died Aug. 7. 1789, aged near 72.   v. Gent. Mag. of that year   page 1074.

[p. 63]   1790.

In a very thin pamphlet printed privately at Paris in 1789,

---

8. Isabella Byron (1721–95), m. 1 (1743) Henry Howard (1694–1758), 4th Earl of Carlisle, 1738; m. 2 (1759) Sir William Musgrave (see above, p. 39). HW's copy of her book is listed Hazen, *Cat.*, No. 2301; the volume, published at London, is actually octavo, not duodecimo. Hazen comments: "In his 'Book of Materials [i.e., *Miscellany*]' ca. 1789 HW entered the volume carefully, perhaps in preparation for a revised edition of his *R&NA* [*Royal and Noble Authors*]."

9. James Paine or Payne (ca. 1716–Nov. 1789), architect, father-in-law of Tilly Kettle (see above, p. 43; *GM* 1789, LIX, Pt. ii. 1153; Thieme and Becker, XXVI, 148). Francis Hiorne (1741–9 Dec. 1789), architect, was one of the first practitioners of the neo-Gothic style in England, and designed the town hall, sessions house, and county jail at Warwick (ibid., XVII, 121); HW seems to have silently corrected the *GM* notice, which calls him "Francis Hiorn . . . son of the architect of those names" (LIX, Pt. ii, 1211), but his misspelling of the name and failure to mention him elsewhere suggest that Hiorne was unknown to him otherwise, and the "correction" inadvertent. William Edwards (1719–89), bridge builder, in 1755 completed a span over the river Taff at Pontypridd. It is described by a correspondent in the *GM*, loc. cit., as consisting "of one very wide and lofty arch, the chord of which is 140 feet, and the height of it 34 feet. This is allowed to be the largest arch in Europe." All three items are printed in *Anecdotes of Painting*, V, 187–88, 190. In the MS, in the item on Paine, "for" has been crossed out after "obituary."

& called *Le Tableau de Famille*,[1] was a parallel between Mirabeau, & *Marcel,* the vile Prevot des Marchands under Charles 5th. to which was this excellent motto.

Tu Marcellus eris.

When Lord North & Col. Barré,[2] who were of different Parties, were both gone blind, the Latter went to visit the Former. Ld North said to him, "Col. B. Every body will believe us both Sincere, if we said, we shoud always be glad to see each other."

Dr Busby[3] sitting between two very ill-tempered married Women, & a Gentleman inveighing against bad Wives, the Dr

1. *Le Tableau de famille. Fragment de l'histoire de France* (Paris, 1789), 8vo, 19 pp. (see Hazen, *Cat.,* No. 3054). The whole pamphlet is taken up with the parallel between Honoré-Gabriel Riquetti (1749–91), Comte de Mirabeau, revolutionary statesman, and Étienne Marcel (d. 1358), French popular leader, provost of the merchants of Paris (see *NBG*). It accuses each of having sacrificed the welfare of his nation to satisfy his own ambition, and ends with the warning to Mirabeau, *Tu Marcellus eris* ("You will be Marcellus," Virgil, *Aeneid,* VI, 883)—i.e., you will share the fate of Marcel (who was assassinated). Marcel was at first in league with the dauphin, afterwards Charles V, but went over to the cause of Charles II of Navarre. In Feb. 1358 he fomented a riot at Paris which forced the execution of two ministers of state. HW thought Mirabeau the only eminent man produced by the Revolution, but called him a "villain," and said of him: "How odious is a reformer who acts from ambition or interest!" (*YWE,* XXXIV, 109, 111, 159, 186). Despite the prophecy, Mirabeau died of natural causes. The wit of the quotation is enhanced by the fact that Virgil's Marcellus was a youth of great promise whose passing was lamented by all.

2. Col. Isaac Barré (1726–1802), army officer and politician. He lost an eye at Quebec in 1759 and went completely blind in 1782; Lord North went blind in 1787, apparently the year he made his remark to Barré (see above, p. 99, n. 6; Namier and Brooke, II, 50–54; *YWE,* XXXIII, 585, and n. 9). HW in a letter to Lord Hertford (12 Feb. 1765) called Barré "the dread of all the vociferous Norths and Rigbys" (ibid., XXXVIII, 508). Barré was an outspoken critic of North during the American war, and, though professing to esteem him "as a private gentleman," claimed that "as a minister he had a right to use and treat him with as severe epithets as parliamentary form would allow" (Namier and Brooke, II, 53).

3. Richard Busby (1606–95), D.D., the famous headmaster of Westminster School. This anecdote is recorded in G. F. Russell Barker, *Memoir of Richard Busby, D.D.* (London, 1895), p. 51, where the two women are identified as the wives of Robert South (1634–1716), D.D., and William Sherlock (?1641–1707), D.D., dean of St. Paul's.

said, "indeed you are too hard upon the Sex: I believe there
are in general many excellent Wives; there may be a bad one
here (turning to his right) & there may be a bad one there (to
his left) but they are not all so."

The Duke of Dorset[4] aged near 45 married Miss Cope of
22. The King asked the Chancellor Thurlow if he did not
think it "a very disproportioned Match! He replied, "S^r,
That is their business, in a year perhaps it will be mine!"
meaning that the Lady might take a young Lover, & the
Divorce come before him.

Old Charles Seymour the proud Duke of Somerset sitting
by the bed of Sarah Dss of Marlborough[5] when She had the

4. John Frederick Sackville (1745–99), 3d Duke of Dorset, 1769, married
(4 Jan. 1790) Arabella Diana Cope (1767–1825), daughter of Sir Charles Cope,
2d Bt.; Edward Thurlow (1731–1806), cr. (1778) Baron Thurlow, was lord
chancellor (with one small break) 1778–92. Before his marriage the Duke
kept a succession of mistresses, among them Nancy Parsons (see above, p. 98
and n. 3). There was no divorce, and his wife, who survived him, later married (1801) Charles, Earl Whitworth (see *GEC*, XII, Pt. ii, 620, and n. *d*).
5. Sarah Jennings (1660–1744), m. (1678) John Churchill, cr. (1702), Duke of
Marlborough, the victor at Blenheim; for Somerset (who unsuccessfully proposed marriage to the Duchess after the death of his first wife) see above,
p. 45, n. 1. The Duchess was an ill-tempered woman who after the death
of her husband spent the remainder of her life in a series of quarrels with
Sir Robert Walpole, among others; Somerset was characterized by Macaulay
as a man "in whom the pride of birth and rank amounted almost to a dis-
ease" (see *GEC*, XII, Pt. i, 77, n. *b*). Somerset's first wife, Elizabeth Percy,
was daughter of Joceline, 15th Earl of Northumberland, who left her the
vast Percy estates (see above, loc. cit.). His second wife, Charlotte Finch
(ibid.), was the third daughter of Daniel Finch, 2d Earl of Nottingham and
7th Earl of Winchilsea (above, p. 88, n. 7). A different version of the anecdote of Somerset's reproach of his second wife, according to which she tapped
him on the shoulder with her fan rather than kissed him, is recorded in
DNB, s.v. Charles Seymour, 6th Duke of Somerset. Anthony Henley (?1704–
48), politician and wit (Sedgwick, II, 126), elder brother of Robert Henley
(ca. 1708–72), cr. (1764) Earl of Northington, lord chancellor, 1761–66, is elsewhere called by HW "as remarkable for his impudence, wit, & cowardice, as
the Duke of Somerset was for pride" (HW's "Commonplace Book of Verses,"
p. 22). The anecdote of his directing a letter to Somerset "over against the
trunkshop" is also recorded, ibid., and was included by HW in his letter to
Lady Ossory 9 Oct. 1776 (*YWE*, XXXII, 322). "Lord Cholmondeley" of the
second Henley anecdote was George Cholmondeley (1703–70), 3d Earl of
Cholmondeley, 1733, who married HW's sister Mary Walpole (ca. 1705–32).
The anecdote of Henry Herbert (ca. 1689–1750), 9th Earl of Pembroke, 1733,

gout, She called for a bottle of Sack, & ordering two glasses to be filled, said, "come, my Lord, I will give you a toast that nobody will drink but ourselves; here is your health and mine."

[p. 64]   That haughty Duke's first Wife was the great Heiress of the Lords of Northumberland; the second, daughter of Lord Nottingham. The Latter one day gave him a kiss voluntarily. He said, "Madam, That is a liberty which was never taken by your Predecessor, tho She was a Percy."

The impudent Anthony Henley (elder Brother of Lord Chancellor Northington) who [had] a great deal of Wit to mortify Somerset, directed a letter to him at Northumberland house *over against the Trunkshop Charing cross.*

That Henley was a great coward; having affronted Lord Cholmondeley at Tunbridge, was beaten by him. Next day Lord Cholm. found Henley beating another Man, & congratulated him on his recovery of Spirit. "Oh my Lord, said Henley, yr Lordship & I know whom we beat."

Henry Earl of Pembroke, who lived in Privy garden by the River, was often swimming; Ld Chesterfield directed a letter to him, *In the Thames over against Whitehall.*

The Memoires of the Duc de Choiseul,[6] published in 1790, were certainly written by him. Monsr Barthelemy, chargè

and the famous Lord Chesterfield is also recorded by HW in his "Commonplace Book," loc. cit., where he notes that Pembroke, besides swimming, was also famous "for architecture . . . for boxing, for playing at tennis, & blaspheming at it"; it was included by him in his letter to Hannah More 29 Aug. 1796 (*YWE*, XXXI, 402). A correspondent to the Yale Walpole Edition suggests that Chesterfield's address might have alluded to Pembroke's promotion of the building of Westminster Bridge (1739–50) rather than to his swimming (ibid., n. 3). HW mistakenly numbered pages 64 and 65 of the MS "62" and "63," and all the subsequent page numbers are consequently off by two; the error has been emended in the transcription. After "was the great heiress" HW first wrote and crossed out "of the heiress."

6. Étienne-François de Choiseul-Stainville (1719–85), Duc de Choiseul, 1758, French statesman, m. (1750) Louise-Honorine Crozat du Châtel (1735–1801); HW knew them at Paris, where they were part of Madame du Deffand's circle. While there HW also met their friend Jean-Jacques Barthélemy (1716–95), abbé, antiquary and numismatist, author of the *Voyage du jeune Ana-*

d'affaires de France, & nephew of the Abbè Barthelemy the author of Anarcharsis, & the great Friend of the [p. 65] Duchess de Choiseul, gave me this account of them jan. 9th. The Dsse & the Abbè being at Chanteloup, often pressed the Duke after his fall, to write his Memoires. At last he did write those printed, & had three copies made. The unfaithfull Amanuensis took a fourth for himself. Being reduced to great poverty by the Revolution in 1789, he sold his copy to a bookseller, to the great vexation of the Duchess & the Abbè.

Epitaph on a great Lyar
while alive.

Were Lingo dead,
Coud more be said,
Than what, while living, each one cries,
Here Lingo lyes!

Moliere's Marriage forcè was founded on the Story of the Comte de Grammont & Mlle Hamilton.[7]

---

charsis (see above, p. 94, n. 3); Barthélemy's nephew, François Barthélemy (1747–1830), cr. (1800) Comte and (1815) Marquis de Barthélemy, was secretary to the French embassy in London 1785–87 and minister plenipotentiary 1787–88, remaining at the embassy as assistant to the new ambassador La Luzerne after the latter's arrival in Jan. 1788 (*YWE*, XXXIX, 450, n. 12 and sources there cited). Choiseul, following his disgrace by Louis XV in 1770, retired to his estate at Chanteloup where in 1778 he had some copies of assorted memoirs printed at his private press. Several years after his death his secretary Jean-Louis Giraud Soulavie (1752–1813) apparently gave a copy of these memoirs and of several other works by Choiseul to the bookseller Buisson, who published them as *Mémoires de m. le duc de Choiseul . . . écrits par lui-même, et imprimé sous ses yeux, dans son cabinet, à Chanteloup, en 1778* (Paris, 1790), 2 vols., 8vo (HW's copy is listed Hazen, *Cat. of HW's Lib.*, No. 3299). According to Claude-Antoine-Gabriel de Choiseul (for whom see *Dictionnaire de biographie française*, Paris, 1933–, VIII, 1218–19) the Duchess disavowed the edition of 1790, but only because of some "plaisanteries de société qui y étaient jointes et qui n'auraient jamais dû y paraître." See Fernand Calmettes, ed., *Mémoires du duc de Choiseul* (Paris, 1904), pp. ii–v and nn.; *NBG*, s.v. Soulavie.

7. Philibert, Comte de Gramont (1621–1707), m. (1663) Elizabeth Hamilton (1641–1708), a great beauty at the Court of Charles II; her brother, Anthony Hamilton, later wrote the *Mémoires du comte de Grammont*, of which HW brought out an edition at Strawberry Hill in 1772 (see above, p. 36, n. 1).

Winstanley[8] in May 1714 advertised Mathem. Waterworks
& other curiosities, to be seen in Piccadilly near Hyde park.
p. 239.
    v. new Edition of Lover & Reader of Steele, by J. Nichols.
1789.
Lucy Countess of Carlisle made close Prisoner again,[9] on
the taking Penruddock & Bamfield.

According to the anecdote (not recorded in the *Mémoires*) Gramont, who had
courted Mlle Hamilton while in England, was returning to France when he
was overtaken by her brothers Anthony and George, who asked him if he
had not forgotten something at London. He replied, "Pardonnez-moi, mes-
sieurs, j'ai oublié d'épouser votre sœur," and returned and did so (*DNB*, s.v.
Elizabeth Hamilton). Antoine Bret (1717–92), in his edition of Molière's
Œuvres (Paris, 1773), III, 138, wrote that this anecdote "est citée par-tout
comme ayant fourni à Moliere le dénouement du *Mariage forcé* [first performed in 1664], mais c'est voir une ressemblance de trop loin." Despite the
disclaimer of Bret and of other editors before and since, the notion has so
persisted that as late as 1962 Robert Jouanny felt obliged to deny it again
in his edition of *Œuvres complètes* (Paris, 1962), I, 544.
    8. Henry Winstanley (1644–1703), engineer and engraver. In Sir Richard
Steele's periodical *The Lover* Nos. 33 and 40 (for 11 and 27 May 1714) is advertised "That Mathematical Water-Theatre, of the late Ingenious Mr. Winstanley . . . Shown for the Benefit of his Widow . . . At the lower End of
Pickadilly towards Hide-Park." HW refers to the "mechanic tricks" of Winstanley in his *Catalogue of Engravers, Works*, IV, 96; for John Nichols's new
edition of Steele's *Lover and Reader* (London, 1789), 8vo, see Hazen, *Cat.*,
No. 1861, and BM Cat.
    9. For Lady Carlisle's imprisonment in the Tower, 1649–50, see above,
p. 34, n. 6. John Penruddock (1619–55) and Joseph Bampfield (fl. 1639–85)
fought on the side of Charles I during the civil war and, after his death,
intrigued on behalf of his son; Penruddock in 1655 led an abortive insurrec-
tion against Cromwell which cost him his life, while Bampfield in 1654 was
dismissed from the service of the Royalists as a suspected double agent. In a
letter from The Hague, 7 Jan. 1650, Elizabeth, Queen of Bohemia, sister of
Charles I (see above, p. 39, n. 7) wrote to James Graham (1612–50), cr. (1644)
Marquess of Montrose, that "Colonel Banfields and Penrudoch are both pris-
oners in the Tower. Upon their taking, my Lady Carlisle is close prisoner
again." The letter is printed in George Monck Berkeley (1763–93), *Literary
Relics: Containing Original Letters from King Charles II. King James II.
The Queen of Bohemia* [etc.] (London, 1789), pp. 21–22 (HW's copy listed
Hazen, *Cat.*, No. 2799). Montrose later in 1650 lost his life in an abortive
invasion of Scotland. *DNB* does not mention Bampfield's or Penruddock's
imprisonment in the Tower, but says that Bampfield was arrested and se-
cured in the Gatehouse at Westminster, afterwards escaping to Holland.

v. letter from Q. of Bohemia to the Marq. of Montrose, in litterary Relics, published by G. Monck Berkeley. Lond. 1789. p. 22.

The Poetry, Paintings, Models, Singing & Playing of several young Women, tho cried up, may properly be called, *Missdoings.*

[p. 66]   Letter from *Earl Stanhope* to the R. H. Edm. Burke containing a short answer to his late Speech on the French Revolution. feb. 1790.[1]

Francis Aliamet[2] *Engraver*, d. in Feb. 1790. v. Gent. Magaz.

1. HW's copy of this *Letter*, dated 24 Feb. 1790, is now *WSL* (Hazen, *Cat.*, No. 1609:53:8). In it Stanhope attacks Burke's speech against the French Revolution (delivered 9 Feb. in the House of Commons), asserting in the final paragraph that "the Revolution in France is one of the most striking and memorable pages in history; and no political event was, perhaps, ever more pregnant with good consequences to future ages" (p. 34). HW, horrified by both the underlying philosophy of the Revolution and by the excesses perpetrated in its name, called Stanhope's *Letter* "the ravings of a lunatic" (*YWE*, XXXIV, 98). When Burke's *Reflections on the Revolution in France* came out in November, he wrote to Mary Berry (8 Nov. 1790): "I have read it twice, and though of 350 pages, I wish I could repeat every page by heart. It is sublime, profound and gay. The wit and satire are equally brilliant, and the whole is wise" (ibid., XI, 132). As a member of the ruling class and believer in the balanced constitution of the English people, HW regarded with loathing the concept of republicanism as it had taken shape in France, equating it with anarchy, a mere "fluctuation of factions" (see below, p. 126). His horror at the events in France intensified with the step-up in executions and reprisals; his letters become filled with epithets against the "butchers" and "hyenas" who have either killed or forced into exile many of his highborn friends and acquaintances. For an extended treatment of HW's reaction to the Revolution, see Robert A. Smith, "Walpole's Reflections on the Revolution in France," in *Horace Walpole: Writer, Politician, and Connoisseur,* ed. W. H. Smith (New Haven, 1967), pp. 91–114.

2. François-Germain Aliamet (1734–90), engraver, died 5 Feb. 1790; "his death was occasioned by a stone falling on his head in Greek-str." (*GM* 1790, LX, Pt. i, 184; see also Thieme and Becker, I, 287). John Brown (1752–87), painter and draftsman, was also author of the posthumous *Letters upon the Poetry and Music of the Italian Opera* (Edinburgh, 1789); "Some Account of the Late Mr. John Brown, Painter," is in the *European Magazine*, Feb. 1790, XVII, 91–92 (see also Thieme and Becker, V, 83). These items and the item on Meyer (for whom see above, p. 92, n. 8) have been printed in *Anecdotes of Painting*, V, 127, 133, 205.

Account of J. Brown *painter,* in Europ. Mag. for febr. 1790
Verses by Carr *Lord* Hervey.[3] ib.
Meyers drawings and prints sold by auct. March 29, 1790.

Mr Turner[4] was sent to the Grand Lama by Hastings &
found a *Child* of 18 Months old, with his *Father* & *Mother*
Standing by him 2 years after he was complimented on his
Resurrection. v. Gentl. mag. for feb. 1790.

Mrs Delany[5] about 3 yrs before her Death showed me a
letter to her fr[om] Q. Charlotte, signed, yr Friend & *Queen!*

3. Carr Hervey (1691–1723), styled Lord Hervey, son of John, 1st Earl of
Bristol and half brother of John, Lord Hervey, author of the *Memoirs* (see
above, p. 54, n. 6). Carr was once the lover of HW's mother, Catherine Lady
Walpole, but the casual insertion of his name here is further evidence against
the allegation that he, and not Sir Robert, was HW's real father. This
claim, first written down in the nineteenth century by Lady Louisa Stuart
and still given currency by historians such as J. H. Plumb, is discussed
and refuted by R. W. Ketton-Cremer, *Horace Walpole,* 3d ed. (London, 1964),
pp. 10–12, and W. S. Lewis, *Horace Walpole* (New York, 1961), pp. 12–15.
The verses HW cites are in the *European Magazine,* Feb. 1790, XVII, 152.
Entitled "To the Memory of Lady E. Mansell, Niece to the Mother of Sir
Hervey Elwes," they are further described as "Written by the first [sic] Lord
Hervey, Brother of Lady Mansell." Since Lady Elizabeth Hervey (1697–1727),
m. (1724) Bussy Mansell, later 4th Baron Mansell, died four years after her
half brother Carr, the Lord Hervey referred to must be her brother John,
author of the *Memoirs.* The verses consist mainly of a 15-line inscription
for Lady Elizabeth's tombstone; conventional and pedestrian, they voice the
obligatory praises of her virtue and expressions of grief at her untimely
passing.

4. Samuel Turner (?1749–1802), lieutenant and later captain in the East
India service, was a kinsman of Warren Hastings who in 1783 was sent by
him on a mission to Tibet to congratulate the infant Teshu Lama on his
reincarnation; the old Teshu Lama, dPal-ldan ye-shes, had died in China on
3 Nov. 1780, and was succeeded by bsTan-pai nyi-ma (1781–1852) (see Günther
Schulemann, *Geschichte der Dalai-Lamas,* Leipzig, 1958, pp. 337, 477, et passim; M. W. Fisher and L. E. Rose, *England, India, Nepal, Tibet, China . . .
A Synchronistic Table,* Berkeley, 1959, pp. 1–8). Turner describes his meeting
with the Teshu Lama 4 Dec. 1783 in a letter to Hastings, dated Patna,
2 March 1784, extracted in the *GM* 1790, LX, Pt. i, 113–16. He there says
that he found the Lama "placed in great form upon his musnud. On the left
side stood his father and mother. . . . Teeshoo Lama is at this time about
eighteen months of age." Turner says nothing about the Lama's having been
complimented two years earlier; the circumstances of the Lama's rebirth naturally seem all the more absurd to HW because of his confusion of *reincarnation* (of the spirit) with *resurrection* (of the body).

5. Mary Granville (1700–88), m. 1 (1718) Alexander Pendarves; m. 2 (1743)
Patrick Delany (?1685–1768), dean of Down. An intimate of the bluestockings

Letter fr. *Lord Petre*[6] to D[r] Horsley Bp of St Davids. March 1790.

I have been told that Ld Bolinbroke[7] after he was deprived of his Peerage, used to sign his letters, H. S. L. B. meaning either, Henry St John Lord Bolinbroke, or H. S. Late Bolinbroke.

In the European Magazine for March 1790 it is said that Israel Mauduit[8] printed but never published 25 copies of Ob-

and favorite of the royal family, Mrs. Delany in her later years became a close friend of HW and left him a self-portrait by Liotard (*Autobiography and Correspondence of Mary Granville, Mrs. Delany,* ed. Lady Llanover, London, 1861–62, VI, 489; "Des. of SH," *Works,* II, 482). Five letters from Queen Charlotte to Mrs. Delany are printed in the *Autobiography,* VI, passim; the letter HW saw may have been the one of 15 Dec. 1781 enclosed in an orna-mented pocketbook given to Mrs. Delany by the Queen and signed, "a very sincere well-wisher, friend, and affectionate Queen. Charlotte" (ibid., VI, 76). The way HW cites the signature makes it seem as if two contradictory terms were being juxtaposed, as if Charlotte's haughty nature had to assert itself even in a note to a friend; his dislike of the Queen characteristically caused him to seize upon real or imagined faults and magnify them (see also above, pp. 75, 99.

6. Robert Edward, 9th Baron Petre (see above, p. 96, n. 8); Samuel Horsley (1733–1806), D.C.L., was bishop of St. David's, 1788–93, of Rochester, 1793–1802, and of St. Asaph's, 1802–06. Petre's *Letter . . . to the Right Reverend Doctor Horsley, Bishop of St. David's* (London, 1790), dated 22 March, was written in response to Horsley's *Review of the Case of the Protestant Dis-senters* (London, 1790) (HW's copies, now *WSL,* listed Hazen, *Cat. of HW's Lib.,* Nos. 1609:53:2–3). In his pamphlet Petre, a Roman Catholic and Freemason, attacks Horsley for discriminating between the case of Protestant dissenters and that of Catholics as regarded their right to toleration (see M. D. Petre, *The Ninth Lord Petre,* London, 1928, pp. 109–13). A bill easing restrictions on Roman Catholics was passed in 1791 (below, p. 123, n. 7); for Dr. Horsley see also below, p. 144.

7. Henry St. John, 1st Viscount Bolingbroke, the famous Tory statesman, opponent of Sir Robert Walpole, and friend of Pope (see above, p. 100, n. 9). His peerage was attainted in 1715 but restored in 1725, although he was not allowed to sit in the House of Lords and thereby return to active political life.

8. Israel Mauduit (1708–87), political pamphleteer. The pamphlet men-tioned in the *European Magazine,* March 1790, XVII, 167, is *An Apology for the Life and Actions of General Wolfe, against the Misrepresentations in a Pamphlet, Called, A Counter Address to the Public. With Some Other Re-marks on that Performance* (privately printed, London, 1765), 8vo; two copies of this pamphlet are in the British Museum, and others are at Yale, the University of Michigan, and the Huntington Library (Nat. Union Cat.). HW's *Counter-Address to the Public, on the Late Dismission of a General Officer*

servations on my Counter Address on dismission of G[en.] Conway.

In the same Magazine is a letter on the fictitious Inscription on Hardiknute,⁹ & comparing it with Rowley's poems, it is signed H. W. I suppose meaning me, but I neither wrote [it] nor know the Author.

Ld Carlisle's¹ verses to Sʳ J. Reynolds. 1790.

[p. 67]   Extract from a MS letter of Dʳ Al. Clarke² to Lady Sundon

(London, 1764) was written in reply to William Guthrie's *Address to the Public* [etc.], which attacked HW's cousin General (later Field Marshal) Henry Seymour Conway (1719–95) at the time of his dismissal from his regiment for voting in Parliament against general warrants (see above, p. 50, n. 8). HW was a lifelong champion of Conway against the calumnies of his political enemies. (Besides being an M.P., Conway was named to the Privy Council in 1765 and served as secretary of state in the first Rockingham and Grafton administrations.)

9. Hardecanute (?1019–42), King of England. The letter signed "H.W." in the *European Magazine*, March 1790, XVII, 181–82, is a satirical "appreciation" of a poem allegedly by Rowley which a correspondent to that magazine had compared with a supposed Saxon epitaph on Hardecanute "discovered" the year before; the whole controversy was evidently an elaborate hoax designed to poke fun at the Society of Antiquaries. The epitaph on Hardecanute translates, "Here King Arthnut drank a winehorn dry and stared about him and died"; Hardecanute in fact died suddenly at a wedding banquet (see ibid., XVII, 177–82; *DNB*).

1. Frederick Howard (1748–1825), 5th Earl of Carlisle, 1758. On 10 April 1790 HW wrote to thank Carlisle for sending him his *Verses to Sir Joshua Reynolds, on his Late Resignation of the President's Chair of the Royal Academy* (London, 1790), 8vo (Toynbee, XIV, 249). Reynolds had resigned in February in disgust at the Academy's opposition to his proposal to name Joseph Bonomi to the vacant chair of professor of perspective, but resumed his post at the Academy's request in March. Carlisle's verses begin, "Too wise for contest, and too meek for strife, / Like Lear, oppress'd by those you rais'd to life," and end, "Accept again thy pow'r—resume the Chair, / 'Nor leave it till—you place an Equal there.'"

2. Alured Clarke (1696–1742), D.D., prebendary of Westminster, 1731, dean of Exeter, 1741; for Lady Sundon, see above, p. 29. Clarke's letter to Lady Sundon is printed in *Memoirs of Viscountess* [sic] *Sundon*, ed. Mrs. K. B. Thomson (London, 1847), II, 140–43, where "whimsical will" is transcribed as "whimsical sort of a will." Philip Wharton (1698–1731), cr. (1718) Duke of Wharton, was the notorious profligate and political and religious apostate pilloried by Pope in his *Epistle to Cobham* as "Wharton, the scorn and won-

Bristol july 23ᵈ. 1733.

—Since I came hither, I have met with an account of a very
peculiar & whimsical Will of the late Duke of Wharton's, in
which he declares himself a Member of the Roman Catholic
Comunion, & a very loyal Subject of the Pretender. Over his
grave he orders the two following Inscriptions, & is very express in his directions about it,

Vixi, & quem dederat cursum Fortuna, peregi.

My Fame shall last, when Pyramids of pride
Mix with the ashes they were rais'd to hide.

How can one guess at the reasons of a God's actions, unless
one had the same degree of understanding that He has!

George 2d walking alone in Kensington garden, was addressed by one of the Workmen, who urged being very poor
& having six children & asking for money. The King put his
hand into his pocket but found he had no money & told the
man so—"no! said the man surprized, then where the Devil
does all the money go, if you are King & have none! The K.
went into the palace & sent him out five guineas.

So few persons now stay at their own houses in the Country
in Summer, but go to Watering places for diversion, that one

der of our days, / Whose ruling Passion was the Lust of Praise [etc.]"
(ll. 180 ff.). Although he was created Duke of Wharton to secure him to the
Whig interest, Wharton subsequently turned Tory, adopted the cause of the
Old Pretender (the titular James III) in 1725, and the following year con-
verted to the Roman Catholic faith upon his marriage to Maria Theresa
O'Neill, maid of honor to the Queen of Spain. Wharton died in Spain in
1731; his monument (in the monastery of the Cistercians at Poblet in Catalonia) does not contain the inscriptions cited by Clarke (the Latin one,
"I have lived, and completed the course which Fortune gave," is from Virgil,
Aeneid, IV, 653), but instead simply lists his titles while noting that he
died "in fide Ecclesiæ Catholicæ Romanæ" (Lewis Melville, *The Life and
Writings of Philip Duke of Wharton*, London, 1913, p. 252; Wharton's will,
dated 1 April 1731 at the Court of Tarragona in Catalonia, was proved
7 Dec. 1736 in the Prerogative Court of Ireland). HW discusses Wharton's
life and writings in his *Catalogue of the Royal and Noble Authors, Works*,
I, 443–45.

may reverse the old proverb, & instead of Home is home, tho never so homely, say, Home is not home, tho never so comely.[3]

It was a brave, cool & excellent answer sent by John Cockburn Gov. of Hume Castle when summoned to render it by Col. Fenwick[4] 1650;

> Rt Hon[ble]
> I have received a Trumpeter of yours, as he tells me, without yr Pass, to render Hume Castle to the L[d] General [p. 68] Cromwell. please you, I never saw your General, nor know your General. as for Hume Castle, it stands upon a rock. given at Hume castle this day before 7 o'clock. So resteth without prejudice of his country
> > yr most humble Servant,
> > John Cockburn.
> v. Heath's Chronicle in that year.

The brave commander having defended his post to extremity, was forced to deliver it at mercy.

Mark Bilford was Limner of pictures to Prince Henry[5] in 1610. v. Collect. of Ordinance for Royal Housholds published by Antiq. Soc. in 1790. Qu⁰. p. 334.

3. HW wrote to Mary Berry 13 July 1790 (in continuation of his letter begun 10 July): "I have nothing to add to my letter but a new edition or correction of an old proverb that I made this morning on . . . everybody's jaunts to watering places—Home is never home, though ever so comely" (*YWE*, XI, 89). For early occurrences of the proverb, see M. P. Tilley, *A Dictionary of the Proverbs in England in the Sixteenth and Seventeenth Centuries* (Ann Arbor, 1950), p. 315.

4. George Fenwick (?1603–57), Parliamentarian, in 1650 took part in Cromwell's invasion of Scotland, and was at the head of a force that captured Hume Castle in Berwickshire on 4 Feb. 1650/51. Cockburn has not been further identified; his answer is recorded by James Heath (1629–64), historian, in his *Brief Chronicle of the Late Intestine Warr in the Three Kingdoms of England, Scotland and Ireland*, "second impression . . . enlarged" (London, 1663), pp. 520–21 (HW's copy of the 1678 folio edition is listed in Hazen, *Cat. of HW's Lib.*, No. 1118).

5. Henry Frederick (1594–1612), Prince of Wales, 1610; eldest son of King James I. Bilford has not been further identified; the work HW cites (not listed by Hazen) is *A Collection of Ordinances and Regulations for the Gov-*

Account of Mr Th. Banks[6] Sculptor in the European Mag. for July 1790. p. 23.

A silly Woman, who was sick, told M[rs] Clive[7] (the celebrated Comedian) that she had *a riot* in her bowels, & asked her what She shoud do for it? Oh! replied Clive, read the proclamation. Instead of understanding the wit of the answer, the Simpleton, probably taking *Proclamation* for *Prescription,* cried, where can I get it?

"Yesterday the King went for Newmarket; whither the Queen also goes to give the Dss of Portsmouth the better conveniency, & for whose divertisement the Queen undertakes that journey."

letter from E. of Huntingdon,[8] in Biblioth. Topogr. Vol. 50. p. 626.

[p. 69]   It was Lady Pomfret,[9] not Lady Lempster, that wrote a life of Vandyck, still MS.

ernment of the Royal Household, Made in Divers Reigns . . . *Printed for the Society of Antiquaries by John Nichols* (London, 1790), 4to.

6. Thomas Banks (1735–1805), sculptor. The "Account" in the *European Magazine,* July 1790, XVIII, 23–24, concludes with a detailed description of the monument to Sir Eyre Coote in Westminster Abbey which Banks completed in 1789. This item has been printed in *Anecdotes of Painting,* V, 140.

7. Catherine Raftor (1711–85), m. (1732) George Clive; actress. Famous for her comic roles, she was a close friend of HW and lived with her brother and sister at "Little Strawberry Hill," a cottage adjoining Strawberry Hill which HW gave her for her life ca. 1754 (see *YWE,* XXXV, 185). By "the proclamation" she was of course referring to the Riot Act (1 George I, st. 2, c. 5).

8. Theophilus Hastings (1650–1701), 7th Earl of Huntingdon, 1656. The letter which HW quotes, dated "London, Pall Mall . . . Sept. 27, 1679," is printed in John Nichols's *Bibliotheca Topographica Britannica* (for which see above, p. 59, n. 4), No. 50 (1790), p. 626. The monarchs referred to are Charles II and his Queen, Catherine of Braganza; the Duchess of Portsmouth was Louise Renée de Penancoet de Kéroualle (1649–1734), cr. (1673) Duchess of Portsmouth, Charles's mistress who exerted great influence on him from 1671 till his death (see above, p. 27, n. 3). Although Catherine in the early days of her marriage refused to countenance Charles's then mistress, Lady Castlemaine, she was soon forced by the helplessness of her situation to submit to his will, and her submission eventually turned to complaisance (*DNB*).

9. Henrietta Louisa Jeffreys (d. 1761), m. (1720) Thomas Fermor (1698–1753), 2d Baron Leominster (or Lempster), 1711, cr. (1721) Earl of Pomfret

at Dulwich College there is a portrait of a Woman painted by Burbage[1] the Actor.

J. K. Sherwin,[2] Engraver to King & Pr. died in Sept. 1790.

Lady Cowper[3] having ordered her Servants never to say *our* house & *our* coach &c & asking one of them who a man was that She saw in her hall, the footman replied, *"yr Lady-ship's* breeches-maker."

A Man who is very nice about trifling facts, may be called, a Matter of factor.[4]

1791.

Abuses must grow & increase in all Governments of Long duration, & will want Reformation, & yet can or scarce ought

---

or Pontefract. HW wrote in *Anecdotes of Painting* (Strawberry Hill, 1762–71), II, 100, that "Lady Lempster, mother of [George, 2d Earl of Pomfret], who was at Rome with her Lord, wrote a life of Vandyck, with some description of his works"; he is evidently referring to Lady Pomfret, but mistakenly calling her by the title of her mother-in-law, Sophia O'Brien (d. 1746), m. (1692) William Fermor (1648–1711), cr. (1692) Baron Leominster. (The correction was not entered in the 1798 edition in *Works*.) *GEC*, X, 573, n. *d*, mentions that Lady Pomfret's diaries and accounts of tours in the Low Countries, France and Italy, 1736–61, were (1879) *penes* G. H. Finch, Esq.; her life of Van Dyck, possibly with these accounts, remains unpublished.

1. Richard Burbage (?1567–1619), the well-known actor and contemporary of Shakespeare who created many of the Bard's tragic roles, was also a successful painter in oils. The portrait at Dulwich College was presented to that institution by William Cartwright, the actor, in the seventeenth century; it is described by Cartwright in his own catalogue as "a woman's head on a boord done by Mr. Burbige, ye actor" (*DNB*). HW paid his only visit to the College on 8 June 1791 (*YWE*, XI, 288).

2. John Keyse Sherwin (?1751–20 Sept. 1790), engraver to the King and to the Prince of Wales, 1785–90. HW pasted a clipping of his death notice in the *Morning Herald* (25 Sept.) in his "Book of Materials," 1771–85, p. 124. This item has been printed in *Anecdotes of Painting*, V, 223.

3. Probably Georgiana Caroline Carteret (d. 1780), m. (1750) William Cowper (afterwards Clavering Cowper), 2d Earl Cowper. She was one of the dowager set whom HW knew at Twickenham and Richmond, while the current Lady Cowper, i.e., Hannah Anne Gore (ca. 1758–1826), m. (1775) George Nassau Clavering Cowper, 3d Earl Cowper, was permanently settled at Florence.

4. I.e., unimaginative or prosaic, with perhaps an allusion to the profession of "factor," or commercial agent. "Nice" here of course means particular or finicky.

to hope for it for these reasons: a total Reformation at once must be unjust, cruel, oppressive, & probably produce more evil than good, as we have seen in France: & Reformation by degrees is seldom or never likely to be perfected, because the Spirit of Reformation never lasts long enough to do good! What good did Mr Burke's place bill[5] effect? by taking away some places, in the King's gift, curtailing others, & lessening Pensions, It reduced the Crown to bribe by multiplying Peerages immoderately.

March 8th. Edwards,[6] the curious Bookseller in Pallmall told me this evening that it costs him 2000£ a year in having his books bound.

I have heard that the Balance to England for sending Priests to foreign Countries is Sixty thousand pds a year.[7]

5. Edmund Burke's bill "for the better regulation of his Majesty's civil establishments, and of certain public officers; for the limitation of pensions, and the suppression of sundry useless, expensive, and inconvenient places; and for applying the moneys saved thereby to the public service," was introduced in 1780 and enacted in June 1782. By curtailing patronage it forced the King to increase the number of grants of peerages in order to reward his supporters; in the eight years following the passage of the bill some sixty new peerages were created (an average of seven or eight per year, eleven in 1790 alone) as compared with thirty-four during the preceding eight years (an average of four). See *YWE*, XXV, 20, n. 1; Carl B. Cone, *Burke and the Nature of Politics: The Age of the French Revolution* (Lexington, 1964), pp. 40–46; Robert Beatson, *A Political Index to the Histories of Great Britain and Ireland* (London, 1806), I, 138–45. Despite HW's misgivings the tactic of multiplying peerages was not sufficient to offset the loss of royal influence which the Place Bill entailed; Burke's measure was yet another step in the long history of the attrition of the powers of the Crown.

6. James Edwards (1757–1816), bookseller and bibliographer. The handsome Bodoni edition of *The Castle of Otranto* was printed for him at Parma and published in 1791; see Hazen, *Bibl. of HW*, 56–63.

7. Presumably the figure is an estimate of the tithes and other revenues that would be taken by Catholic priests had they not been forced out of England; in a letter to Sir Horace Mann of 28 Dec. 1781 HW branded Cosimo III, Grand Duke of Tuscany, as a "proud silly bigot, who impoverished his subjects to enrich the clergy" (*YWE*, XXV, 223–24). In Feb. 1791 a bill was introduced in Parliament "to relieve, upon conditions and under restrictions, persons called protesting Catholic dissenters, from certain penalties and disabilities to which papists, or persons professing the popish religion, are by law subject"; this bill was passed by the Commons on 20 April, by the Lords on 7 June, and received the royal assent 10 June (*Journals of the House of*

[p. 70] March 7th. 1791. d. Rich. Paton,[8] marine Painter in Wardour street Soho. v. Lond. Chronicle.

If the East was the Cradle of Science, at least it never grew to Manhood there.[9]

Thomas,[1] Son of George Ld Lumley, married Elizabeth Plantaginet, natural Daughter of Edward 4th. by Elizabeth Lucy. v. Collins in Scarborough.

Sir Amias,[2] father of Sir H. Poulet to soften Wolsey whom

Commons, XLVI, 206, 442, 707; Journals of the House of Lords, XXXIX, 251–52, 257).

8. Richard Paton (1717–91), marine painter (see Thieme and Becker, XXVI, 297). In his "Book of Materials," 1771–85, p. 17, HW pasted a newspaper cutting, which he dates 21 Feb. 1775, describing Paton's "waiting on his Majesty at the Queen's palace with some of his pictures, viz. two representing different periods of the royal naval review at Portsmouth, and two others, being views of the royal dockyards at Deptford and Chatham." Paton's death notice is in the London Chronicle 5–8 March 1791, s.v. 8 March. This item has been printed in Anecdotes of Painting, V, 106.

9. See above, p. 49, n. 6.

1. Thomas Lumley (d. ?1487), son and heir of George (d. 1507), 2d Lord Lumley (baron by writ), 1485, father of Richard, 3d Lord Lumley. According to Collins, Peerage, III, 703 (in the article on the Earls of Scarborough), Thomas Lumley "dying in the lifetime of his father, left issue by Elizabeth Plantagenet, his wife, (natural) daughter of Edward IV. (by the Lady Elizabeth Lucy)"; see, however, GEC, VIII, 274, n. e. Nothing is known of Lady Elizabeth Lucy beyond the fact that she was a mistress of Edward IV, the mother of his natural son, Arthur, and possibly of his natural daughter, Elizabeth (see R. S. Sylvester, ed., Complete Works of St. Thomas More, II, New Haven, 1963, 243–44); for Elizabeth Plantagenet (b. ?1464), see ibid., II, 243. HW owned the second edition of Collins's Peerage (London, 1714), 2 vols., 8vo, and also an edition of 1756, 5 vols.-in-6, 8vo (Hazen, Cat. of HW's Lib., Nos. 652–53); Hazen believes that HW's notes here were taken from the latter edition.

2. Sir Amias (or Amyas) Paulet (or Poulet) (d. 1538), soldier, father of Sir Hugh Paulet (or Poulet) (d. ?1572), military commander and governor of Jersey. "In the reign of Henry VII. when Cardinal Wolsey was only a schoolmaster at Limington in Somersetshire, Sir Amias Paulett, for some misdemeanour committed by him, clapped him in the stocks: which the Cardinal, when he grew into favour with Henry VIII. so far resented, that he sought all manner of ways to give him trouble, and obliged him . . . to dance attendance at London for some years, and by all manner of obsequiousness to curry favour with him. During the time of his attendance, being commanded by the Cardinal not to depart London without licence, he took up his lodging in the great gate of the Temple towards Fleet-street. And . . . when the Cardinal was made lord-chancellor, he re-edified the said gate (now called

he had early set in the Stocks, rebuilt the middle Temple gate on the Cardinal being made Ld Chancellor, & adorned it with his arms & other Devices. ib. in Earl Poulet.

A Gentleman, who had no particular partiality for Truth hearing a person relate some remarkable effects of lightning s^d "Oh! That is nothing to What happens in the West Indies, where they are so used to its violence that they scare mind it. I knew a Gentleman & his Sister there, who were sitting on each side of the Chimney, when a great Storm happening, the lightning fell & reduced the Sister to a heap of ashes. The Brother rang the bell, & said to the Footman, send the Maid hither to sweep away my Sister."

When a Founder of a new Religion enjoins his Disciples as a chief merit to believe in his Mission, it is presumption that he has no Mission; for tho Faith may be a merit towards him it is no merit in the believer; for if he believes on conviction he cannot help believing, & then has no merit: if he believes without being convinced, he tells an Untruth.

[p. 71]　　Account of Mr Richd Dalton,[3] Engraver & librarian to the King, in Gentlem. Magaz. for March 1791.

the Middle-Temple gate) and sumptuously beautified it on the outside with the Cardinal's arms, cognizance, badges, and other devices, in a glorious manner, thereby hoping to appease his displeasure" (Collins, IV, 3, in the article on the Earls Poulett). According to John Collinson, *History and Antiquities of the County of Somerset* (London, 1791), III, 219–20, Wolsey's misdemeanor consisted in his "getting drunk and making a riot at a fair." *DNB* observes that Paulet was free in 1524, as in that year he was a commissioner to collect the subsidy in Somerset.

3. See above, p. 97, n. 1. Dalton died 7 Feb. 1791; the account in *GM* March 1791, LXI, Pt. i, 195–98, describes him as having been "King's librarian" in 1764, and discusses various works of engravings by him. The auction of his collection at Christie's 9 and 11 April, which was done "for the benefit of his servants" (ibid., p. 198), is noticed in the *Daily Advertiser* for those dates. There the collection is described as consisting of "pictures of the Italian, French, Flemish, and Dutch schools, highly finished miniatures, enamels, crayons by Rosalba, marble bustos, capital bronzes, curious carvings in ivory, models in terra cotta, Roman ware, &c." HW bought "the original portrait of Samuel Cooper, the miniature painter, from the royal collection," and a "head of a gentleman, by Rosalba" ("Des. of SH," *Works*, II, 512); for

His collection sold by auction at Christie's in Pallmall
April 9 & 11. 1791.

A Republic is not a Government, but a fluctuation of factions.

Good letter of R. E. of Salisbury[4] to Archbp. of York in the
Talbot & Howard papers. Vol. 3ᵈ. p. 259.
Sʳ Th. Sherley committed to Tower. ib. 325.

Lines from Tickell's[5] Epistle from a Lady to a gentleman
at Avignon (v. Dodsley's Collect. of Poems, vol. 1. p. 67)
which being written on the old Pretender in 1715, have
proved a Prophecy on his Son.

the portrait of Cooper, see below, Appendix A. This item has been printed
in *Anecdotes of Painting*, V, 209.
    4. Robert Cecil (1563–1612), cr. (1604) Viscount Cranborne and (1605) Earl
of Salisbury; statesman. His letter to Matthew Hutton (1529–1606), archbishop
of York, 1596–1606, endorsed 1 Feb. 1604, is printed in Edmund Lodge, *Illustrations of British History, Biography, and Manners . . . from the Manuscripts of the Noble Families of Howard, Talbot, and Cecil* (London, 1791),
III, 259–63 (HW's copy listed Hazen, *Cat.*, No. 455). Written in response to
the Archbishop's suggestion that the prosecution of Puritans be relaxed,
Salisbury observes prophetically that "although manie relligious men of moderate spiritts might be borne wth, yet such are the turbulent humors of
some that dreame of nothinge but a newe hyerarchy, directlie opposite to
the state of a monarchy, as the dispensation wth such men weare the highway to breake all the bonds of unytie to nourishe schisme in the Church &
Comonwealthe" (Lodge, III, 260). Sir Thomas Shirley or Sherley (ca. 1564–
?1630), adventurer and privateer, was imprisoned in the Tower in Sept. 1607
on a charge of illegal interference with the operations of the Levant Company (see *DNB*; Foster, *Alumni Oxon.*). His imprisonment is mentioned in a
letter of Rowland Whyte to Gilbert, 7th Earl of Shrewsbury (17 Sept. 1607),
printed Lodge, III, 324–26.
    5. Thomas Tickell (1685–1740), poet (see R. E. Tickell, *Thomas Tickell
and the Eighteenth Century Poets*, London, 1931, p. 15 et passim). His
"Epistle from a Lady in England; to a Gentleman at Avignon" was originally published in 1717 as a folio pamphlet; HW owned the second edition
of Dodsley's *Collection of Poems by Several Hands* (London, 1748), 3 vols.,
where the poem is reprinted, I, 63–70 (see Hazen, *Cat.*, No. 2370). By the Old
Pretender's "son" HW is thinking mainly of his younger son, Henry Benedict Maria Clement (1725–1807), styled Duke of York, who actually became
a cardinal in 1747. Except for the last line, however, Tickell's passage is
equally applicable to the elder son, the Young Pretender Charles Edward
Stuart (1720–88), who ended his days a drunkard at Rome.

> To Rome then must the Royal Wand'rer go,
> And fall a Suppliant at the papal toe:
> His life in Sloth inglorious he must wear,
> One half in luxury, and half in pray'r.
> His life perhaps at length debauch'd with ease,
> The proffer'd Purple & the Hat may please.

Lines in the Mysterious Mother[6] that have proved to be a Prophecy of what has happened in France since the Revolution of 1789;

> Ev'n stern Philosophy, if once triumphant,
> Will frame some jargon, and exact Obedience
> To metaphysic nonsense, worse than Ours.
>
> Act 4th.

[p. 72]   1792.

Mr Frederic North,[7] 3[d] Son of Fred. Earl of Guilford, staying a long time in Corfou in 1792 to learn modern Greek, & somebody asking the Earl where his Son was, he answered "en

6. HW's tragedy of double incest, first printed at Strawberry Hill in 1768 but because of the "revolting" theme (HW's word) not published until 1791 (see Hazen, *SH Bibl.*, 79–85; *Works*, I, 125; below, p. 130). The lines HW quotes are in Act IV, scene i.

7. Frederick North (1766–1827), 5th Earl of Guilford, 1817, third and youngest son of Frederick North, 2d Earl of Guilford, 1790 (better known as Lord North, George III's prime minister; see above, p. 99, n. 6, 110). The younger Frederick was received into the Greek Church in 1791, remaining in it till his death, and was an accomplished linguist, speaking French, German, Spanish, Italian, and modern Greek; he later became secretary of state in Corsica (1795–97), governor and vice admiral of Ceylon (1798–1805), and chancellor of the University of Corfu (1819–27). "Mr Douglas" was Sylvester Douglas (1743–1823), cr. (1800) Baron Glenbervie, married (1789) Catherine Anne North (1760–1817), eldest daughter of Lord Guilford (see *GEC;* Collins, *Peerage*, IV, 484; *YWE*, XII, 116, n. 12); Louis-Jules-Barbon Mancini-Mazarini (1716–98), Duc de Nivernais, diplomat and writer, was an old friend of HW who translated his *Essay on Modern Gardening* into French (1785). Nivernais's bon mot was presumably uttered on 7 Oct. 1791, as the National Assembly's decree against addressing Louis XVI as "Sire" or "Majesté" was passed on 5 Oct. and reversed on the 6th (see *Procès-Verbal de l'Assemblée Nationale*, Paris, 1791–92, I, 34–36, 39–40). *Corcyra* is the Latin form of the ancient Greek *Kerkura*.

Corfou," or by a pun, "encore Fou." Mr Dougas, Son in law
of Lord Guilford, being at Paris in 1791, told that pun to the
Duc de Nivernois on the day after the National Assembly had
reversed their decree which forbad their King to be called
Sire; on which the Duke immediately said, "Et le Roi est
encore Sire," or "le Roi est en Corcyre"; *Corcyra* being the
old name of *Corfou*—astonishing quickness of Wit & recol-
lection in a Man that [is] Seventy five.

Mad. de Genlis,[8] alias Sillery, alias Brulart, being in England in 1792, desired to see the palace of the Prince of Wales
with Mademoiselle d'Orleans: the Prince consented, & received them himself, & offering his hand to the first: She
waved it, & pointed to Mlle, but the Prince s^d with an ironic
Sneer, "Oh! I thought you were Equal now."

A play being acted at the Haymarket by the Players from
Drury lane on *Jan. 30*^th^., the King at his next Levèe asked
the Marquis of Salisbury[9] Ld Chamberlain, how he came to

8. Stéphanie-Felicité Ducrest de Saint-Aubin (1746–1830), m. (1763) Charles-
Alexis Brulart, Comte de Genlis, later Marquis de Chastres; dramatist and
educational writer. HW in a letter to Lady Ossory (8 Jan. 1793) calls her
"Mrs Genlis, *alias* Sillery, *alias* Brulart, as she would be styled at the Old
Baily" (*YWE*, XXXIV, 177; see also ibid., n. 21). Madame de Genlis was
governess to the Duc d'Orléans ("Philippe Egalité") and formerly his mistress. She arrived in England in the autumn of 1791 with his daughter
Louise-Marie-Adélaïde-Eugénie de Bourbon d'Orléans (1777–1847), and HW
notes her arrival at London in a letter to Lady Ossory of 4 Feb. 1792; he
there calls her "that scribbling trollop" in allusion to her affair with Orleans
and to her Rousseauesque educational writings (which he detested). Although
she declared herself in favor of the Revolution at its outset, Madame de
Genlis was probably not so thoroughly republican in her sentiments as HW
and the Prince seem to have thought. See *YWE*, IV, 284; XI, 303, n. 39;
XXXIII, 475–76, 483, n. 26; XXXIV, 138; *NBG*.

9. James Cecil (1748–1823), 7th Earl of Salisbury, 1780, cr. (1789) Marquess
of Salisbury; lord chamberlain of the Household, 1783–1804, in which post
he was responsible for the licensing of plays. In 1791 the Drury Lane Theater
was pronounced unsafe and had to be pulled down and rebuilt; this forced
the company, managed by Richard Brinsley Sheridan (1748–1816), the statesman and dramatist, to temporarily relocate, not in the "Little Theater" or
Theater Royal in the Haymarket, but in the King's Opera House there. On
30 Jan. 1792 Sheridan staged a performance of David Garrick's *Cymon* in
apparent defiance of the traditional ban on theatrical representations on that

Suffer Sheridan (the Manager) to have a play on that day—
The fact, I was told, was this: Ld Sal. had allowed a play to
be acted at the little Theatre in the Haymarket, but had not
adverted to the day being the 30th. of January—but it being
advertised, the Chamberlain forbad it, & ordered it for another day, but Sheridan seeing it advertized by leave of the
L. Chamberlain & unwilling to lose the profits of a night, and
probably [p. 73] glad to please the Presbyterians, whom he
courted, did act on that night, & was not forbidden from
oversight or fear.

Account of a singular custom at Metelin by the Earl of
Charlemont;[1] in European Magazine for Jany. 1792, p. 49.

Full accounts of Schnebelie,[2] the Engraver, & of Sr Josh:
Reynolds, in Gentleman's Magazine for february 1793.

date, the anniversary of the martyrdom of Charles I. The performance had
apparently not been expressly forbidden beforehand, but on 3 Feb. Lord
Salisbury wrote to Sheridan reprimanding him and ordering him "to cause
the practice to be discontinued in future" (*London Stage 1660–1800 . . .
Part 5: 1776–1800,* ed. C. B. Hogan, Carbondale, 1968, II, 1422–23). Sheridan's
"courting the Presbyterians" is presumably an allusion to his enlistment by
the Scottish royal boroughs in 1787 to plead their grievances in Parliament,
which he did without success until 1794; the Lord Chamberlain's fear sup-
posedly would be of a riot by spectators cheated out of the play at the last
moment, whose ranks might be swelled by anti-government or anti-
monarchical elements. HW's two spellings of "advertised" are so in the MS.
For "profits of a night" he originally wrote "profits of a first night," but
crossed out "first."

　　1. James Caulfeild (1728–99), 4th Viscount Charlemont, cr. (1763) Earl of
Charlemont; Irish statesman. "Metelin" or Mytilene is another name for
Lesbos, the island of Sappho on the Aegean sea. Charlemont's "Account" in
the *European Magazine,* Jan. 1792, XXI, 49–50, was originally published in
Vol. III (1790) of *Transactions of the Royal Irish Academy* (of which he was
founder and first president) and describes the "singular custom" of matri-
lineal descent still practiced in Lesbos in 1749, the year he visited there (see
M. J. Craig, *The Volunteer Earl,* London, 1948, pp. 59–60, 210).

　　2. Jacob C. Schnebbelie (1760–92), topographical draftsman and engraver,
died 21 Feb. 1792 (see Thieme and Becker, XXX, 188). The accounts of him
and of Sir Joshua Reynolds, who died 23 Feb., are in *GM* Feb. 1792 ("1793"
is so in the MS), LXII, Pt. i, 189–91; descriptions of the burial of Sir Joshua
and his character by Burke (see below) are to be found, for example, ibid.,
March 1792, LXII, Pt. i, 273–74, and in the *European Magazine,* March 1792,
XXI, 213–14. These items have been printed in *Anecdotes of Painting,* V, 72,

In the Second Volume or Annèe des Antiquitès Nationales
de France,[3] cf. livraison, Collegiale d'Ecouis, p. 6 is an
Enigmatic Epitaph, with others Similar, on a Subject like
that of my Tragedy of the Mysterious Mother.

Burial of S[r] J. Reynolds in St Pauls, & his Character by
Burke. v. Magazines for feb. & March 1792.
Do. of R. Adam[4] Archit. in Westm. abbey.

Ld Muncaster[5] pamphl. on Slave trade.

It was s[d] of a young Lady of Spirit, spoiled and ill educated,
that it was heads or tails whether she wd turn out well or ill—

223, as also the notice of the auction at Greenwood's of Sir Joshua's models
casts, etc. (see below, p. 131), p. 72; *DNB* notes that the contents of his studio
were sold there in 1796.

3. HW's reference is to Aubin-Louis Millin, *Antiquités nationales ou
receuil de monumens pour servir à l'histoire générale et particulière de l'empire françois* (Paris, 1790), 4 vols., 4to (his copy is listed Hazen, *Cat. of HW's
Lib.*, No. 3721). In the article on the Collégiale d'Ecouis, p. 6 (bound into
Vol. III in the copy at Yale), is the following epitaph said to have been transcribed from a marble plaque in the church:

> Ci gît l'enfant, ci gît le père,
> Ci gît la sœur, ci gît le frère,
> Ci gît la femme et le mari,
> Et ne sont que deux corps ici.

Millin explains: "La tradition est qu'un fils de Madame d'Ecouis avait eu
de sa mère, sans la connaître et sans en être reconnu, une fille nommée Cécile.
Il épousa ensuite, en Lorraine, cette même Cécile qui étoit auprès de la
duchesse de Bar. Ainsi Cécile étoit fille et sœur de son mari. Ils furent en-
terrés dans la même tombeau, en 1512, à Ecouis" (pp. 6–7). Millin cites several other similar epitaphs, pp. 7–11. HW had been collecting instances of the
theme of double incest ever since treating that subject in the *Mysterious
Mother* (1768) (see above, pp. 127, n. 6; *YWE*, I, 186; IV, 93–94; VIII, 363,
366; XXXIX, 103).

4. Robert Adam (1729–92), the noted architect, died 3 March and was in-
terred in Westminster Abbey on 10 March. Among the accounts in periodicals
are those in *GM* March 1792, LXII, Pt. i, 282–83, and in the *European Magazine*, March 1792, XXI, 239–40.

5. John Pennington (1737–1813), cr. (1783) Baron Muncaster. A supporter
of Wilberforce in the latter's crusade against slavery, he published *Historical
Sketches of the Slave Trade, and of its Effects in Africa* (London, 1792).

no, it was not an even wager; it was but one head against many Tails.

Lord Salisbury poems;[6] ⟨Yorick's⟩ journey to ⟨Weymth⟩

Sr Josh. Reynolds's models, casts & duplicate Prints Sold by auction at Greenwood's Leic. fields april 16–17. 1792.[7]

The Marquise de Coigny,[8] a French Lady of Wit, aged about thirty, came to England in 1791 & staid several [p. 74] months. She was much liked, but had a very disagreeable hoarse Voice; She said, "dans ce pais cy il n'y a qu'une voix contre moi, & c'est la mienne."

The Abbe de St Fare, a natural Son of Louis XV, or of the late Duke of Orleans, I forget which, was here at the same time. They were dining with the Prince of Wales: his R.H. or one of his Brothers, told a Story not quite decent. It was observed that Princes were more apt than other Men to take such liberties before Women. Soon after the Abbè told such a Story; on which Madame de Coigny cried out, "Voila comme il se legitime!"

F. Drope[9] preb. of Lincoln, being ejected fr. his College in 1648, taught School at Twickenham. he was author of a

6. HW quotes a poem by Salisbury below, p. 142, and mentions a volume of his poetry which he had privately printed in 1792. "Yorick's journey to Weymouth" (if that is the correct reading) may have been the title of a poem in this collection, of which no copy or other record has been found.

7. See above, p. 129, n. 2.

8. Louise-Marthe de Conflans d'Armentières (1759–1825), m. (1775) François-Marie-Casimir de Franquetot, Marquis de Coigny (*YWE*, XXXIV, 155, n. 19). The *Morning Chronicle* 31 Dec. 1791 reports her departure for Paris the day before, but she was back in London the following August, when HW sent another bon mot by her to Lady Ossory: "On hearing that the mob at Paris have burnt the bust of their late favourite Monsieur d'Eprémenil, [Madame de Coigny] said, 'Il n'y a rien qui brûle sitôt que les lauriers secs'" (letter of 18 Aug. 1792, *YWE*, XXXIV, 155). "The Abbe de St Fare" was Louis-Étienne (1759–1825), Abbé de Saint-Farre, natural son of Louis-Philippe de Bourbon (1725–85), Duc d'Orléans, by Mlle Le Marquis, a *danseuse* of the Italian comedy at Paris (ibid., XXXIV, 175, n. 10).

9. Francis Drope (?1629–71), prebendary of Lincoln, 1669–70, canon, 1670–71, was a demy of Magdalen College, Oxford, 1645–48, 1660–61, and a fellow,

132   HORACE WALPOLE'S *Miscellany* 1786–1795

treatise on fruit trees. v. Topogr. Miscell[an]ies, qu⁰. 1790.
Vol. 1. p. 3 of Collect⁸. for Berkshire.

Born's travels thro Bannat of Temesvar. by *Raspe*.¹ 1777.

Ferbers travels thro Italy, by D⁰. 1779.

Sᵗ Ciprian's sweet & devout Sermon, englished by Sʳ Thom.
Elliot,² printed by Berthelet. 1539.

1661–71 (*DNB;* Foster, *Alumni Oxon.*). The article "Collections for Berkshire," p. 3, in *Topographical Miscellanies,* I, ed. Sir Samuel Egerton Brydges
(London, 1792), notes that Drope was ejected from his college "by the Parliamentarian Visitors in 1648, he then being Bachelor of Arts. Afterwards he
assisted Mr. William Fuller in teaching a private school at Twickenham in
Middlesex, where continuing till the King's return in 1660, he was restored to
his place. . . . He wrote . . . *A short and sure guide in the practice of
raising and ordering fruit-trees.* Oxon. 1672, Oct[avo]." *DNB* suggests that
Drope was ejected from Magdalen for having borne arms for the King; his
work on fruit trees was praised the year it came out in the Royal Society's
Philosophical Transactions, VII, No. 86, p. 5049, as written from the author's
own experience. HW's copy of *Topographical Miscellanies,* now *WSL* (listed
Hazen, *Cat.,* No. 3795), was sold at the Strawberry Hill Sale (London 933) in
1842. Its later history was unknown until Dec. 1975, when the present editor
discovered it in the Beinecke Library at Yale while doing research for this
note. (It had been purchased by the Yale College Library in 1882, but lacked
the original binding with HW's bookplate and pressmark; it is identifiable
by the scattered notes in HW's hand.) "1790" as the date of the work is so
in the MS.

1. Rudolf Erich Raspe (1737–94), German-English writer and mineralogist;
author of *Baron Munchausen's Narrative of His Marvellous Travels and Campaigns in Russia* (London, 1785) (*YWE,* XXIX, 5, n. 12). HW paid for the
publication of his *Critical Essay on Oil-Painting* (London, 1781), 4to, which
supports HW's theory that the use of oil colors was known long before the
Van Eyck brothers (see below, p. 138; Hazen, *Cat.,* No. 2459). The works referred to here are Raspe's translations (from the German) of Ignaz, Edler
von Born (1742–91), *Travels through the Bannat of Temeswar, Transylvania,
and Hungary, in the Year 1770* (London, 1777), 8vo, first published at Frankfurt and Leipzig in 1774, and Johan Jacob Ferber (1743–90), *Travels through
Italy, in the Years 1771 and 1772* (London, 1776), 8vo, first published at
Prague in 1773; for Born and Ferber, who were respectively German and
Swedish mineralogists, see Constantin Wurzbach, *Biographisches Lexikon des
Kaiserthums Oesterreich* (Vienna, 1856–91), II, 71–74, and *Svenskt Biografiskt
Lexikon,* ed. B. Boëthius et al. (Stockholm, 1918–56), XV, 589–95. 1779 as
the date of publication of Ferber's *Travels* is so in the MS but is perhaps
an error, no such edition being listed in the BM or Nat. Union Cat.

2. Sir Thomas Elyot (?1490–1546), diplomat and author. His *Swete and
Devoute Sermon of Holy Saynt Ciprian of Mortalitie of Man,* a translation

Lady S—— having been reported to be with child by her Footman, & being very rude to the Margravine of Anspach, the Prince of Wales s^d he was not surprized as he supposed She had got her breeding from her Footman.[3]

[p. 75] Lord Lothian[4] being asked what he had approved most at a play acted by some people of quality, replied, "the Prompter, for I heard him best, & saw him least."

A person having s^d curosity for curiosity, as soon as he was gone, another s^d, "how strangely that gentleman murders the language! "No, sd a Third, he only knocked an *I* out."

eye

Extracts from a MS. book in the Remembrancer's Office, almost every page of which is signed by Henry 7th.[5]

of *De Mortalitate* by St. Cyprian (d. 258), bishop of Carthage, was first published at London in 8vo in 1534 by Thomas Berthelet (fl. 1528–54, d. by 1559), who published all of Elyot's books that were issued in his lifetime; HW cites the second printing, also 8vo, 1539. In his "Book of Materials," 1759–70, p. 65, HW compiled a bibliography of eight works by Elyot, five of which he owned; he apparently did not acquire this one. See *DNB;* BM Cat.; Nat. Union Cat.; E. G. Duff et al., *Hand-Lists of Books Printed by London Printers, 1501–1556* (London, 1895–1913), Pt. III, "Thomas Berthelet."

3. HW amplifies and corrects the details of this anecdote below, p. 153, where he identifies "Lady S——" as Lady Salisbury, i.e., Mary Amelia Hill (1750–1835), m. (1773) James 1st Marquess of Salisbury. The Margravine of Anspach or Ansbach was the former Lady Craven (above, p. 6, n. 5).

4. William John Kerr (1737–1815), 5th Marquess of Lothian, 1775.

5. Henry VII's books of payments, 1495–1509, formerly in the King's Remembrancer's Office (Court of Exchequer), are now in the Public Record Office (4 vols., 1495–1502, 1505–09) and the British Museum (1 vol., 1499–1505); an earlier volume for the years before 1495 is now missing (see S. B. Chrimes, *Henry VII*, London, 1972, p. 332). HW's extracts here were copied in turn from extracts made by Thomas Astle (1735–1803), antiquarian and HW's correspondent, which are printed as an appendix to Robert Henry's *History of Great Britain* (London, 1771–93), VI, 724–26 (HW's copy listed Hazen, *Cat.*, No. 543). The items through "to a Woman for a red rose——2s." are dated by Astle as from 13–14 Henry VII (1497–99) and those after as from 9 Henry VII (1493–94). However, a more detailed and scrupulous copy of the original books by Craven Ord (1756–1832), now BM Add. MSS 7099, fols. 1–96, suggests that most, if not all, of the latter group of extracts date from 7 Henry VII (1491–92). The right-hand column here has been normalized somewhat for the sake of appearance. See the following notes.

To a Woman for 3 apples _____ 12d.

for 2 pair of bellows _____ 10 pence[6]

for the King's loss at Tennis _____ 10d.[7]

for apples _____ 20d.[8]

to a strange Tumbler _____ 20s.

for finding 3 hares _____ 6s.8d. frequently

To the Players of London_____ 10s.

To Tumblers _____ 20s. twice[9]

To a Scotch Fool _____ 13s.4d.

To Master Barnard,[1] the blind

Poet_____ 100s.

to a Man & Woman for Straw-

berries_____ 8s.4d.

to Bishop of Bangors cheeses_____ 6s.8d. frequently

to a Woman for a red rose_____ 2s.

for apples & cakes _____ 6s.8d.[2]

To Cart for writing of a book_____ 6s.8d.[3]

To a Spy_____ 20s.[4]

To two monks, Spies_____ 40s.[5]

[p. 76] p[d] for two plays in the hall_____ 26s.8d.

to the King's players[6] _____ 100s.

6. HW apparently first wrote "10d." but accidently blotched the pence sign and spelled it out as a correction.

7. Astle has "12d."

8. "Item, a rewarde given for apples by Thomas Foteman homeward, 20d." (ibid.).

9. "Item, to a tumbuler at my lord Bathe's, 20s." "Item, to the tabouretts and a tumbuler, 20s." (ibid.).

1. Bernard Andreas or André (d. ?1521), poet laureate to Henry VII.

2. "Item, to Robert Forst for appaules and cakes, 6s. 8d." (ibid.). Ord, copying the same item, dates it "Jan:2 7. H:7th [1492]" (fol. 3).

3. Ord, loc. cit., has "Jan:2 [1492] HM to Carter for writing of a Boke o 7 4." Cart or Carter, like Ashby below, was probably a scribe who copied a book for the King.

4. "26th Dec. Item, to a fellow with a berde, a spye, in reward, 20s." (Astle). See next note.

5. This item is dated 24 Dec. 1491 by Ord, fol. 2. Astle notes at the end of his extracts: "The several items are not following each other, but copied from various places in the book."

6. According to Glynne Wickham, *Early English Stages 1300 to 1660* (London, 1959–63), I, 267, in Henry VII's household provision was made for a company of six actors.

to him that brought the prog-
nostication_____6s.8d.[7]
to the King to play at cards_____100s.
to a Spy_____13s.4d.[8]
to him that brought the King
a Lion _____33s.4d.[9]
to a Spy that dwelleth in the West
Country_____20s.[1]
to the King at tables, chefs,
glasses &c_____56s.8d.[2]
to players that begged by the way____6s.8d.
to Pechie the Fool_____6s.8d.[3]
lost to my lord *Morging*[4] at Butts ____6s.8d.
to Ashby for writing of a book_____3s.4d.[5]
to Sʳ Edw. Borough which the K.
lost at butts with his Crossbow____13s.4d.[6]
to a Spaniard that played the fool____40s.[7]
to Diego, the Spanish fool_____20s.
to Dᵒ._____6s.8d.[8]
to a Scotch Spy_____40s.

7. This and the following item are dated 8 Jan. 1492 by Ord, fol. 3.
8. "Item, to John Ibye, a spye, in reward, 13s 4d." (Astle). Also dated 8 Jan. 1492 by Ord.
9. Astle has "53s. 4d." Dated 16 Jan. 1492 by Ord.
1. Dated 18 Jan. 1492 by Ord.
2. Dated 24 Jan. 1492 by Ord, who has "cheese" for "chefs."
3. Dated 12 Feb. 1492 by Ord.
4. There was no "Lord Morging" in the peerage at the time of Henry VII. The reference in the original MS may have been to John Morgan (d. 1504), a favorite of the King, who was dean of St. George's, Windsor, and bishop of St. David's, 1496 (see *DNB*; Chrimes, pp. 39 and n. 2, 42, n. 3, 43).
5. Dated 21 May 1492 by Ord, fol. 4. Ashby is perhaps to be identified with George Ashby (d. 1515), clerk of the signet to Henry VII and Henry VIII (see *DNB*).
6. Dated 4 June 1492 by Ord, fol. 5. Edward Aborough or Borough was knighted by Henry at the battle of Stoke-on-Trent, 16 June 1487 (W. A. Shaw, *The Knights of England*, London, 1906, II, 24).
7. Dated 10 June 1492 by Ord.
8. "2d Oct. . . . Item, to Dego, the Spaynyshe foole, in rewarde, 6s. 8d." (Astle). Ord also has "Dego" (fol. 7).

to one that presented the K. with a
Mule ————————————————20s.[9]
to one that brought a Lamprey ————4s.[1]
to Henry Pyning [Poines] the K[s].
Godson ————————————————20s.[2]
to the Fool [called] the Duke of
Lancaster
to Pudesay, the Bagpiper ————————6s.8d.

This little abstract is a tolerable picture both of Henry
& the times; of his Avarice & of the general dearth of elegant
amusements, & of the rarity of common fruits and flowers.
With all his boasted policy he was less liberal to Spies, than
to Fools & Tumblers, & p[d] less for Intelligence [p. 77] than
for senseless diversions—a presumption that his Ambition
& vaunted Wisdom coud not save him from Innui, nor his ex-
torted riches purchase rational pleasures. Thro what scenes
of Injustice & blood did he wade to enjoy the supreme Power
of laughing at Ideots & rope-dansers! The poor young Earl of
Warwick was sacrificed that he might glut his rapacity, & ex-
amine the daily accounts of the six & eight pences that he
so niggardly parted with to gratify his taste in eatables or
fooleries![3]

9. Ord has "Aug:11th 9. H:7th [1494] HM to the Priour of Shene [sic]
servant for a Mule o 20 o" (fol. 11).
    1. Cf. Ord, loc. cit.: "Nov:20th [1494] . . . HM to Nicol Grey for a freshe
lamprey o 4 o."
    2. "Items, to Harry Poyning, the king's godson, in reward, 20s." (Astle; the
insertions in this and the next item are HW's). This godson has not been
further identified. Astle's transcription suggests that he was an offspring of
Sir Edward Poynings (1459–1521), a prominent follower of Henry VII (see
DNB), but there is no record of Sir Edward's having had a son named Henry,
and Ord transcribes the name as "Pymago" (fol. 71 et passim).
    3. HW in his *Historic Doubts on the Life and Reign of King Richard the
Third* (1768) suggests that historians have been unfairly prejudiced against
Richard III by the Henry-inspired Lancastrian accounts of that monarch,
adding that "under all the glare of encomiums which historians have heaped
on the wisdom of Henry the seventh," it is easy to perceive "that he was a
meant and unfeeling tyrant" (*Works*, II, 109). Edward, Earl of Warwick (1475–
99), was executed by Henry after a fourteen-year imprisonment; though innocent of any machinations himself, as the last of the male line of the House

Hist. of the principal Transact[s]. of the Irish Parl. from 1634 to 1666, &c. Oct[vo]. by Lord Mountmorres.[4] 1792.

A rosy Clergyman cutting a slice of a Sirloin, s[d] Charles 2[d] made Beef a Knight—yes, s[d] a Gentleman present, & you make it a Baronet by putting a red hand to it.[5]

Accts of Fournier, Chatelain, Tull, Worlidge, Hollar, Hekel, Perry, & Smith, Artists, in Capt. Grose's[6] Olio, p. 166. 1792.

In the Catalogue des tableaux de la Galerie Imp. & roiale de Vienne, printed in Oct[vo]. at Basle 1784 by Chretien de Mechel[7] of Basle, are mentioned several pictures by Holbein,

of York he had represented the single most serious threat to Henry's claim to the throne. For mitigations of Henry's reputation for avarice, see Samuel Bentley, *Excerpta Historica* (London, 1831), p. 86, and S. B. Chrimes, pp. 305–13; for a recent treatment of the question of Richard III's villainy (which unequivocally confirms it), see Alison Hanham, *Richard III and His Early Historians 1483–1535* (Oxford, 1975).

4. Hervey Redmond Morres (ca. 1743–97), 2d Viscount Mountmorres of Castlemorres, 1766. HW's copy of his *History of the Principal Transactions of the Irish Parliament, from the Year 1634 to 1666 . . . to which is Prefixed, a Preliminary Discourse on the Ancient Parliaments of that Kingdom* (London, 1792), 2 vols., 8vo, is listed Hazen, *Cat. of HW's Lib.*, No. 2909.

5. The first allusion is to the apocryphal story of Charles II's being so delighted by a loin of beef that he knighted it (hence the name "sir-loin"); the second is to the "baronet's hand" or "bloody hand," i.e., the hand gules in a field argent granted by James I to English baronets to be borne on their shields. The dubbing of a loin of beef has also been attributed to James I and Henry VIII. See *OED*.

6. Francis Grose (?1731–91), antiquary and draftsman. HW's copy, now *WSL*, of his *Olio: Being a Collection of Essays, Dialogues, Letters* [etc.] (London, 1792), 12mo, is listed Hazen, *Cat.*, No. 3923. Grose's "accounts," pp. 165–72, are brief biographical sketches or anecdotes of the artists Daniel Fournier (ca. 1711–ca. 1766), draftsman and engraver; Jean-Baptiste-Claude Chatelain (ca. 1710–ca. 1771), engraver; N. Tull (d. 1762), painter and draftsman; Thomas Worlidge (1700–66), painter and etcher; Wenceslaus Hollar (1607–77), engraver; Augustin Heckel (ca. 1690–1770), painter and engraver; Francis Perry (d. 1765), engraver; and John Smith (?1652–1742), mezzotint engraver. For Chatelain, Tull, and Heckel, see Thieme and Becker, VI, 427–28; XVI, 208–09; XXXIII, 476; HW discusses Worlidge, Hollar, and Smith in his *Anecdotes of Painting* and *Catalogue of Engravers, Works*, III, 451; IV, 37, 99–100.

7. Christian von Mechel (1737–1817), engraver, art dealer, and writer on art (see L. H. Wüthrich, *Christian von Mechel: Leben und Werk eines Basler*

by his Father, by his Son Sigismond & his friend Amerbach. In the same book are proofs of pictures in oil painted above a Century before the pretended Invention by Van Eyck.

A person sent a present to a *Schoolmaster* of a *Tea-chest* with this Motto, *Tu doces—Thou Teachest.*

The rights of juries defended by *Ch. Earl Stanhope.* Sept. 1792.[8]

[p. 78]   Scrap.

Dryden great Master of th'harmonious art
Coud charm our ear, but seldom touch'd our heart:
Spontaneous numbers flow'd so fast, he caught
The polish'd couplet eer he weigh'd the thought.[9]

Kupferstechers und Kunsthändlers, Basel, 1956); HW's copy of his *Catalogue* is listed Hazen, *Cat.,* No. 2417. (In the MS HW first cited "Vienne" as the place of publication, but crossed it out and wrote in "Basle" above.) The *Catalogue* lists fifteen pictures by Hans Holbein the younger (pp. 242–60), two by his father Hans Holbein the elder (d. 1524) (pp. 240, 250), and two by his uncle (not son) Sigmund (d. 1540) (p. 250). "Amerbach" is so in the MS, but is evidently a slip for Christoph Amberger (d. 1561 or 62), eight pictures by whom are listed, pp. 243–57 (see also Thieme and Becker, I, 387–88; XVII, 333–58; *Anecdotes of Painting, Works,* III, 58–100). In the Preface, p. vi, Mechel mentions "une découverte bien intéressante relativement à la date de l'invention de la peinture à l'huile, qu'on attribue communément aux frères van Eyck de Bruges, et dont on fixe la date au commencement du XV siècle. . . . On a découvert en Boheme au Château de Karlstein . . . des peintures à l'huile d'une date bien antérieure. Ce sont celles de Thomas de Mutina, de Théodoric de Prague, et de Nicolas Wurmser de Strasbourg." HW had questioned the invention of oil painting by the Van Eycks in his *Anecdotes of Painting (Works,* III, 30) and paid for the publication of a work by Raspe supporting his doubts (see above, p. 132, n. 1; also *YWE,* XXIX, 5–6, and nn. 14–23).

8. Charles, 3d Earl Stanhope, *The Rights of Juries Defended together with Authorities of Law in Support of those Rights and the Objections to Mr. Fox's Libel Bill Refuted* (London, 1792), 8vo. For Stanhope, see above, pp. 85, 115.

9. See above, p. 91, where HW credits Pope with having "introduced good sense into verse." Although "polish'd couplet" apparently refers to Dryden's heroic verse, HW was especially impressed by the musical quality of Dryden's odes; he claimed the harmony of *Alexander's Feast* to be diminished by Handel's setting of it (*YWE,* XXVIII, 345, 354). Elsewhere he comments on Pope's inability to write an ode (ibid., XVI, 257; *Catalogue of the Royal and Noble Authors, Works,* I, 549*–550*), but would like Johnson rate him the

Charade made impromptu by Mr Gibbon[1]
the historian at Lausanne.

Sur votre doigt mon premier se met,
Mon Second est l'heureux Secret
Que Tu possedes sans mystere;
Mon Tout, Tu ne scauras le faire.
The word is Deplaire. Dè is a thimble.

At Burford near Tenbury in the Church is a Painting on
board of the Father & Mother of Edmund Cornwall Baron
of Burford,[2] & of himself in armour, all large as life; the doors
which cover the Painting have Saints in compartments, & the
Pediment histories from Scriptures; the outsides of the Doors,
arms & matches. At the feet of the principal Figures, the
Painter's name, Melchior Salaboss fecit anno Domini 1588.
In the Church of Lydiard Tregoze Wiltshire, is a similar

superior craftsman; "polish'd" here should be taken to mean spontaneously
mellifluous, rather than in its more usual sense of finely fashioned or re-
worked. See the Introduction. HW cites a pedigree of Dryden in Bridge's
History . . . *of Northamptonshire*, below, p. 140.

1. Edward Gibbon (1737–94), author of the *History of the Decline and Fall
of the Roman Empire*, lived intermittently at Lausanne from 1753 and was
proficient in the French language. His charade may have been brought back
to England by Lord and Lady Sheffield, friends of his who visited him at
Lausanne in 1791 (see *YWE*, XI, 335).

2. Edmond Cornwall (ca. 1535–85), styled Baron Burford, son of Richard
Cornwall (ca. 1493–1568) by his wife Janet, née Wogan (ca. 1507–47). The
monument to Cornwall and his parents in the church at Burford, one mile
west of Tenbury in Shropshire, was erected in 1587 by his brother Thomas;
it is described, with particulars of the Cornwall family, in Vol. II (published
1796) of Richard Gough's *Sepulchral Monuments*, pp. 79*–82* (see above,
p. 10, n. 1). HW thanked Gough for his "account . . . of the Cornwall monument" in a letter of 14 Nov. 1792 (printed Toynbee, XVI, 163–64), where he
says that he has "never met with the painter's name"; the painter Salaboss
has not been further identified. Gough does not mention the monument at
Lydiard Tregoze in *Sepulchral Monuments*. It was erected in 1615 by Sir
John St. John (d. 1648), cr. (1611) Bt., to commemorate his parents Sir John
St. John (d. 1594), m. Lucy Hungerford (d. 1598), and is described in *A History of Wiltshire*, ed. R. B. Pugh and E. Crittal, Victoria History of the
Counties of England (London, 1955–), IX, 88–89. The two central doors of
the triptych open to reveal the life-size figures of Sir John and his wife kneeling upon a tomb. "Matches" in "arms and matches" means heraldic representations of matrimonial alliances (*OED*).

Monumental Painting for Sr J. St John & his Lady, 1594 & 1598, ⟨tho⟩ no Painter's name.

From Mr Gough.

Excellent bon mot. Nov. 1792.

Ld Henry Fitzgerald,^{3} a warm Republican, told Lord Darnley that he had blotted out the Supporters to his arms on his chariot, & asked him if he w^d not do the same? "No, s^d Ld D. not unless my Supporters were Monkies"—Which Ld Henry's were.

[p. 79]   1793.

Notices from Brydges'^{4} *Hist. of Northampt.* fol. 2 vols 1793.

In Stene Chapel monument of Temperance Browne D^r of Sir T. Crewe, by J. & Mathias *Christmas* Fratres 1635. Pedigree of *Dryden*. p. 226. Vol. 1.

3. Lord Henry Fitzgerald (1761–1829), 4th son of the 1st Duke of Leinster (*YWE*, XVI, 266, n. 37); Lord Darnley was John Bligh (1767–1831), 4th Earl of Darnley, 1781. Fitzgerald's blotting out the supporters to his arms was of course a symbolic repudiation of his noble status (for an illustration of the Leinster arms and supporters, see *Burke's Peerage*, p. 1579). HW sent this bon mot to Lady Ossory in his letter of 8 Jan. 1793 (*YWE*, XXXIV, 177).

4. John Bridges (1666–1724), topographer. HW's copy of his *History and Antiquities of Northamptonshire* (Oxford, 1791), 2 vols., folio, is listed Hazen, *Cat. of HW's Lib.*, No. 1; this work was compiled from Bridges's materials by Peter Whalley. ("1793" as the date of publication is so in the MS.) The monument in Steane Chapel of Temperance Crewe (ca. 1609–34), m. John Browne, 3d daughter of Sir Thomas Crewe (ca. 1565–1633), described Bridges, I, 201, is also described in *GM* 1786, LVI, Pt. ii, 933, and George Baker, *History and Antiquities of the County of Northampton* (London, 1822–41), I, 688; it was executed by John and Mathias Christmas, carvers and statuaries, sons of Gerard Christmas (d. 1634), carver to the royal navy and the lords of the admiralty. HW believed that Dryden was a great-uncle of his, which explains his interest in the poet's pedigree. (Dryden was actually a first cousin three times removed; see *YWE*, I, 375, and n. 9.) Sir Francis Crane (d. 1636) was director of the tapestry works established at Mortlake under the patronage of James I; his letter, addressed to James, describes the difficulties and expense of that undertaking. Willem Wissing (1656–87), portrait painter, was buried in St. Martin's Church in the parish of Stamford Baron St. Martin Without; Bridges, loc. cit., reproduces the inscription on his monument there. HW discusses Crane and Wissing in his *Anecdotes of Painting, Works*, III, 162–63, 323 (for Wissing, see also Thieme and Becker, XXXVI, 111).

Letter of Sr Francis *Crane*. 328.
Wissing. Vol. 2. 583.

Anecdote of Charles Mordaunt Earl of Peterborough[5] in the reign of Q. Anne, from General Mordaunt Feb. 9. 1793.

Ld Peterb. walking down St James's street, was followed by a Troop of beggars, crying, God bless yr Grace! the Earl asked for whom they took him? "Oh! God bless yr grace! we know you, you are the Duke of Marlborough! "no, That I am not, s^d Lord P. and I will give you two convincing proofs; I have but two guineas in my pocket, & Those I will *give* amongst ye."

A Short Address to the Public &c on his Dismission from the Army. by Hugh Lord Sempill.[6] Lond. Jan. 1793.

Carlos[7] being asked if it woud not be very becoming in the Queen to give a thousand pound to the Subscription by

5. Charles Mordaunt (ca. 1658–1735), cr. (1689) Earl of Monmouth; 3d Earl of Peterborough, 1697; admiral, general, and diplomat; Gen. Mordaunt was Thomas Osbert Mordaunt (ca. 1729–1809), Maj. Gen., 1782, Lt. Gen., 12 Oct. 1793 (*GM* 1809, LXXIX, Pt. i, 279; *Army Lists*, 1793, p. 4, 1808, p. 4). Lord Peterborough was a political enemy of John Churchill (1650–1722), cr. (1689) Earl and (1702) Duke of Marlborough, the victor at Blenheim; his bon mot alludes to the charges of avarice brought against Marlborough by his foes. Another version of this anecdote is given in *DNB*, according to which the mob, mistaking Peterborough for Marlborough, were about to drag him through the kennel when apprized of their error. For another bon mot attributed to Peterborough, see below, p. 143.
6. Hugh Sempill (1758–1830), 14th Baron Sempill, 1782. A lieutenant and captain in the 3d Foot Guards, he was deprived of his commission on 30 Nov. 1792 for corresponding with the "Friends of Freedom in France" (*GEC*, XI, 629); in a vain attempt to get his commission back, he published *A Short Address to the Public, on the Practice of Cashiering Military Officers without a Trial; and a Vindication of the Conduct and Political Opinions of the Author* (London, 1793), 8vo.
7. Perhaps Carlos Cony (fl. 1774–?93), who had been the attorney of HW's nephew George, 3d Earl of Orford (d. 1791); the bon mot alludes to Charlotte's supposed avarice and niggardliness (see above, p. 99, n. 7; *YWE*, XXVI, 261). Following the execution of Louis XVI on 21 Jan. 1793, the French National Convention on 1 Feb. declared war on Great Britain and Holland (see *GM* 1793, LXIII, Pt. i, 181; *Annual Register*, 1793, "State Papers," pp. 139–41). On Feb. 8 Catherine the Great (see the epigram below) read an edict to her senate by which she ordered the termination of all inter-

several Ladies for the Widows of Soldiers & Sailors that shall be killed in the War; said, "yes—but She will not." Q. why not?" Q. why not? Answ. Because she will not give so bad an example to the rest of her money."

[p. 80]   Epigram
on the Manifesto of the Empress of Russia
against the French on their Murder of their King.

When Catherine weeps o'er murder'd Louis' tomb,
Catherine, who plann'd her own Petruccio's doom,
Who says, that Charity begins at home?

Extract from a poem by the Marquis of Salisbury.[8]

> Poor little Tommy had a pain;
> She thought the same woud come again,
>   Unless She brought assistance.
> Tho scarcely rising four years old,
> He had a tooth, as I am told,
>   That pain'd him at a distance—

His Lordship in 1792 had printed a few copies of a thick quarto full of equally excellent poetry, some of which he gave away. At the end was what he too ⟨readily⟩ called an

course with France, branding the delegates to the National Convention as "monsters" who have laid there "parricidal hands on the life of the Lord's anointed, of their lawful master, cruelly and inhumanly immolated" (*Annual Register*, pp. 224–25). Among other satirical sobriquets HW nicknamed the Empress "Catherine Slayczar" in allusion to the widespread suspicion that she had been responsible for the assassination of her husband, Peter III, whom she succeeded to the throne in 1762; the question of her guilt or innocence has never been resolved. See *YWE*, X, 38–39; XI, 242, 288; XXXI, 162; XXXIV, 87, 153, et passim.

8. See above, pp. 128, n. 9, 131, n. 6. These verses seem to contain a ribald allusion to the "toothache" or "Irish toothache" (defined by Partridge as a "priapism"), though the expression is dated by Partridge from the late nineteenth century. No copy of Salisbury's volume of poetry has been traced. HW's description of Salisbury's poetry as "excellent" is probably ironic, since he elsewhere refers to him as "poor Lord Salisbury" and calls him a "stately simpleton" (see *YWE*, XXXIX, 495, and n. 4).

Index: it was a List of the poems & the number of verses contained in each.

Charles Earl of Peterborough in the reign of Queen Anne being at Rheims was shown the Sainte Ampoulle; the Priest who Showed it, said, "Milor, est'ce que vous sacrez vos Rois?" he replied, "Non, Monsr, nous les massacrons."[9]

[p. 81]   Contrast.

Mrs. W. an affected learned Lady, whose Husband was a meer Lawyer, who had studied nothing but in his profession, being ill, sent for him to her bedside to take leave, & said to him, "I am dying, but, Pætus, it is not painfull"[1]—he rushed out of the room & said to the Servants, "why, you did not tell me She is lightheaded: She talks of Peter & Paul!"

Mrs Fr. R. a silly devout Gentlewoman, s^d. "I must rise very early tomorow morning, so I will read my morning prayers over night."

Dr Hoadley[2] Archb. of Dublin had Wit as well as his Brother Benjamin Bp of Winchester, but more roughness. A dull

---

9. HW included this anecdote in his letter to Sir Horace Mann 5 June 1775 (*YWE*, XXIV, 112–13); a slightly different version was told to Joseph Spence by the Chevalier Ramsay in 1729 (Spence's *Anecdotes*, ed. J. M. Osborn, Oxford, 1966, I, 451). The Sainte Ampoulle was the phial at Rheims containing the holy oil with which French kings were anointed at their coronations (*YWE*, XXIV, 113, n. 25).

1. When Caecina Paetus was ordered by the Emperor Claudius to end his life (A.D. 42), his wife Arria stabbed herself first, declaring, "Paete, non dolet" (see *Oxford Classical Dictionary*, 2d ed., ed. N. G. L. Hammond and H. H. Scullard, Oxford, 1970, s.v. Caecina Paetus; *YWE*, V, 424; XXXIII, 230; XXXV, 466).

2. John Hoadly (1678–1746), D.D., 1717, archbishop of Dublin, 1730, and of Armagh, 1742 (*DNB;* Venn, *Alumni Cantab.*); for his brother Benjamin see above, p. 29, n. 6. Richard Marlay (ca. 1728–1802), D.D., was bishop of Clonfert, 1787–95, and of Waterford, 1795–1802; HW mentions meeting him at Paris in 1775, and is mentioned by him in letters to the Earl of Charlemont in 1782 and 1796 (*YWE*, VII, 351; Henry Cotton, *Fasti Ecclesiæ Hibernicæ*, Dublin, 1848–51, I, 133–34, IV, 173; *Alumni Dublinenses*, ed. G. D. Burtchaell and T. U. Sadleir, Dublin, 1935, p. 554; Great Britain, Historical

Clergyman having published a dull book, sent it to the Former, & soon after waited on him to ask if his Grace had redde it. "Sr, s^d the Prelate; it is a rule with me never to look a gift horse in the mouth."

from Dr Marley Bishop of Clonfert.

Speech of the *Earl of Abingdon*³ on his Ldsp's motion for postponing the farther consideration the abolition of the Slave trade, with some strictures on the Speech of the Bp. of St David's.

by Debret April 1793.

I was saying, that the Publication of Th. Paine's⁴ Pamphlets had turned out to be of the greatest Service, for they had produced such excellent answers and such plain discussions of the blessings of our Constitution that It is become infinitely better known to the simplest understandings [p. 82] than it had ever been, & more endeared to all ranks of people. "yes, s^d Lady Louisa Macdonald (wife of the Chief Baron) It has resembled the discovery & effects of Inoculation."

Manuscripts Commission, 12th Report, Appendix, Part X [*Charlemont Manuscripts*, Vol. I], London, 1891, p. 396; 13th Report, Appendix, Part VIII [*Charlemont Manuscripts*, Vol. II], London, 1894, p. 274). "Redde" is so in the MS (see above, p. 98, n. 5).

3. Willoughby Bertie (1740–99), 4th Earl of Abingdon, 1760. His speech in the House of Lords on 11 April was published as a separate octavo pamphlet by John Debrett (d. 1822), publisher and compiler, and is also summarized in the *Parliamentary History of England,* ed. W. Cobbett and J. Wright (London, 1806–20), XXX, 652–58; in his speech he argues against the abolition of the slave trade as a movement founded upon the same meretricious principles as the French Revolution. His motion was opposed by Lord Stanhope, Lord Grenville, and Samuel Horsley, bishop of St. David's (for whom see above, p. 117, n. 6), and he agreed to withdraw it (*Parliamentary History,* XXX, 659–60).

4. Thomas ("Tom") Paine (1737–1809), the radical pamphleteer, was in Dec. 1792 while in France tried *in absentia* and found guilty of seditious libel for having authored *The Rights of Man: Being an Answer to Mr. Burke's Attack on the French Revolution,* published at London in two parts, 1791 and 1792; the BM Cat. mentions some 25 answers to this work, which was adopted as a manifesto by the pro-Revolution parties in England. Lady Louisa Leveson-Gower (1749–1827), married (1777) Sir Archibald Macdonald (1747–1826), Kt., 1788, cr. (1813) Bt.; Macdonald was attorney general, 1788–93, and lord chief baron of the Exchequer, Feb. 1793–1813 (*YWE,* XXXII, 409, nn. 1a–2).

Excellent Calembour on le Marechal de Villeroi,[5] the incapable & unsuccessfull General & Favourite of Louis 14;

Villeroi, Villeroi
a bien servi le Roi—
Guillaume, Guillaume.

We scarce know anything at all of Berengaria,[6] Queen of Richard 1st.—In the new History of Somersetshire by Collinson it is said, in Vol. 3[d]. p. 498. that Geoffry Luttrell, in 17. John, had a particular Commission of adjusting the disputes between King John & Berengaria Queen Dowager of Richard the first at that time referred to the Pope's arbitration, & was empowered in the King's name to swear to the performance of such an Establishment as shoud be then agreed to.

This Shows that Berengaria outlived her Husband many years and looks as if John had withheld her jointure.

In one of the three Volumes of that History I found that

---

5. François de Neufville (1644–1730), Duc de Villeroi; maréchal de France. The "calembour" or pun refers to Villeroi's ineffective campaign against William III in the Low Countries, 1695–97. In 1702 he was captured before Cremona by the Imperial army, which however failed to occupy the town, a set of circumstances which gave rise to the following quatrain (cited *NBG*):

Français, rendez grâce à Bellone,
Votre bonheur est sans égal:
Vous avez conservé Crémone,
Et perdu votre général.

6. Berengaria of Navarre (d. after 1230), m. (1191) Richard I, King of England. John Collinson (?1757–93), country historian, wrote *The History and Antiquities of the County of Somerset* (Bath, 1791), 3 vols., 4to; HW's copy is listed Hazen, *Cat. of HW's Lib.*, No. 3164. Geffrey Luttrell (d. 1217 or 18) was a minister under King John (Collinson, loc. cit.); Pope Innocent III wrote John in 1204, 1207 and 1213 protesting his withholding of Berengaria's jointure, and a composition was finally made in 1215 of which the Pope approved. (In the MS HW wrote "adjusting the disputing the disputes," an obvious slip which has been emended.) A careful scanning of Collinson by the editor has failed to turn up the other mention of Berengaria; Agnes Strickland, *Lives of the Queens of England* (London, 1885), I, 319, notes that she received as part of her dower the royal revenues from the tin mines in Cornwall and Devon, but says nothing of a grant of lands to her in Somersetshire or elsewhere in England. (HW may have been remembering lands assigned to some other queen; see, e.g., Collinson, III, 3.) For Berengaria, see also below, p. 146 and n. 8.

Queen's name again, but lost the place & can not find it now, tho I think it named some Lands assigned to her.

An Irish Peer, very apt to romance on the antiquity of his family, boasted of possessing a house built by William *Rufus*.[7] A Gentleman told him, he supposed it had only been repaired by William Roof-house.

[p. 83]   In Dr Ducarel's[8] hist. of the Hospital of St Catherine, in the second Vol. of the Bibliotheca topograph. Britann. it is said that Q. Berengaria was living even to the tenth year of Henry 3^d. but that it is not known when She died. Probably She never came to England.

In the 2^d Vol. of Les Anecdotes des Reines de France pp. 68. 69. the Author says he has proved in the bibliotheque de Poitou Tom. 1. p. 300. that Berengaria was living in 1229 au Mans which had been given to her for her jointure, & that She had founded there the Abbey de l'Espau les le Mans & that in 1216, she assisted at a Judgment by single combat.

Lady Euston,[9] 2^d Daughter of James Earl Waldegrave by Maria Duchess of Gloucester, being at a ball in May 1793,

7. William II (d. 1100), King of England, 1087–1100, was nicknamed "Rufus" ("the Red") in allusion to his ruddy complexion.
8. Andrew Coltee Ducarel (1713–85), D.C.L., civil lawyer and antiquary. His *History of the Royal Hospital and Collegiate Church of St. Katharine*, published at London, 1782, as No. 5 of John Nichols's *Bibliotheca Topographica Britannica*, was bound into Vol. II of the collected set (published 1790; see above, p. 59, n. 4). The item on Berengaria is in an account of the queen consorts of England, p. 44; the queen consorts were by law the perpetual patronesses of the hospital, which was regarded as part of their dower (p. 42). HW is correct about Berengaria's having never come to England. His copy of *Mémoires historiques, critiques, et anecdotes de France* (Amsterdam, 1764), 4 vols., 12mo (better known by the running title: *Anecdotes des reines et régentes de France*) is listed Hazen, *Cat.*, No. 1303; it was apparently edited by Jean-François Dreux du Radier (1714–80), who was also author of *Bibliothèque historique, et critique du Poitou* (Paris, 1754), 5 vols., 12mo (see *NBG; Dictionnaire de biographie française*, Paris, 1933–, XI, 757–58). Berengaria received Le Mans and the county of Bigorre as the continental part of her dower (see above, p. 145, n. 6). On 23 Aug. 1216 she presided over a trial by combat there, and in 1230 founded the Cistercian monastery called "Pietas Dei" at Espau in Maine.
9. HW's grandniece; see above, pp. 27, n. 3. Frederick, Duke of York, was in February appointed commander in chief of the British forces in the United

where were some young French Aristocrates Emigrès, one of them said to her, "What woud you do, now that yr young men are gone to Flanders, if *We* were not here to dance with you?" "yes, said She, *They* are fighting for *you,* & *you* are dancing for *them.*"

Mr Hare[1] said of one of the *Legges,* who was much less sensible than the rest of his family, "He is the only *Leg* I ever knew, who was all *Calf.*"

In the Church of great Malvern, said to have been decorated by Henry 7th. but more probably by Sir Reginald Bray,[2]

Provinces, and an item in the *Daily Advertiser* 30 April 1793, dated Bruges, 17 April, announces his arrival there at the head of 4,000 troops; the allied army proceeded to drive the French army out of Belgium, defeat it at Tournai and Famars, and take Valenciennes (on 26 July). Lady Euston's husband, George Henry Fitzroy, styled Earl of Euston and later 4th Duke of Grafton, was colonel in the army (during service), 1794 (*GEC*).

1. James Hare, the politician and wit (see above, p. 87, n. 4). The Legge family included the Earls of Dartmouth and Henry Bilson Legge (1708–64), chancellor of the Exchequer. Which Legge Hare was referring to has not been determined.

2. Sir Reginald Bray (d. 1503), statesman and architect. HW's copy, now *WSL,* of the *Antiquarian Repertory: A Miscellany,* ed. Francis Grose et al. (London, 1775–84), 4 vols., 4to, is listed Hazen, *Cat.,* No. 3850. Of the church of Great Malvern in Worcestershire the *Repertory* comments: "There is some reason to believe that the noble prince King Henry the Seventh was a benefactor. . . . It is reported that the windows of this church were beautified by this prince; his effigy is yet remaining in the third lower pane in the north aile, called Jesus Chapel. . . . In the pane behind, his great favorite Sir Reginald Bray" (III, 11–12). "Poutie of Harley Castle" has not been further identified. The will of "William Denyson, clerk, provost of the Queen's College, Oxford," dated 18 Nov. 1558, is reproduced ibid., III, 221–22; "Denyson" was presumably William Dennys (or Denysse or Dennes), M.A., B.D., who was named provost of Queen's College in 1534 and was afterwards canon of Windsor and of Canterbury (Foster, *Alumni Oxon.*). Thomas, styled "of Woodstock" (1355–97), 6th son of Edward III, cr. (1377) Earl of Buckingham and (1385) Duke of Gloucester, was reappointed constable of England during pleasure after the accession of Richard II (1377). His "Orders for the Office of Constable of England," printed *Antiquarian Repertory,* IV, 273–82, are addressed to Richard and call "battayles within lists" the "greateste acte that may be in armes" (p. 273), but HW is wrong in saying that his remark, "yt is very apparainte that many ought to have ben," alludes to Richard's interruption of the trial by combat between Henry of Lancaster, cr. (1397) Duke of Hereford, afterwards Henry IV, and Thomas de Mowbray (1366–99), cr. (1383) Earl of Nottingham and (1397) Duke of Norfolk: the aborted duel

as his portrait is placed there [p. 84] along with the King's, the altar piece is said to have been painted by one Poutie of Harley Castle in com. Worc. v. Antiq. Repertory. Vol. 3. p. 13.

W. Denyson Provost of Queen's Coll. Oxford, in 1575, left 100 marks to the College to buy plate, particularly 13 Silver *spoons*, with Christ & the 12 Apostles at the ends. ib. p. 221.

A striking Symptom of the malevolence of Thomas of Woodstock Duke of Gloucester to his nephew Richard 2ᵈ. may be found in the Duke's orders for the Office of Constable of England, for speaking of Lists for Single Combat (*which he approves*) which he says have been in England, in presence of Edward 3ᵈ. as in this yʳ Time, *and it is very apparent that many ought to have been.* This evidently alludes to the Single Combat between the Dukes of Hereford & Norfolk, which was appointed to be fought before King Richard, but which Majesty forbad to proceed. Antiq. Repert. vol. 4. p. 273.

> Letters to Absence can a Voice impart,
> And lend a tongue when Distance gags the heart.³

A Mʳ Nellican⁴ being at Lady Guilford's at Bushy park, it was thought very difficult to rhyme to his [p. 85] name; Mʳ Francis North made the following;

(made famous by Shakespeare in the first scene of *Richard II*) took place on 16 Sept. 1398, a full year after Gloucester's death.

3. These lines were perhaps inspired by the absence of the Berry sisters (see above, pp. 79, 93, 101), who in Sept. 1793 went to visit relations and friends in Yorkshire. HW wrote to them, 17 Sept. 1793: "My beloved Spouses. . . . I lament that the summer is over, not because of its uniquity, but because you two made it so delightful to me, that six weeks of gout could not sour it" (*YWE*, XII, 4).

4. Perhaps William Swinney Neligan (d. 1795), whose death "at his house at Exmouth, co. Devon" is recorded in *GM* 1795, LXV, Pt. i, 351. Lady Guilford, i.e., Anne Speke (ca. 1740–97), who married (1756) Frederick, Earl of Guilford (better known as Lord North) (d. 1792), was ranger of Bushey Park in Middlesex and lived at Bushey House; Francis North (1761–1817), her second son, succeeded his brother George Augustus as 6th Earl of Guilford, 1802, while her daughter Lady Anne North (1764–1832) married (1798) John Baker-Holroyd, cr. (1781) Baron and (1816) Earl of Sheffield. HW mentions visits to the Norths at Bushey in 1790 and 1795 (*YWE*, XI, 114; XII, 167),

> Poor Mr Nellican, poor Mr Nellican
> he hurt his rump
> against the pump
> And woud go no more near the well again.

And it was then s^d to be still more difficult to rhyme to Lord Hawksbury's name *Jenkinson:* Lady Anne North sd She thought She coud, & produced this;

> Happy Mr Jenkinson, happy Mr Jenkinson,
> Your Wife to you,
> I am sure was true,
> For you have got a Winking Son.   (⟨true⟩ in both
>   Father & *Son*

Epigram on Ld Howe,[5] from the newspapers.

> When Cesar triumphed o'er his Gallic Foes,
> Three Words concise his galant acts disclose:
> But Howe still more concise will use but one,
> And Vidi tells us all that he has done.

On taking the Arsenal at Toulon. from the newspapers.

> The Sans Culottes, those Sons of Bitches,
>   At length beneath their Conquerors fall;

and in a letter of 30 Nov. 1793 thanks Lady Anne for verses sent to him, probably composed by her brother Frederick (Toynbee, *Supplement,* III, 341); for another witticism by Francis North, see below, p. 152. Charles Jenkinson, Lord Hawkesbury, cr. (1796) Earl of Liverpool (see above, p. 36, n. 2), was secretary at war under Lord North; the rhyme seems to allude to a nervous tic inherited from him by his eldest son, Robert Banks Jenkinson (1770–1828), 2d Earl of Liverpool, 1808, statesman and prime minister, whose mother, Amelia Watts (ca. 1751–70), was twenty-two years younger than her husband.

    5. Richard Howe (1726–99), 4th Viscount Howe, 1758; cr. (1788) Earl Howe; vice admiral of Great Britain; commander in chief in the Channel, 1793–97. Though in search of the enemy fleet in the latter part of 1793, he was often forced by adverse weather to take shelter in Tor Bay, and was represented by scurrilous writers as doing so in order to avoid contact. *DNB* cites a Latin version of this epigram, ending: "Howe sua nunc brevius verbo complectitur uno, / Et 'vidi' nobis omnia gesta refert." See below, p. 151. The arsenal at Toulon was taken by Vice Admiral Samuel, Lord Hood in Aug. 1793, but by the end of the year had fallen again to the French.

Before, they only lost their breeches,
But now they've lost their Arse-nal.

[p. 86]   1794.

Mrs Damer[6] having sent her Statue of the King to S[r] Ashton Lever's museum before the crown was finished, was one
morning modelling the cap from a piece of red Velvet. Lord
Derby (violent in opposition) & Miss Farren the Actress came
in: he s[d] ironically to Mrs Damer "So I see even you are making the red Cap of Liberty!" "yes, s[d] Miss Farren admirably,
but yr Lordship will observe That it's within the limits of the
Crown."

This winter the Women showing much of their necks &
shortening their stays, M[r] Th. Onslow[7] said, there is great
plenty, & no waste—waist.

He said he once saw a young Woman who had no hands,
but cd do every thing with her feet—"I was afraid, said he,
that She woud ask me for a pinch of Snuff.

6. Anne Seymour Conway (1748–1828), m. (1767) John Damer (d. 1776);
sculptress. The only daughter of HW's cousin Field Marshal Henry Seymour
Conway, she was a favorite of HW, who made her his executrix and residuary legatee (see the Introduction); her marriage to Damer was an unhappy
one (he shot himself) and her MS journals, now *WSL*, reveal her to have had
a lesbian passion for Mary Berry. After the death of Sir Ashton Lever (1729–
88), collector, his museum was shifted to a building called the Rotunda on
the Surrey side of Blackfriars Bridge; Mrs. Damer's oversize statue of
George III, after being exhibited there, was placed on permanent display in
the Register Office of Scotland at Edinburgh. Edward Smith Stanley (1752–
1834), 12th Earl of Derby, 1776, in 1797 married as his second wife Elizabeth
Farren (ca. 1763–1829), the noted actress; Mrs. Damer did a bust of Miss Farren which was exhibited at the Royal Academy in 1789. See Percy Noble,
Anne Seymour Damer: A Woman of Art and Fashion (London, 1908),
pp. 78–79 et passim; Thieme and Becker, VIII, 318. This item has been
printed in *Anecdotes of Painting*, V, 238. In the MS HW mistakenly numbered p. 84 (corrected to 86 by the editor; see above, p. 111, n. 5) as "94";
the slip was undoubtedly influenced by the "1794" date written on the same
line.
7. Thomas Onslow (1754–1827), 2d Earl of Onslow, 1814. *GEC* notes that
he was well known from 1780 to 1800 as "little Tom Onslow" for his practical jokes, and that he appears to have possessed "an infinity of wit which
too frequently degenerated into buffoonery" (see also Namier and Brooke,
III, 230). HW records a visit by him to Strawberry Hill in Sept. 1793 in his
"Book of Visitors" (*YWE*, XII, 245).

Ld Howe having been censured for lying so long at *Torbay*[8] & Somebody toasting him at a great dinner in the City, a Gentleman said, "I have no objection to drinking his Lordship's health, but I will not drink him in *Port*.

It was said too, "that one might not only have a peep into Brest (Breast) but a naval Review (navel).

Pedantry is the Sublime of Vulgarism.[9]

[p. 87]   On M[r] Addison's Opera of Rosamond.[1]

So bright was Addison, so fix'd his fame,
That ev'n his Rosamond scarce soil'd his name:
Yet ah! ye Demigods, how insecure
Your Lot, when Clay divine & Mud impure
In the same Mess can blend! when he who drew
Good Coverley, coud spawn S[r] Trusty too!

8. See above, p. 149, n. 5. Howe put into port in the middle of December and did not venture out again until April. On 1 June 1794, following a blockade of Brest, he silenced his critics by winning a great victory over a fleet of 27 ships under the French admiral, Villaret-Joyeuse. On 1 July 1794 Richard Newton published a print entitled "A Peep into Brest with a Navel Review!"; this print satiries the currently fashionable low-cut French chemise gown while the punning title alludes to Howe's blockade (see J. C. Riely and D. R. Roylance, *The Age of Horace Walpole in Caricature*, New Haven, 1973, No. 62).

9. See above, p. 64.

1. Addison's *Rosamond*, an opera in three acts with music by Thomas Clayton, was first produced in 1707 at Drury Lane; its last performance had been in 1767 at Covent Garden, in a truncated version with the music by Samuel Arnold. (It was also set to music by Dr. Thomas Arne.) The "low buffoonery and vulgar jest" of Sir Trusty, keeper of Rosamond's bower, are exemplified in his opening song and speech: after singing, "For of us pretty fellows, / Our wives are so jealous, / They ne'er have enough of our duty," he exclaims, "I smell a shrew! / My fears are true, / I see my wife" (Act I, scene ii). HW evidently forgot about Sir Trusty when he wrote to John Pinkerton (26 June 1785) that Addison never dropped "into an approach towards burlesque and buffoonery" (*YWE*, XVI, 269). He writes in his "Book of Materials," 1771–85, p. 6, that "Addison in some of his Spectators approaches nearest to Shakespeare's natural humour, that is character. . . . Sir Roger de Coverley is the best drawn character next to Falstaff" (printed in *Notes . . . on Several Characters of Shakespeare,* ed. W. S. Lewis, Farmington, 1940, p. 4). See *Catalogue of the Royal and Noble Authors, Works,* I, 550*, n.; Peter Smithers, *The Life of Joseph Addison*, 2d ed. (Oxford, 1968), pp. 118–23; *London Stage 1660–1800 . . . Part 4: 1747–1776,* ed. G. W. Stone, Jr. (Carbondale, 1962), II, 1237.

And with a pencil fit for Shakespear's hand
(If e'er a second Falstaffe He had plann'd)
Coud stain a Canvas pure as Dian's breast
With low buffoonery and vulgar jest!

1795.

Sr Peter Burrell² taking up a very melancholy air, & wearing his hair very long & lank, Frank North said, "Peter went out and wept."

Lady Mary Duncan³ talking Italian with the Sardinian minister, told him She had been out of order, "ma che aveva preso un purgatorio."

Wilkes dining with the Prince of Wales, & some persons singing after dinner, the Prince insisted that Wilkes Should Sing too. He protested that he had no voice nor knew a note of music. The Prince persisting, & bidding him sing anything, whatever he woud—on which Wilkes sung "God save great George our King!" The Prince surprized said, "pray, Mr Wilkes, "how long have you *been* so loyal? he bowed, and replied, S^r, ever since I have had the honour of knowing your Royal Highness."⁴

As soon as the ceremony of the marriage of the Prince [p. 88] & Princess of Wales [was over],⁵ all the Bishops in the

2. Sir Peter Burrell (1754–1820), Kt., 1781, 2d Bt., 1787, cr. (1796) Baron Gwydir. North's words are a quotation from Luke xxii. 62. "Frank" is so in the MS, though perhaps a slip; "lank" has been written over "Curld."

3. Lady Mary (Tufton) Duncan, widow of Sir William Duncan, physician to George III (see above, p. 26, n. 2); the Sardinian minister was Filippo di San Martino, Conte di Front, envoy extraordinary and minister plenipotentiary at London, ca. 1789–ca. 1812 (Arturo Segre, *Vittorio Emanuele I,* Turin, 1928, p. 316; *Royal Calendar,* 1789–1812, passim). The Italian means "but had taken a purgatory"; Lady Mary confused *purgatòrio* ("purgatory") with *purgante* ("purgative").

4. This anecdote is recorded in "Anecdotes, Bon Mots, &c. &c. of the late Alderman Wilkes" in the *European Magazine,* April 1798, XXXIII, 226 (see also Horace Bleackley, *Life of John Wilkes,* London, 1917, p. 376 and n. 3); in the latter years of his life Wilkes (see above, p. 48, n. 5) forsook his radical politics and became a supporter of the King.

5. The Prince of Wales on 8 April 1795 married his cousin Caroline Amelia Elizabeth of Brunswick-Wolfenbüttel (1768–1821); the ceremony took

Chapel went up to the Prince to congratulate him—the Last that got up to him was his old Tutor the Archbishop of York: the Prince shook him by the hand & s^d.—"tho last, not least in love"—Somebody who overheard only the last words—or pretended to have heard no more, s^d to another Person, "think how shocking the Prince's behaviour was! he told the A. of York that he was not the least in love!"

On Lady Salisbury's first pregnancy, which was late, it was scandalously laid to her footman in a newspaper, for which the Printer was justly prosecuted & punished.[6] Some time after, that Lady being very rude to Mrs Fitzherbert, the Prince said he did not wonder at her Ladyship's behaviour, as She had had her *breeding* from her Footman.

A remarkably good German Trumpeter being presented to the Prince of Wales & producing some extraordinary sounds, the Person who introduced him, asking the Prince in admiration if his R.H. had ever heard such notes before—no, s^d the Prince, but I have *behind*.

Treatise on connection between Agriculture & Chymistry &c by L: of Dundonald.[7] Quarto 1795. European Mag. for May, p. 320.

place in the Chapel Royal at St. James's (see *YWE*, XII, 107, 139). William Markham (1719–1807), archbishop of York, 1777, was preceptor to the Prince of Wales and to his brother Frederick, afterwards Duke of York, 1771–76.

6. See above, p. 133 and n. 3. Though Lady Salisbury married the Marquess in 1773, their first child, Lady Georgina Charlotte Augusta, was not born until 1786. (An account of the christening is in *GM* 1786, LVI, Pt. i, 436; see also Collins, *Peerage*, II, 495.) For Mrs. Fitzherbert, see above, p. 48.

7. Archibald Cochrane (1748–1831), 9th Earl of Dundonald, 1778; naval officer and chemical manufacturer. His *Treatise, Shewing the Intimate Connection that Subsists between Agriculture and Chemistry, Addressed to Cultivators of the Soil* [etc.] (London, 1795), 4to, anticipates many of the ideas expressed in Sir Humphry Davy's *Elements of Agricultural Chemistry* (1813); it is praised by the reviewer in the *European Magazine*, May 1795, XXVII, 320–21, as having "opened a field of discovery, and of the judicious application of well-founded theory to efficient practice, which we do not recollect to have been even attempted by any other writer on this most important subject." This item is entered under 1794 in the MS (bottom of p. 86) but has been shifted to its approximately correct chronological position.

Geo. 2ᵈ Lord Harcourt[8] begging of his Father one *Acre* out of the park for a flower garden, & placing several busts of poets in it with inscriptions, and keeping an Album there for Persons to write some sentence, Sʳ Josh. Reynolds the Painter wrote, "This is a Wiseacre!"

It is said in Vol. 3ᵈ. p. 206 of Lyson's Environs of London[9] that Leibnitz asserted that Catherine Finch *Css of Conway* wrote Opera Philosophica. the ⟨sister of sr⟩ Heneage.

W. Peckitt[1] Glass Painter of York d. Oct. 1795, aged 65.

Some remarks on the apparent circumstances of the War in the 4ᵗʰ Week of October 1795. by *Lord Auckla[n]d*.[2]

---

8. HW's friend and correspondent, identified above, p. 47, n. 3; his father was Simon Harcourt (1714–77), 2d Viscount Harcourt, 1727, cr. (1749) Earl Harcourt. Nuneham Park was a seat of the Harcourts in Oxfordshire.

9. Daniel Lysons (see above, p. 105), *The Environs of London* (London, 1792–96), 4 vols. royal 4to. The work was dedicated to HW; his copy, now *WSL*, is listed Hazen, *Cat. of HW's Lib.*, No. 3859. "Catherine" is a slip for Anne Finch (1631–79), m. (1651) Edward Conway, 3d Viscount Conway, cr. (1679) Earl of Conway, half sister of Sir Heneage Finch (1621–82), cr. (1681) Earl of Nottingham, lord chancellor. Lysons states, loc. cit., that "this Countess of Conway is said to have written a Latin work, entitled *Opuscula Philosophica*," and gives as his authority a letter in the *GM* Oct. 1784, LIV, Pt. ii, 728, which in turn cites a statement by Leibnitz in a "German literary journal." The work in question was originally written in English but translated into Latin and published posthumously at Amsterdam, 1690, as *Opuscula Philosophica Quibus Continentur Principia Philosophiae Antiquissimae et Recentissimae;* a retranslation into English, entitled *The Principles of the Most Ancient and Modern Philosophy*, was published at London in 1692. See *Conway Letters*, ed. M. H. Nicolson (New Haven, 1930), pp. 4, 453–56, et passim.

1. William Peckitt (1731–95), glass painter. HW employed him for windows at Strawberry Hill in 1762 and 1773 (see *YWE*, XXVIII, 213, n. 21); his death is noticed, e.g., in *GM* Oct. 1795, LXV, Pt. ii, 885. This item has been printed in *Anecdotes of Painting*, V, 136.

2. William Eden (1744–1814), cr. (1789) Baron Auckland, statesman and diplomat. His pamphlet (summarized in the *GM* Nov. 1795, LXV, Pt. ii, 938–41) paints an optimistic picture of England's military and economic situation vis-à-vis France; it aroused considerable interest because of Auckland's close connection with Pitt, and was thought to be an expression of Pitt's own views.

[p. 89]   In Murphy's[3] Travels in Portugal in quarto 1795 it is said p:44 but not positively that the fine Gothic Church of Batalha was built after a Design of Stephen Stephenson, an Englishman. Mr Murphy gives a reason that makes it probable, tho not very, he supposing that Philippa Queen of Portugal Daughter of John of Gaunt might have introduced English Architects into Portugal; but I think She lived too long before the Erection of Batalha.

3. James Cavanah Murphy (1760–1814), architect and antiquary. In 1788 he was commissioned to make drawings of the famous Dominican church and monastery of Batalha in Estremadura; after his return to England he published *Plans, Elevations, Sections and Views of the Church of Batalha . . . To Which is Prefixed an Introductory Discourse on the Principles of Gothic Architecture* (London, 1795), imperial folio, and *Travels in Portugal . . . in the Years 1789 and 1790, Consisting of Observations on the Manners, Customs, Trade, Public Buildings, Arts, Antiquities, &c. of that Kingdom* (London, 1795), 4to. HW's copies of these works are listed Hazen, *Cat.*, Nos. 2910, 3247, 3650; he mentions Murphy's *Travels* in a letter to Mary Berry 22 Nov. 1795 (*YWE*, XII, 178). Stephen Stephenson is apparently not named in any other work on Batalha, but Philippa (1360–1415), daughter of John of Gaunt (1340–99), Duke of Lancaster, m. (1387) John I, King of Portugal, did live at the time of the erection of the monastery, and may have been instrumental in bringing over workmen and plans from England. See Thieme and Becker, XXXII, 1; Albrecht Haupt, *Die Baukunst der Renaissance in Portugal* (Frankfurt, 1890–95), II, 9–11; T. W. E. Roche, *Philippa: Dona Filipa of Portugal* (London, 1971), p. 2 et passim.

Appendix A
Walpole's Pencil Notations at the Back of the *Miscellany*

Entered on the verso of the last leaf of the *Miscellany* are four memoranda in pencil by Walpole. A comparison of these with similar memoranda in ink on a detached scrap of paper, now in the Lewis Walpole Library at Farmington, suggests that they were written in 1786 or 1787.

1. *Mr Dalton has the Original of Cooper.* For Richard Dalton, engraver and antiquary, see above, p. 97, n. 1, and p. 125. HW bought "the original portrait of Samuel Cooper [1609–72], the miniature painter, from the royal collection" at the auction of Dalton's collection at Christie's in 1791 (see p. 125, n. 3); this was a self-portrait done about 1650. It was engraved by Thomas Chambers for the first edition of Walpole's *Anecdotes of Painting* (1762–71), where it is found at III, 61, and was reengraved by W. Raddon for the Dallaway edition of 1826–28 (III, 116). Sold with other works by Cooper at the Strawberry Hill Sale in 1842, it is now in the Dyce Collection in the Victoria and Albert Museum. See Thieme and Becker, VII, 362–65.

2. *Parallel of Mrs Hastings & Mad. la Motte.* On the scrap of paper mentioned above HW wrote "Mad. de la Motte & Mrs Hastings Procure pres[ents] of diamonds for both Qs." For Mrs. Warren Hastings and her closeness to Queen Charlotte, see above, p. 75, n. 8; Walpole alludes to a rumor of her being bribed with diamonds to carry ladies to Court in a letter to Mary Berry, 26 Feb. 1791 (*YWE*, XI, 207). Jeanne de Saint-Rémy de Valois (1756–91), who married (1780) Marc-Antoine-Nicolas Lamotte, called Comtesse de la Motte, was imprisoned in 1786 for her complicity in the famous affair of the Diamond Necklace; she and her husband apparently

tricked the Cardinal de Rohan into ordering a necklace for
Queen Marie Antoinette to enable them to seize and sell the
diamonds (see ibid., XII, 4–5, n. 3; XXV, 603, n. 6). The
"Comtesse" escaped and joined her husband in England in
Aug. 1787, and published *Mémoires justicatifs* at London
early in 1788. Another item on the scrap of paper alludes to
her presence in England and to the forthcoming publication
of her book, which suggests that the memoranda on the scrap
were written late in 1787.

3. *St Bedlam's Day*. On the scrap of paper Walpole wrote
"St Bedlam's day, the 10th." It is possible that this is a jocu-
lar reference to the incarceration of Margery Nicholson in
Bedlam in Aug. 1786 after her attempted assassination of the
King (see above, p. 31, n. 8).

4. *Ungalant affair of Livia. Tacitus*. This is a conjectural
reading; only "gal . . . fa . . . of Livia. Tacitus" is clear.
On the scrap of paper Walpole wrote "Pr. [of Wales] presented Ld Charlemont to Mrs Fitzherbert, 'tho not young, he
is a man of galantry'—this did not sound like presenting him
to his Wife" (for the Prince's secret marriage to Mrs. Fitzherbert in Dec. 1785 see above, p. 48, n. 5). Possibly Walpole
thought of drawing a parallel between the Prince's ungallant
(in a different sense) treatment of Mrs. Fitzherbert and the
equally ungallant behavior of Tiberius Claudius Nero, husband of Livia Drusilla (58 B.C.–29 A.D.), who divorced her so
that she might become the wife of the Emperor Octavian
(Augustus); this episode is mentioned in Tacitus, *Annals*, V,
1. See *The Oxford Classical Dictionary*, 2d ed., ed. N. G. L.
Hammond and H. H. Scullard (Oxford, 1970), s.v. Livia
Drusilla.

Appendix B
Walpole's Spellings in the *Miscellany*

The following is a list of Walpole's spellings in the *Miscellany* that differ from modern usage. A number of them (e.g., *Arrian, redde, Sarazins, syrop*) were already archaic in Walpole's time and suggest the influence of his antiquarian studies.

advertized
Arrian
beautifull, gracefull,
   ungratefull, etc.
Cesar
chymistry
cloathed
clumsey
compleatly
cotemporaries
coud, shoud, woud
dansers
embassador
filigraine
galant
grosly
groupes
holyday
housholds
ideots
innui (ennui)
lilly
litterally
litterary
lyar (liar)
lye, lyes

meer (mere)
neice
occurrencies
offerred
origine
Phebus
pitt
Plimouth
pomgranates
quere
redde (read)
relicks
Rhingraves
Sarazins
staid (stayed)
strait (straight)
surprize
syrop
tho, thro
tomorow
trowzers
unsuccesful
wave (waive)
wrapt
yeild

Index

This index contains names, selected subjects, and titles of works mentioned, quoted, discussed or alluded to in the Introduction and Horace Walpole's text. Except for periodicals, anonymous works, and works by Walpole, titles are given under the author or editor.